James River Chiefdoms

James River Chiefdoms

The Rise of Social Inequality in the Chesapeake

Martin D. Gallivan

University of Nebraska Press
Lincoln and London

Library of Congress Cataloging-in-Publication
Data
Gallivan, Martin D., 1968–
James River chiefdoms : the rise of social
inequality in the Chesapeake /
Martin D. Gallivan.
p. cm.
Includes bibliographical references and index.
ISBN 0-8032-2186-x (cloth : alk. paper)
1. Powhatan Indians–Kings and rulers.
2. Powhatan Indians–First contact with
Europeans.   3. Powhatan Indians–
Antiquities.   4. Excavations (Archaeology)–
Virginia–James River Valley.   5. Chiefdoms–
Virginia–James River Valley.   6. Indians of
North America–History–Colonial period,
ca. 1600–1775.   7. Virginia–History–Colonial
period, ca. 1600–1775.   8. James River Valley
(Va.)–Antiquities.   9. Great Britain–
Colonies–America.   I. Title.
E99.P85G35 2003
975.5004'973–dc21
2003042699

Contents

Figures

Tables

Preface: The Arrival of the Tassantasses

On 24 July 1608 John Smith and 12 of his men pushed a small barge into the James River and floated downstream for the Chesapeake Bay. Powered by sail, oars, and a desperate need for provisions, the Englishmen set out to learn what they could of the area surrounding James Fort and its inhabitants. This was Smith's second expedition on the Bay, and by this time his contacts with the Native societies of eastern Virginia assumed a familiar pattern. At the northern reaches of the Chesapeake, Smith's men encountered a large force of armed Tockwoghs who surrounded the Englishmen. Quickly though, their hostile posture gave way to an exchange of goods, after which the two parties returned to the Tockwoghs' village, where the Tockwoghs entertained the visitors with a lavish feast (Smith 1686c:171).

During the early years of the Jamestown Colony, Smith and other colonists described a number of similar encounters throughout the Tidewater region with diverse groups of Algonquin-speaking Indians who comprised the Powhatan paramountcy.[1] The colonists also provided fleeting accounts of contact with other Native groups, including the Monacans of the Virginia Piedmont. Frequently, local groups initiated these encounters with the English through threats, intimidation, and hostilities, occasionally involving the shedding of blood and the loss of life. After a brief show of force, the Powhatans often assumed a less belligerent posture, offering the Tassantasses, or strangers, gifts and a feast hosted by the *weroance*, whom the English described variously as king, commander, or chief. We catch a glimpse of Native political dynamics in these events and the situational tactics through which the diverse Native societies in the Chesapeake region sought to probe the intentions of the English and to absorb them into their world. During the early seventeenth century, the Native world of the Virginia Coastal Plain was centered on the overwhelming authority of the individual named Powhatan, the Mamanatowick, or "great king," of the Powhatans. The Powhatans' social organization was defined by sharp inequities of status, authority, and wealth that included *weroances*. Across the fall line in the Piedmont, a powerful Monacan polity marked by chiefs' towns and tributary villages loomed as a persistent threat to the coastal Algonquins.

By Smith's second trip on the Bay, his encounters with Native groups

have the feel of social theater, with both the Powhatans and the English playing recurrent roles drawn from culturally defined categories of warfare and
trade. After brief hostilities, the Powhatans sought to obtain copper objects,
glass beads, and iron implements from the English. During these encounters,
Native leaders demanded and received these items from the English in return
for the food, hospitality, and knowledge critical for the colonists' survival during Jamestown's tenuous early years. In orchestrating such exchanges with
the English, *weroances* enhanced their renown by building social ties with
strangers who offered gifts that resonated in Powhatan society for their color
symbolism and exotic provenance.

As the Mamanatowick, Powhatan dominated this interaction and in the
process controlled an impressive social network through which gifts, tribute,
and power flowed. When the English sought to crown Powhatan as a vassal
of King James and to present him with symbols of authority at James Fort,
Powhatan responded, "If your king have sent me presents, I also am a king and
this my land: eight days I will stay to receive them. Your father is to come to
me, not I to him nor yet to your fort, neither will I bite at such a bait" (Smith
1986d:183). Powhatan was by no means alone in seeking to frame relations
with the Tassantasses on his own terms. While on their way to visit Powhatan
in his village at Werowocomoco, Smith and his men spent several nights with
a *weroance* who sought to dissuade Smith from his mission, arguing that "you
shall find Powhatan to use you kindly, but trust him not, and be sure he have
no opportunities to seize your armes; for he hath sent for you onely to cut
your throats" (Smith 1986d:193). Powhatan never actually did cut Smith's
throat due partly to the role that Smith, as an English *weroance*, began to
play in the social networks through which Powhatan controlled important
sources of power.

Even as *weroances* assembled networks of power centered on themselves,
Native communities in the Chesapeake also shared sacred knowledge and
decision-making authority across different segments of their societies. The
huskanaw, a male rite of passage, brought together Powhatans from villages
throughout the Coastal Plain to produce men qualified to exercise authority
in sacred, political, and military affairs. During the *huskanaw*, Powhatan boys
left the village and the social order entirely to acquire the sacred knowledge
and experience necessary to assume a new status as men capable of being
councilors, priests, or *weroances*. Though less apparent to the English colonists,
corporate bodies of such men steered decision making in Powhatan com-

munities, exerting an influence over *weroances* and even the Mamanatowick himself.

These early accounts of Native societies in Virginia reflect a cultural tension between authority structures focused on men of renown and decision-making institutions with a corporate orientation. While the overwhelming tenor of Native political dynamics in the Contact era Chesapeake centered on the authority of *weroances*, the men who placed themselves between Powhatan communities and the outside world, power also resided within cultural structures and social relationships of a more collective nature.

The Chesapeake region's precontact archaeological record likewise reflects a long-term culture history rife with complex ambiguity. Archaeological sites of the Late Woodland period (A.D. > 900–1500) immediately preceding the colonial era reflect the first focusing of settlement in large, horticultural communities with substantial houses, palisades, and midden deposits. Without an understanding of Native cultural practices drawn from documentary accounts, though, archaeologists would have a dim sense of the Powhatans' centralized authority, the Monacans' system of tribute, and the flows of prestige goods throughout the Chesapeake.

The sharp disjunction between the documentary record of the colonial era and the Chesapeake region's archaeology serves as the point of departure for this study. Ethnohistorical analyses have begun to recapture Native worldviews reflected in the events of the Contact period (e.g., Rountree 1989; Hantman 1990; Gleach 1997; Kupperman 2000; Axtell 2000). A remaining challenge is to link these worldviews to a reconstruction of the long-term historical trajectories and cultural practices of the Chesapeake, practices centered on residential settlements that lined the region's principal rivers. As detailed in the following chapters, the residents of riverine settlements reproduced and altered their practices—daily routines that put into action a mastery of the cultural order—to profound effect during the Late Woodland period. A fuller comprehension of the Chesapeake region's late prehistoric archaeology is critical to understanding the towering personalities of the Contact period and Native culture history that underlay the colonial encounter. This is the challenge taken up in *James River Chiefdoms: The Rise of Social Inequality in the Chesapeake.*

Acknowledgments

This work behind this book, a revision of my doctoral dissertation, reflects the efforts and support of many people and several institutions.

I would first like to thank the members of my doctoral committee—Jeffrey Hantman, Stephen Plog, Patricia Wattenmaker, and Fred Damon—for the insights and training they offered me at the University of Virginia. I owe a tremendous debt to Jeff Hantman, my dissertation committee chair, who provided me with the essential foundations of anthropological archaeology and the support that allowed me to meet the challenges of interpreting the prehistoric James River Valley. Whether I needed a tighter research design or a good meal, Jeff (and the whole Hantman family) have given repeatedly without hesitation. Steve Plog has also been especially supportive of my research and instrumental in shaping my approach to the archaeological record by encouraging a consideration of social change grounded in quantitative analysis. Pati Wattenmaker and Fred Damon furnished me with critical guidance in conducting anthropological research. I thank Fraser Neiman of the Thomas Jefferson Memorial Foundation, and now the University of Virginia's Department of Anthropology, who served as the outside reviewer on my dissertation committee.

The research presented here may be placed, I hope, within the tradition of an integrative approach to anthropology that thrives within the University of Virginia's Department of Anthropology. Several archaeologists from this tradition played an important role in shaping my understanding of North American archaeology. Michael Klein's research provided a model for this study by demonstrating the interpretive power that flows from a regional data set in which archaeological features serve as a fundamental unit of analysis. In response to my countless queries, Mike patiently steered me to the rich archaeological resources of the region and the principles needed to interpret them. Much of this research springs from Mike's efforts to develop a systematic ceramic chronology for the region and from his study of architectural patterning in the Chesapeake. Other influential "ancestors" who have pursued the archaeological study of Virginia's Indians alongside Mike at the University of Virginia include Gary Dunham and Thomas Klatka.

I have benefited from my continuing conversations with the University of Michigan's Debra Gold regarding North American prehistory and from her unparalleled grasp of the Chesapeake region's bioarchaeology. Dennis Blanton, Director of the William and Mary Center for Archaeological Research, was instrumental in helping me refine the basic questions that drive this research. As channeled (literally) through the voice of Jeff Hantman, Kent Lightfoot of the University of California at Berkeley has provided a blueprint for my approach to the archaeology of social change, largely without his knowledge. The University of Maryland's Mark Leone, who brought me into the field of archaeology, deserves my special thanks for providing an articulate voice in the archaeological pursuit of meaning and for serving as my advocate when I have needed one. I am indebted to Fred Plog, mentor to Jeff Hantman and Kent Lightfoot, whose innovative approaches to the regional and village archaeology of the American Southwest strongly influence my research.

This study would not have been possible without the benefit of fieldwork conducted at several sites under the auspices of the University of Virginia archaeological field school. Barbara and Jimmy Wood supplied unwavering support by allowing our field school crews to excavate at the Wood site, by protecting the site, and by safeguarding the field crew during the occasional flash flood or electrical storm. Whether we needed a house to sleep in, a water heater, or a backhoe, both Carolyn and John Wright went to extraordinary lengths to ensure that our excavation on their Elk Island property was a success. Steadfast graduate student assistance at the Wood and Wright sites came from Debbie Gold, Mintcy Maxham, Chris Fennell, Heather Lapham, Adrienne Lazazzera, and Lauren Silver. Led by Giovanna Klein, Jared Bryson, Corrinne Hollin, and others, a dedicated group of University of Virginia undergraduates deserves much of the credit for this study's field research.

I am also indebted to literally hundreds of field archaeologists who have worked in Virginia. In this research I draw on the results of excavations by avocational archaeologists, university-based researchers, cultural resource management firms, and state archaeologists. My citation of their publications does not sufficiently acknowledge the importance of their work for this study. I thank Randolph Turner and David Hazzard of the Virginia Department of Historic Resources (VDHR), whose stewardship of Virginia's archaeological record has allowed me to produce a broad regional study of Virginia prehistory. By granting ready access to the state's collections, VDHR's Keith Egloff offered me key pieces of the late prehistoric puzzle. Keith's keen understanding of Virginia's archaeological resources and his willingness to guide researchers through them make him a vital asset to Virginia archaeology. Howard MacCord's enthusiastic pursuit of the Native American past in Virginia for more than fifty years laid much of the groundwork for this study. Vincas Steponaitis and Steve Davis of the Research Laboratories of Anthropology at the University of North Carolina allowed me free access to data sets that proved to be critical in my reconstruction of prehistoric developments in the James River basin.

I am grateful to archaeologists at the William and Mary Center for Archaeological Research and to the faculty at William and Mary's Department of Anthropology. While working at the center and in the department, I "field tested" many of the ideas in this study with researchers, faculty, and students who offered perceptive insights and constructive criticism.

I thank Virginia's Native communities for their willingness to share knowledge and understanding of their past. Consultation and partnership with the descendant community represent an important obligation for students of Native culture history. Virginia's Indians have endured a difficult history since 1607 and have persevered despite efforts to eliminate their existence. Though Native communities in other parts of North America prefer the label "Native American," I use the term "Indian" in this study out of respect for the preferences and current practice of Virginia's Indians.

Finally, I owe much to my family. John and Catherine Gallivan offered encouragement and support through years of courses, fieldwork, teaching, and writing. My sisters, Maryann and Sara, have prevented me from either taking myself too seriously or doubting myself when I have stumbled. Most of all, my wife Ramona Sein's dogged confidence in my abilities has proven to be integral to any successes that I achieve. Mona has clarified my thinking on topics ranging from the dynamics of prehistoric political economies to the construction of an outdoor field shower. She has never hesitated to advise when I needed advice or to coax me forward when I needed cajoling—for both I am grateful.

James River Chiefdoms

Chapter 1

Understanding the Native Worlds
of the Chesapeake

Late-sixteenth and early-seventeenth-century encounters between European colonists and Native societies in the Chesapeake region constitute events at the historical roots of the modern world. In the cultural strategies and historical tactics that surrounded the colonial outposts of an expanding Europe we see the origins of a modern world ordered by capitalist ventures, globalized institutions, and creolized identities. Despite centuries of scholarship aimed at explaining these early contacts, the perceptions, motives, and strategies of most American Indian participants remain opaque.

One unresolved issue related to these encounters involves rather striking inconsistencies between archaeological evidence and written descriptions related to the Native societies met by settlers of the first permanent English colony in the New World at Jamestown. Ethnohistorical interpretations of the Powhatans and Monacans often diverge in important ways from conceptions of these societies drawn from the region's archaeological record. Where the Powhatan chiefdom of early-seventeenth-century colonial accounts was a society organized in terms of centralized decision making, hierarchical political organization, and social inequality, the archaeological record of the late precolonial and early colonial eras conspicuously lacks the typical hallmarks of such multicommunity polities. Unlike portions of the adjacent Southeast and North American interior, no clear site-size hierarchies appear in regional surveys, burials generally lacked wealth items or exclusionary ritual distinctions, and no truly monumental architecture marked the landscape. Similarly, recent archaeological research concerning the Monacans of the Virginia Piedmont and culturally related groups immediately west of the Blue Ridge Mountains has found little to match Jamestown colonists' descriptions of Monacan kings' houses, chiefs' villages, and tribute relations.

How did the Powhatans and the Monacans conceive of and organize their worlds, particularly the inequality and solidarity, the authority and submission, the self-aggrandizement and defiance so eloquently witnessed by English colonists? In seeking answers to this question, one must confront the distinct cultural and historical character of late precolonial Virginia. This study strives to do so by developing a set of interpretive strategies concerning the organization of Native households, communities, and regional polities and applying these to excavation data and ethnohistorical accounts centered in Virginia's James River Valley. My intention is to shift the focus of research concerning the origin and development of complex polities in the Chesapeake region toward evidence of the regularized, daily practices of the residential setting. Such a focus may produce a better understanding of Native political relations that incorporated a paradoxical blend of individual aggrandizers and institutions of corporate authority.

Analysis of the household, community, and regional scales allows an interpretation of late precontact cultural developments central to the political hierarchy and social inequality of the colonial encounter. The focus on the archaeology of settlement organization adopted for this study provides a frame of reference for understanding culture change that is rooted in relations of production and social reproduction. In an effort to synthesize materialistic and ideational approaches to the study of social change, I seek to combine an archaeology of economic transformation with a study of long-term social dynamics (cf. Weber 1993, 1996). During the fifteen centuries leading up to colonial contact, Native societies in the Chesapeake altered practices related to subsistence and settlement and, in the process, transformed the organization of production and social reproduction. By exploring the means through which political strategies drew from these developments in the villages of the James River Valley, I strive to place the social actor at the center of culture change. The social arrangements described by Jamestown colonists were created by human agents who originated, reproduced, and transformed cultural structures through practices that shaped the archaeological record of residential settlements. With a fluency in cultural structures and the situational tactics to improvise upon these structures, an individual's practices may conform to prescribed patterns or may transform them (Bourdieu 1977; Giddens 1979). Meaning arises as a consequence of such historically situated activity and not as an abstract code apart from practice (Mintz 1985:14), such that culture may be conceived of "not simply a product but also a production, not simply as socially constituted but socially constituting" (Roseberry 1982:1026).

I will argue that the apparent disjunction between ethnohistorically and archaeologically derived conceptions of Virginia's Indians largely disappears in the context of evidence recording a wholesale reorganization of Native social practices between A.D. 1200 and 1500. During these centuries, Native communities throughout the James River Valley improvised upon traditional cultural patterns by establishing villages with settlement populations and residential permanence that greatly transcended the size and sedentariness of the smaller hamlets that previously lined the region's principal rivers. Detailed archaeological analysis of residential communities indicates that with the establishment of larger, more permanent villages, individuals throughout the river basin initiated changes in their daily routines that resulted in the reorganization of social relations at several scales. The social dynamics spawned by these developments produced a political economy containing funds of power largely absent from preceding eras. During the subsequent colonial encounter, *weroances* of the coastal region tapped these funds to enhance their social mediacy. These *weroances* implemented strategies that accorded with culturally sanctioned practices even while subverting the collective symbols dominant during the preceding centuries of the late precontact Chesapeake. Nonetheless, a close reading of the colonial accounts hints at the importance of Native tactics that averted the expanding hegemony of powerful *weroances* during the Contact era (cf. Certeau 1988).

The long-term precontact archaeology of the Middle Atlantic region hints at an oscillating pattern whereby the intensity of prestige-good exchange, large-scale feasting, and elite mortuary ceremony rose and fell in periodic cycles (Hantman and Gold 2000). During the Woodland period (1000 B.C.– A.D. 1500), exchange and communal ritual in the Middle Atlantic focused on a shifting set of symbols and resources that produced sporadic cycles of ranking and collapse. Yet with the establishment of substantial villages after A.D. 1200, Virginia Indians crossed a historical and cultural threshold beyond which social inequality assumed an institutionalized role in daily interaction. With this development, cycles of political centralization produced powerful, though unstable, polities that eventually included the multitiered Powhatan paramountcy, a chiefdom that has become a part of American folklore and an important archetype of hierarchical society in North America.

The culture history of the Powhatans, Monacans, and other complex Native American societies encountered by English colonists in the Chesapeake cannot be explained solely as the result of long-term cultural evolution (cf. Binford 1964) or the upheavals generated by a "tribal zone" surrounding colonial contact (cf. Ferguson and Whitehead 1992). Nor were the political dynamics of the fifteenth- and sixteenth-century Chesapeake region exclusively the peripheral developments of a world system defined by European centers of political and economic power (cf. Wallerstein 1974). Rather, the Powhatan and Monacan societies of the colonial encounter appear to be the product of social dynamics generated by the late precontact establishment of village communities placed in a transformative historical conjuncture of the early colonial era (cf. Sahlins 1985).

The Late Precontact and Early Colonial James River Valley

In order to frame these developments in a regional context, I examined archaeological evidence from the James's headwaters near the Appalachian Plateau to its mouth 340 miles (550 kilometers) to the east in the lower Chesapeake Bay (figure 1-1). The selection of a river valley as a study area breaks with the conventional use of physiographic provinces and state boundaries to define units of archaeological analysis. My analysis of James River archaeology crosses what was traditionally three different study areas: the Virginia Coastal Plain, populated by Algonquin Indians and dominated by the Powhatan chiefdom during the early seventeenth century; the Virginia Piedmont, inhabited by the Monacans during the colonial era; and the Ridge and Valley province, most likely occupied by a range of Native American societies, including Siouan-speakers culturally affiliated with the Monacans.

The James River Valley represents the geographic area for this study due to the importance of river drainages in directing social interaction and indications that technological and stylistic innovations crossed physiographic boundaries as often as they were impeded by them. Beginning with the Late Archaic period (3000–1000 B.C.), a shift in the spatial focus of settlement patterns toward the floodplains of major rivers resulted in the creation of a riverine social landscape throughout much of the Eastern Woodlands (Mouer 1990). Waterways began to channel social interaction within the Chesapeake region. Physiographic provinces bounded a shifting set of material culture at different points during prehistory, yet the sharing of stylistic innovations (e.g., ceramic decorative motifs) and cultural practices (e.g., mass interment of human remains) across physiographic provinces demonstrates that even when social boundaries appeared in the Chesapeake, they were quite porous. By the colonial era interaction between the Coastal Plain Powhatans and the Monacans of the interior played a formative role in early colonial political dynamics. Immediately prior to the colonial era, Monacans served in an intermediary role in the elite exchange networks that drove the political economy (Hantman 1990, 1993). Thus the use of a river basin as an analytical universe avoids the assumption that physiographic provinces bounded cultural units and allows me to address questions concerning social relationships organized along a nested series of spatial scales, from household to community to region.

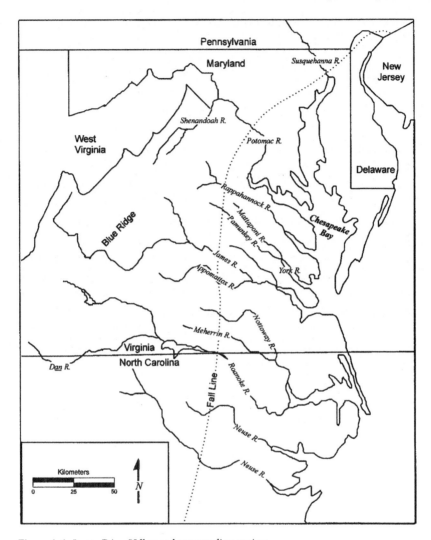

Figure 1-1. James River Valley and surrounding region

The archaeological data from the James River Valley considered in this study result from archaeological excavations conducted over the past 30 years by the members of the volunteer Archaeological Society of Virginia, by university-based researchers, and by private firms working within a cultural resource management context. The systematic archaeological research conducted as part of the cultural resource management process during the final decades of the twentieth century has provided the breadth and depth of information critical to understanding culture change in the late precontact Chesapeake. The large-scale excavation of many of these sites, the accumulated results of multiple radiocarbon assays, and the development of a powerful means of dating archaeological assemblages based on ceramic attributes (Klein 1994) together allow comparative analysis of the internal organization of residential settlement in the region for the first time.

The Internal Organization of Residential Settlements

A central aim of this study is to identify and interpret the changing composition of residential settlements of the late precontact and early colonial Chesapeake. Researchers have accumulated an understanding of long-term regional settlement patterns through systematic surveys (e.g., Turner 1976; Potter 1982; Hantman 1985; Custer 1980). Analyses of ceramic design have allowed for more precise temporal control over culture histories (e.g., Klein 1994; Egloff and Potter 1982). Studies of late precontact mortuary archaeology have examined the spatial and temporal distribution of mass interments (e.g., MacCord 1986; Boyd and Boyd 1992; Curry 1999), the sacred and political implications of these burials (e.g., Dunham 1994; Jirikowic 1990; Hantman 1990), and the biological information gleaned from mortuary contexts (e.g., Gold 1998; Trimble 1996; Chase 1988). A critical area of research left largely unaddressed concerns the internal organization of residential settlements located along river floodplains and their adjacent bluffs. It is in this context that pivotal social relationships were negotiated, manipulated, and transformed. By writing of this context, Europeans ranging from Spanish missionaries to English colonists offer us insights into critical elements of Powhatan and, to a more limited extent, Monacan social relations during the colonial encounter. This evidence, combined with the archaeological record of changes in the routinized practices of late prehistory, allows us to conceive of the village dwellers of the James as agents who selected from a range of strategies and tactics to shape their own culture history.

In an effort to link the James River Valley's archaeological record to the practices of residential communities, I have made archaeological features the fundamental units of analysis in this study. Although hardly elegant, pit features provide the primary sealed contexts of Native American social life in the Eastern Woodlands. Pits reflect the construction, use, and modification of settlement infrastructure and material culture more directly than any other context in the archaeological record. I have gathered information concerning more than 600 late precontact and early colonial pit features in order to classify and compare their contents, spatial contexts, and morphological characteristics. Evidence of domestic architecture in the form of approximately 150 postmold patterns complements these data by providing an entrée into the practices of the domestic group. In applying the "household cluster" concept (Winter 1976) from Mesoamerican archaeology to the architectural and pit feature data collected for this study, I will consider these features in terms of the changing practices of the domestic sphere. The James River Valley's data set of architectural and pit features allows empirical assessment of a diverse range of issues, most immediately those relating to settlement population and residential permanence. Developing methods for more precise characterization of these two variables, both of which are fundamental to precontact social change, serves as the initial task of this study.

The Social Dynamics and Political Strategies of Middle Range Societies
The late precontact archaeology and ethnohistory of James River Valley societies raise issues fundamental to contemporary anthropological archaeology, particularly those concerning the organization and transformation of middle range societies (Feinman and Neitzel 1984). Middle range societies may be classified as intermediate in scale and complexity between the mobile hunter-gatherer bands that dominated all but the last 10,000 years of human history and state societies that permeate the modern world. As in the James River Valley, archaeological contexts worldwide reflect the cultural transformations of middle range societies following the adoption of food production. These societies settled down, populations rose rapidly, and new technologies appeared. In many of these contexts, a reorganization of social relations accompanied these changes through which social heterogeneity, inequality, and hierarchy eclipsed the structuring principles of kinship and of egalitarianism.

Archaeologists have come to recognize that models of cultural evolution seeking to explain these developments that emphasize forces "external" to society have achieved only limited success. Approaches to culture change now generally incorporate transformations "internal" to social and political systems (Preucel and Hodder 1996:205). While the external constraints of the natural environment, climate, and human biology undoubtedly shape culture change, models emphasizing solely these externalities have failed to provide the cross-culturally consistent explanations promised by their advocates. "Internal constraints" (Trigger 1991:557) related to knowledge, beliefs, values, and socially conditioned habits create cultural traditions with an equally influential impact on trajectories of social change. Social dynamics, or the transformative social relationships influenced by these traditions, profoundly shape the historical development of middle range societies (e.g., Plog 1995a:193).

A focus on the social dynamics and internal constraints of middle range societies confers upon humans a more active role in social change. Several innovative studies (e.g., Blanton et al. 1996; Pauketat 2001, 1994; Brumfiel 1992) apply such an approach to the archaeology of social change by focusing on the physical products of political strategies and authority structures. These authors assume that some persons in any social setting will attempt to influence institutions of authority as they pursue socially valuable resources (Blanton et al. 1996:2). Such political strategies have the potential to instigate social change, yet they play against internal and external constraints that limit what political agents may accomplish.

For this study, I draw upon archaeological data concerning the organization of residential sites to identify changes within households and communities and across a river basin. This multiscalar analysis reveals the introduction of a different set of social dynamics during the final precontact centuries following the creation of relatively large and permanent village communities. These new social dynamics provided opportunities for the pursuit of novel political strategies by the end of prehistory. In examining the products of such strategies, I seek evidence for changes in the orientation of the political economy as defined by the production, consumption, and distribution of material and ideal sources of power. Researchers have raised the possibility that abrupt changes in the orientation of the Chesapeake political economy accompanied the late sixteenth and early seventeenth centuries as elites sought to dominate the networks of power produced by the colonial context (e.g., Feest 1978:254; Fausz 1985:235; Axtell 1988:181; Rountree 1989:149–151; Gleach 1997:22). As demonstrated outside the Chesapeake by numerous studies (e.g., Sahlins 1985; Ferguson and Whitehead 1992; Bragdon 1996), culture change may result when radically different cultural structures are put into play by different groups during the events of the colonial encounter. The possibility that Native cultural structures in the Chesapeake were altered in fundamental ways during the colonial encounter may be evaluated against archaeological data reflective of changes in political strategies during late prehistory and the early colonial era.

Organization of the Study

The remainder of this study outlines the cultural and physical landscape of James River communities, details the theoretical and methodological framework for the analysis, and evaluates historical developments in settlement structure, domestic economic practices, community organization, and regional interaction. My interpretation of this evidence relies heavily on quantitative methods, ethnohistorical analysis, and regional comparison. A concluding chapter reevaluates events of early colonial contact in the Chesapeake in light of insights produced by the archaeological analysis of residential settlements.

In chapter 2 I summarize the social setting of the late precontact and early colonial Chesapeake and describe the region's environmental context. Ethnohistorical records offer vivid accounts of social interaction in the Indian "towns" of the Chesapeake region, though they provide only a historically shallow sense of this interaction. As noted by others (e.g., Kupperman 2000), these accounts often mirror Englishmen's conceptions of themselves as much as they reveal Native cultural patterns. For the precolonial era, archaeologists' use of survey data to address the emergence of complex societies in the Chesapeake has produced a solid understanding of trends in regional settlement patterns and environmental variation. However, researchers' emphasis on cultural ecology and functional explanations of these patterns has left important questions concerning the origin and development of complex societies largely unaddressed.

In chapter 3 I describe the theoretical and methodological approaches followed in this study. I present a model of social change within middle range societies drawn from Chesapeake ethnohistory and from studies of other Native North American contexts. The model emphasizes social transformations and novel political strategies that followed the establishment of village communities (cf. Flannery 1972; Plog 1990a; Blanton et al. 1996). Also addressed in this chapter are the methods of data collection, chronology construction, and feature classification used for this study. Appendix 1 provides additional details regarding the sites in the study, including a discussion of chronology construction.

In chapter 4 I evaluate the sedentariness and settlement population of excavated floodplain communities in the James River Valley. Drawing on models of artifact and feature accumulation that results from a lengthy and repeated floodplain presence (e.g., Lightfoot 1984; Varien 1999), I construct a gauge of sedentariness that is applicable to James River sites using the feature and artifact data collected for this study. With a measure of sedentariness in place, settlement size may be estimated through a model of pottery use and discard behavior (cf. Schiffer 1975; Pauketat 1989; Kohler and Blinman 1987; Warrick 1988).

In chapter 5 I analyze archaeological patterning related to the domestic scale. The architecture and pit features of households are compared within a settlement, across the drainage, and through time. Issues concerning domestic control of surplus production are considered through an evaluation of the spatial organization of houses and pit features (particularly storage facilities) (cf. Flannery 1972; Plog 1990a; DeBoer 1988). Variation in the architecture and storage features of the household cluster serves as a means of detecting social differentiation within residential settlements.

In chapter 6 I consider the community organization of Native societies in the James River Valley. To assess the changing spatial structure of residential settlements I examine evidence of settlement nucleation, elite architecture, and the use of communal facilities. As the primary setting upon which Native societies staged the social transformations of the late precontact and early colonial eras, residential settlements offer important insights into social dynamics fundamental to the emergence of complex polities.

In chapter 7 I evaluate regional interaction and social organization at the scale of the river drainage. I analyze the geographic distribution of stylistic elements in ceramics and domestic architecture for evidence of social boundaries within the James River Valley. This evaluation draws on an approach to stylistic variation that considers style as a means of conveying information nonverbally (e.g., Wobst 1977; Conkey 1978; Hantman and Plog 1982; Plog 1990b, 1995b). The regional distribution of fine-grained (i.e., cryptocrystalline) lithic artifacts in the James River interior also allows me to identify changes in exchange patterns tied to alterations in the regional social relations of late prehistory.

In chapter 8 I examine the ways in which Native societies of the colonial Chesapeake drew upon funds of power originally generated by late precontact social transformations. By considering this political action in the context of long-term social changes in the region, we arrive at a new understanding of the motivations and strategies of Native participants in the events of the early colonial era. It becomes apparent that the intercultural contact and the historical events of the colonial era Chesapeake played an important role in the reiteration and modification of Native cultural structures (cf. Sahlins 1985).

Chapter 2

The Natural and Social Landscapes of Tsenacomoco

After departing the Tockwoghs' village on his second effort to reconnoiter the area surrounding Jamestown, John Smith and his men traveled south on the Chesapeake Bay and up the Patuxent and Rappahannock rivers (Smith 1986d:172–177). As they made their way up the Rappahannock, the colonists met several groups of Virginia Algonquins, some of whom feasted the strangers, others of whom sniped at them. Eventually, the English traveled far enough west to encounter a group of Mannahoacs, Piedmont Indians allied with the Monacans during the early colonial era. During hostilities between the English and the Mannahoacs, which lasted 30 minutes, the English wounded and captured a Mannahoac named Amoroleck. Amoroleck reported that he came from Hassinanga, one of four Mannahoac villages on the Rappahannock, each of which was headed by a "king." When the English asked why the Mannahoacs had attacked them, "[h]e answered, they heard we were a people come from under the world, to take their world away from them. We asked how many worlds he did know, he replyed, he knew no more but that which was under the skie that covered him, which were the Powhatans, with the Monacans, and the Massawomecks, that were higher up in the mountaines. Then we asked him what was beyond the mountaines, he answered the Sunne: but of anything els he knew nothing; because the woods were not burnt" (Smith 1986d:175–176).

Amoroleck's brief description of the cultural landscape offers a glimpse of Native categories that ordered conceptions of Tsenacomoco, the Algonquin term for the "densely inhabited land" that was Virginia during the early seventeenth century (Feest 1966:69). Amoroleck conceived of three Native "worlds": the Powhatans', the Piedmont world of the Monacans and Mannahoacs, and the world of the Massawomecks, presumably an Iroquoian group from the northeastern interior. Amoroleck's knowledge of the social and natural landscape faded beyond the mountains Quirank—the Blue Ridge—though he was well aware of the English presence near the coast.

Smith's (1986b) *Map of Virginia* similarly reflects a world of social connections surrounding the Chesapeake Bay. The map comprises a remarkably

accurate rendition of geographic and cultural features stretching from the Atlantic to the Blue Ridge and from the Roanoke Valley to the upper reaches
of the Susquehanna River. As a hybrid of Native knowledge systems and a
colonizer's experience as he moved through the cultural landscape, the map
aims to totalize knowledge about and expectations of a particular space (cf.
Certeau 1988). I will first describe Tsenacomoco's ecological setting before
turning to an outline of the Native social context drawn from a careful reading of Smith's map, other colonial accounts, and the region's archaeological
record.

Environmental Setting

With the world's emergence from the glacial conditions of the Pleistocene
between 15,000 and 10,000 years ago, warmer temperatures and rising sea
levels triggered changes responsible for the physiographic settings of the
Chesapeake region (Carbone 1976; Brush 1986; Dent 1995). Worldwide sea
level rise associated with glacial melting during the Holocene, or recent, geological epoch resulted in the creation of the Chesapeake Bay and its estuarine
system. By 3,500 years ago (1500 B.C.) the region's physiographic and climatological conditions approximated their modern state (Brush 1986:151), with
only limited vegetational changes after this time (Kraft and Brush 1981). The
Chesapeake drainage system comprises the largest estuary in North America,
extending from the Finger Lakes to the Dismal Swamp and from the Eastern
Shore to the Appalachian Plateau.

The Chesapeake region was both rich and diverse in resources useful to
Native American populations, a richness that has substantially declined only in
recent centuries. The near stabilization of water levels in the Chesapeake Bay
and its associated estuaries roughly 3,500 years ago fostered the development
of shellfish beds, wetlands, and anadromous fish runs critical to late precontact subsistence regimes throughout the region (Dent 1995:85). A temperate
climate and generally predictable rainfall produced rich and varied upland
forests. The wide range of floral and faunal resources available to foragers and
hunters as well as soil, temperature, and seasonality factors conducive to agriculture allowed for highly productive subsistence economies throughout the
late precontact era from the James's headwaters adjacent to the Appalachian
Highlands to its mouth at the Chesapeake Bay.

The English referred to the James River (figure 2-1) as the Powhatan
River during Jamestown's early years, a nod to the Mamanatowick's initial
dominance of the river on which the English settled. This dominance appears

to have precluded the possessive renaming of the landscape that accompanied other European colonial efforts (Kupperman 2000), at least in the earliest years of the colony. The Powhatan/James River is a principal tributary of the Chesapeake drainage system and Virginia's longest river at 340 miles (550 kilometers). It drains a basin of over 6 million acres (2.4 million hectares), or approximately a fourth of what is today Virginia. Less than 300 feet (100 meters) wide in the Ridge and Valley, the James widens to 500 feet (150 meters) in the Piedmont and spreads dramatically after passing through the falls, the boundary between the Coastal Plain and the Piedmont. Near its mouth in the lower Chesapeake Bay, the James River ranges up to 5 miles (8 kilometers) wide. The extensive Roanoke River drainage, which empties into Albemarle Sound, borders the James River basin on the south. The James and three large Chesapeake Bay drainages to the north—the York, Rappahannock, and Potomac—are arranged in a fan-shaped system in which the large interfluvial distances of the Piedmont decrease after the rivers pass through the fall line (Mouer 1990:51). At Jamestown, a narrow peninsular expanse of approximately 12 miles (20 kilometers) separates the James from the York River.

Unlike all Virginia rivers save the Roanoke and the Potomac, the James extends through the Ridge and Valley, Blue Ridge, Piedmont, and Coastal Plain physiographic provinces. From its headwaters to the Chesapeake Bay, altitude generally decreases along the James's easterly course. As one moves east, rainfall and average temperature increase modestly (Gardner 1987:53). Historically, forest variation included an oak-chestnut association in the Ridge and Valley and the Blue Ridge, an oak-hickory association in the Piedmont and inner Coastal Plain, and an oak-pine association for the remainder of the Coastal Plain (Braun 1950). An overall diversity and richness of natural resources relevant to American Indian societies is apparent across the river basin, with the Coastal Plain containing productive estuarine areas associated with tidal rivers, while the interior provinces feature greater variation in relief and extensive uplands that are more limited in the Coastal Plain.

At the James's origin in the Ridge and Valley province, north-south–oriented valleys separate ridges that extend from the Hudson Valley to central Alabama. Historically, extensive grasslands that supported elk and bison bordered mast forests that drew large numbers of deer, squirrels, and turkeys. Lithic materials ideal for stone tool production are at their most abundant and varied in the Ridge and Valley portion of the drainage with local access to fine-grained materials, which occur sporadically in the Piedmont and

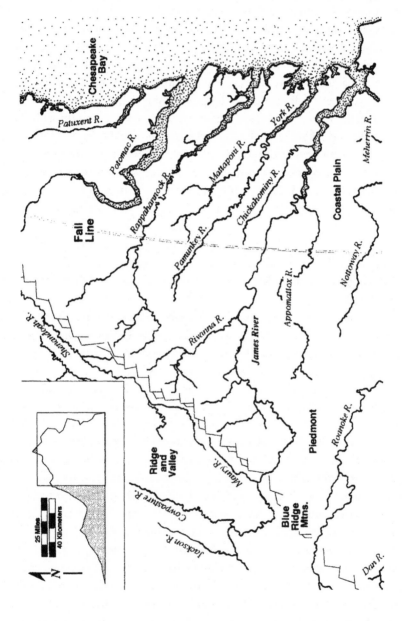

Figure 2-1. James River Valley

are virtually absent from the Coastal Plain. Fine-grained lithics—including jasper, chalcedony, and chert—attracted Native Americans to Ridge and Valley locations throughout prehistory. The James River basin portion of the Ridge and Valley province lies less than 20 miles (30 kilometers) from three river drainages linked prehistorically to diverse cultural traditions. Relatively short portages separate the James from the Shenandoah River, which flows north and east to the Potomac; the Roanoke River, which flows southeast to Albemarle Sound; and the New River, which flows north and west as part of the Ohio River system. The Clinch River, beginning approximately 50 miles (80 kilometers) southwest of the James River basin, linked southwest Virginia to the Tennessee River drainage and (during the late precontact era) to the cultural traditions of the Mississippian world.

East of the Ridge and Valley, the Blue Ridge Mountains held no settlements of any permanence during the late precontact era, although resources there did draw Native Americans who resided in neighboring areas. The Blue Ridge's topographic variation, from 1,000 feet (300 meters) above sea level along the James to over 2,500 feet (750 meters) on nearby ridges, produced a range of forest habitats that supported abundant wildlife. Copper deposits also occur in the Blue Ridge between the Potomac and James rivers. As an embodiment of sacred authority, copper played a fundamental role in elite interaction in the Chesapeake region by late prehistory and during the early colonial era (Potter 1989; Hantman 1990). Soapstone, another material with symbolic resonance for Native Americans (Klein 1997), occurs in the Blue Ridge along with rhyolite, jasper, green stone, quartz, and quartzite, materials useful in stone tool production (Hantman and Klein 1992).

The Piedmont region, bounded by the Blue Ridge and the fall line, consists of rolling surfaces drained by dendritic rivers. The Virginia Piedmont widens progressively to the south, extending 150 miles (240 kilometers) east-west in the central portion of the state. Once cleared, Piedmont floodplain soils provide fertile, easily tilled surfaces well suited to agriculture. Fauna similar to the Blue Ridge's in diversity and richness were present historically in the Piedmont, with deer particularly abundant in interfluvial uplands. Anadromous fish runs reached the Piedmont during the spring, providing substantial quantities of protein in an easily obtained form. Widely available lithic resources suitable for flaked tools are limited to quartz and quartzite. Float chert, cobbles present in river gravels, provides some direct access to cryptocrystalline lithics (Hantman 1987).

To the east within what is today Richmond, a fall line separates the Piedmont from the Coastal Plain. The Atlantic coast's fall line is the point at which east-flowing rivers cross from the hard, igneous and metamorphic rocks of the Piedmont into the softer, unconsolidated sediments of the Coastal Plain. Marked by the sharp fall off of rivers at the fall line, a north-south running zone immediately surrounding the falls played a critical role in late precontact social interaction as a locus of contact between Piedmont Siouan-speaking groups and Algonquin groups of the Coastal Plain. The fall zone may have served as an access window for the capture of anadromous fish (Binford 1983:215), as a game preserve for deer (Turner 1978), or as a political buffer zone between Monacan and Powhatan polities (Mouer n.d.). Ethnohistorical and archaeological evidence reflects the permeable and dynamic nature of the fall line as a social boundary, implying that at different points in time any of these alternatives may correctly characterize the area (Hantman 1993).

To the east, much of Virginia's Coastal Plain is an estuarine environment with diverse flora and fauna. The Chesapeake Bay estuary entails rivers and wetlands with a range of shifting salinity levels that historically supported a remarkable array of fish, shellfish, and wetland plants. Immediately below Jamestown, a fluctuating zone of brackish water divided the saline and fresh portions of the river. Along with intermittent wetland areas, highly productive soils capable of supporting considerable agricultural yields line the Coastal Plain's major rivers. The Chesapeake region's drainage system draws from freshwater marshes in the inner Coastal Plain and the upper reaches of streams. During the late precontact era, great runs of anadromous fish reached these areas in the spring, which provided a critical resource for the Powhatans (Rountree 1989:25). The saltwater and brackish marshes in much of the remainder of eastern Virginia supported oysters, a variety of fish, and migratory birds. The dune forests and beach zones of the eastern edge of the Coastal Plain sustained fewer potential subsistence resources, although shell mound sites along the shore attest to the importance of shellfish from this area in the subsistence regimes of Coastal Plain groups. The particularly productive inner Coastal Plain provided an optimal environmental setting that supported the densest populations of Virginia Indians during the late precontact era. Proximity to flat land, deciduous forest, anadromous fish runs, and freshwater marshes generated year-round abundance accessible to the groups living there (Rountree and Turner 1994:356).

Researchers have argued that the richness, diversity, and spatial/seasonal variability of coastal Virginia fostered the emergence of complex polities (e.g., Binford 1964; Turner 1976; Rountree 1989:29). Complementary subsistence resources clearly played a critical role in the increasing populations of Tsenacomoco. The notion that the uniquely rich and diverse resources of eastern Virginia, particularly those of the inner Coastal Plain (Rountree and Turner 1994:356), led to population pressure and social circumscription that was absent in other areas is less clear. Although lacking the highly productive estuarine environments of the Coastal Plain, the Piedmont, Blue Ridge, and Ridge and Valley provided environmental settings similarly rich and diverse with regard to potential subsistence resources and considerably richer with regard to the lithic and mineral deposits critical to exchange relations (Hantman and Klein 1992). Anadromous fish central to arguments concerning the productivity of the inner Coastal Plain ecology (e.g., Binford 1964) also reached the Piedmont in large numbers. Recent analysis of bioarchaeological evidence has demonstrated that late precontact horticultural economies in the Piedmont and Ridge and Valley included substantial maize production capable of producing considerable surpluses (Gold 1998; Trimble 1996). Additionally, the extensive uplands, vertical zonation, and Blue Ridge access characteristic of the interior portion of the Chesapeake region provided natural resources largely absent from the Coastal Plain.

While the year-to-year climatological variation during the late precontact and early colonial era covered in this study was less dramatic than the environmental changes that created the physiographic setting described above, climatological conditions did continue to fluctuate during the late precontact era. Some researchers see direct links between social change and this environmental fluctuation, most notably with regard to the "Medieval Warm Interval," the "Little Ice Age," and severe droughts of the early historical era. During the Medieval Warm Interval of A.D. 1000–1300, relatively warm and dry conditions prevailed across much of the region. The overlap between this interval with the widespread appearance of maize-based horticulture in the Middle Atlantic region suggests to some that climate change provided an impetus for turning to food production by placing stresses on wild food resources (Potter 1993:143). Explaining the adoption of agriculture during this particular warm and dry interval rather than during others that appear in the Holocene's ecological record demands consideration of socially driven and historical factors. Increasing regional population densities played an important role in this development. The circa A.D. 800–1000 availability of productive cultigens, particularly maize, to Middle Atlantic groups from sources to the west and south also introduced historical conditions critical to the adoption of agriculture.

The subsequent Little Ice Age, when northern hemisphere temperatures averaged 3.5 degrees Fahrenheit below modern conditions (Grove 1990), provides a second example of climatological variation that may have triggered social change in the Chesapeake. This linkage is complicated, though, as climatological experts do not agree on the timing, duration, or severity of the Little Ice Age, and data regarding the extent of climatological change in the Chesapeake region remain equivocal. The Little Ice Age, generally assigned the fourteenth through nineteenth centuries, was not simply a global cold snap. Rather, the episode represents a cooling trend that began at different times in different regions of the world, interrupted by periods of relative warmth. In the Chesapeake region, the extent to which the Little Ice Age impacted cultural developments remains unclear. Nevertheless, several researchers tie cooler temperatures to archaeological evidence of intergroup competition during the final precontact centuries in the Chesapeake region. In one scenario, the cool and dry conditions between A.D. 1350 and 1750 led to lowered agricultural productivity, increased reliance on hunting, and competition and conflict over hinterland hunting territories (Gardner 1986:88–89; cf. Potter 1993:154). Paleoclimatological data from the same geographic region, though, point to modest temperature change and increased effective moisture (Carbone 1976:88).

Lastly, a recent study has demonstrated that the worst droughts of the past 800 years coincided with the failures of the late-sixteenth-century Roanoke Island's "Lost Colony" and the early-seventeenth-century "starving time" at Jamestown (Blanton 2000). Researchers analyzed bald cypress tree rings recovered from southeast Virginia to construct a temperature and precipitation history during the period from A.D. 1185 to 1984 (Stahle et al. 1998). According to Blanton (2000), extreme drought must be considered as one of the factors in the failure of the Roanoke colony and the starvation of the early Jamestown colony. Documentary accounts point to the sensitivity of Tidewater Indians' subsistence system to prolonged periods of low rainfall. Droughts forced Roanoke and Jamestown colonists to depend upon a badly strained Native subsistence economy for provisions, as alluded to in colonial histories. The recent tree-ring research adds a detailed climatological context for the Roanoke Colony's failure and the high mortality rates at Jamestown.

Although the above examples allow us to assign ecological conditions an important role in late precontact and early colonial cultural developments in the Chesapeake, the use of climatological factors to explain cultural developments faces several challenges. Synchronizing environmental changes with cultural developments is difficult in most regions of the world (Plog and Hantman 1990), and uncertainty regarding the precise sequence of environmental and cultural developments remains a problem in the Chesapeake. Studies such as Blanton's (2000) that tie tree-ring evidence of environmental fluctuation to the documentary record of historic events represent an innovative solution to this problem.

In fact, that study demonstrated that year-to-year fluctuations in temperature and rainfall have long characterized the Chesapeake region, fluctuations that required Native Americans to develop social means of alleviating resource shortfalls. The bald cypress tree-ring record that Blanton and colleagues evaluated indicates that substantial annual fluctuation in rainfall has characterized the most recent 800 years in the region. Short-term climatic events, such as the droughts identified by Blanton and his colleagues, become critical in the detailed analysis of historical sequences captured by the documentary record of the late sixteenth and early seventeenth centuries. Spanish Jesuit missionaries' descriptions of Virginia in 1570 as a land "chastened" with famine and death (Lewis and Loomie 1953:89) offer a glimpse of the impact of periodic droughts in the region. While such events may be implicated in long-term culture change, they must be viewed in tandem with evidence from the social environment. As in other regions (e.g., Braun and Plog 1982), technological and social practices related to storage, intergroup alliance, and regional exchange played a role in limiting the impact of unusual climatological conditions, since a considerable degree of temperature and precipitation variance was normal in the region.

Generally, the precontact centuries following the establishment of the Chesapeake estuarine system circa 1500 B.C. entail a period of less radical ecological change than occurred during the preceding 10,000 years. Concurrently, cultural change accelerated. Given this contrast, climatological variation cannot be assigned a singular role in the rearrangement of social life that marked the late precontact era. Environmental conditions placed constraints on communities in the region, as they do today, and climatological events affected historical developments in both subtle and profound ways. These developments, though, ultimately demand explanation in cultural terms.

The Cultural Context
In 1607 roughly 100 Englishmen disembarked 40 miles (64 kilometers) upstream from the James River's mouth to establish the Jamestown Colony. Colonists including John Smith (1986a, 1986b, 1986c, 1986d), William Stra-

chey (1953), George Percy (1998), and Henry Spelman (1998) recorded their impressions of the early colonial encounter, focusing on Indians of the surrounding Coastal Plain. These impressions form the basis of ethnohistorians' interpretations of the people known to the English as the Powhatans (e.g., Mooney 1907; Feest 1966; Rountree 1989; Gleach 1997; Kupperman 2000; Axtell 2000; Rountree and Turner 2002). In the northern Virginia Coastal Plain, Indians speaking Algonquin dialects related to the Powhatans' engaged in a shifting set of relations with the Powhatans and their paramount chief (Potter 1993). The Monacans and Mannahoacs, probable Siouan-speakers referred to collectively as the Monacans in some contexts, resided in the Virginia interior, west of the fall line (Hantman 1990). Fleeting contacts with English colonists and the brief textual references to these encounters confirm that the early-seventeenth-century Monacans lived in settlements lining the Piedmont portion of the James and Rappahannock rivers. Archaeological evidence suggests strong cultural affiliations and close exchange ties between the Monacans and the Indians of the Ridge and Valley, who are not named or described in early colonial records (Hantman 1998; Gardner 1986). To the south of the Powhatans, Iroquoian-speaking Nottoway and Meherrin settlements lined the rivers still named for these groups (Binford 1964). In North Carolina, coastal Algonquin and Iroquoian groups and Piedmont Siouans paralleled the linguistic contrasts that marked Virginia's early historic cultural landscape (Ward and Davis 1999; Merrell 1991).

Before Jamestown
From the accounts of European contacts with Indians of the Virginia Coastal Plain prior to 1607, it is clear that hierarchical political systems preceded the establishment of Jamestown. Intermittent encounters between Europeans and Virginia Indians occurred throughout the sixteenth century, with contact after 1586 generally ending up violently. In 1561 Spanish colonists captured the son of an Algonquin chief near the mouth of the James (Lewis and Loomie 1953; Gradie 1993:165), a man they christened Don Luis. As I will discuss in the final chapter, Don Luis represented the first of several culture brokers in coastal Virginia who influenced Native groups' strategies in the face of the colonial encounter (cf. Fausz 1985:239). By the 1580s English colonists on the North Carolina Outer Banks heard of a wealthy and powerful king on the James River, most likely Powhatan, who "would be loathe to suffer any strangers to enter his Countrey, and [who] was able to make a great many of men into the fielde, which . . . would fight very well" (Lane 1955:60–61). In

the North Carolina Coastal Plain surrounding the Roanoke colony, *weroances* led affiliated Algonquin villages by the 1580s.

Equivocal evidence of the impact of European-introduced diseases prior to Jamestown's settlement may be drawn from Powhatan's opaque remark that he had "seene the death of all [his] people thrice" (Smith 1986c:247). Documentary accounts do indicate that epidemics ravaged the North Carolina Algonquins in contact with the Roanoke colonists during the 1580s (Hariot 1972:28). By 1617, following a period of intensive contact between Jamestown colonists and Powhatans, a "great mortality" gripped the Powhatans (Strachey 1953:46), caused by an epidemic of probable European origin. Archaeological evidence of earlier epidemics has not been identified. In the North Carolina Piedmont, probably the best-understood Contact era archaeological context in the Middle Atlantic, evidence of depopulation triggered by European diseases does not occur until the latter half of the seventeenth century (Ward and Davis 1991). Ward and Davis (1991) found no indications of "virgin soil" pandemics preceding direct face-to-face encounters between Europeans and Indians that some researchers hypothesize (e.g., Dobyns 1983; Ramenofsky 1987; Smith 1987; Barker 1992), although evidence of deadly diseases does occur with subsequent, intensive European-Indian contact. The recent research indicating that drought had a devastating impact on Native societies of the Chesapeake region during the late sixteenth and early seventeenth centuries (Blanton 2000) provides what may be a more parsimonious explanation for Powhatan's reference to waves of death.

Powhatan Society

The English referred to the Virginia Algonquins surrounding their Jamestown settlement as the Powhatans, applying the commonly used name of the Virginia Algonquins' paramount chief. Although most researchers have followed this practice (cf. Feest 1978), the Powhatans were an evanescent social entity and a complex polity lasting less than a century and just beyond the life of its charismatic founder. Like other Native societies on the edge of the colonial endeavor (e.g., Merrell 1991), the Powhatans of ethnohistorical accounts represented a "new world" of social possibilities during the Protohistoric and early colonial eras rather than a society whose cultural practices had withered from a more vibrant precolonial past. It is easy to forget the extent to which Native societies exerted control over the field of intersocietal interaction during the early years of the struggling English colonies in Roanoke, Jamestown, and New England (Kupperman 2000). In many ways the early years of the colonial encounter in the Chesapeake represent the ultimately doomed efforts of Native societies and English people to civilize one another (Gleach 1997).

Archaeological evidence of an identifiably Algonquin presence in the Virginia Coastal Plain extends to as early as A.D. 200 (Potter 1993), and the descendants of the constituent tribes of the Powhatan chiefdom continue to reside in eastern Virginia and play a prominent role in contemporary cultural and political life (Rountree 1990; Moretti-Langholtz 1998). Reconstructions of early colonial Powhatan population from colonial references indicate that approximately 13,000 Powhatans resided in 6,500 square miles (16,800 square kilometers) of the Virginia Coastal Plain (Turner 1976, 1978). The Powhatans' settlement pattern included substantial "towns" lining the major rivers of Virginia populated during the warm-weather months and smaller, less permanent settlements away from the riverine environment occupied during hunting forays after the agricultural cycle. Within Powhatan settlements social distinctions led the English colonists to differentiate between the "better sort" and common folk (Smith 1986b:160–161). A mixed horticultural-foraging-fishing-hunting economy permitted the Powhatans to produce enough surpluses in the early years of Jamestown to support the colony with large quantities of maize. Powhatan economic relations hinged on the complementary production of engendered labor (male hunting and female foraging and horticulture) that came together in the household, the fundamental unit of production. Based on colonial descriptions of chiefly succession, the Powhatans appear to have reckoned descent through the matriline.

Powhatan Authority

In 1607 the man referred to as Powhatan was the Mamanatowick. At that time Powhatan dominated or influenced Coastal Plain groups from the James River basin to the Potomac's southern shores and from the fall line to the Eastern Shore. Powhatan's "empire," as the English referred to it, began with inherited authority over six groups residing near his natal village, also named Powhatan, located in the inner Coastal Plain near the James River fall line. By the early seventeenth century Powhatan had extended his authority from a core area along the inner Coastal Plain of the James and York rivers to more than 30 named groups in the Virginia Coastal Plain through military action or its threat. A *weroance* held authority within each "district" or petty chiefdom of the Powhatan paramountcy, and the principal towns within districts each had their own lesser *weroance*. Generally glossed as "chief," John Smith suggests that the name *weroance* more accurately implied a military commander (Smith 1986b:174). This status helps contextualize the tenor of Powhatan political dynamics circa 1607, defined as they were by a fluid tangle of alliances, military threats, and intermittent hostilities.

Although some controversy formerly attached itself to the appropriate label for the Powhatan polity, most researchers accept Binford's (1964) use of the term "chiefdom." Given the ethnohistorical indications of a three-tiered political hierarchy, the Powhatans appear to have been an almost archetypal complex, or paramount, chiefdom (Earle 1978; Wright 1984). As envisaged in Smith's (1986b) *Map of Virginia*, the Powhatan political landscape consisted of "Kings' Howses," where *weroances* resided, and "Ordinary Howses," which lined the rivers of the Virginia Coastal Plain. Tribute, recorded by Strachey (1953:87) as comprising 80 percent of all production, flowed from commoners to *weroances* and from *weroances* to the Mamanatowick. This proportion appears to reflect more closely Strachey's rhetorical excesses, and possibly those of Powhatan himself, regarding the harshness of the Powhatan regime rather than any actual tribute payments. English notions of tribute and exchange never fully grasped the social context of the Powhatan gift economy, resulting in intersocietal misconceptions that frequently ended in hostilities (Mallios 1998). *Weroances* dominated prestige-good exchange networks through which these materials moved and which provided the material expression of chiefly social status. In mortuary rituals reserved exclusively for *weroances*, the Powhatans interred remains with prestige goods such as copper or shell beads in temples constructed for this practice (Smith 1986b:169).

The authority of chiefly leaders in the Powhatan polity and of paramount chief Powhatan's power appears to have been multifaceted. Strachey (1953: 60–61) emphasized the Mamanatowick's power to coerce: "It is strange to see with what great fear and adoration all these people do obey this Powhatan, for at his feet they present whatsoever he commands, and at the least frown of his brow, the greatest will tremble; that may be because he is very terrible, and inexorable in punishing such as offend him." Historical events indicating that some Virginia Algonquins resisted, or at least avoided, Powhatan's demands and that others pursued agendas at odds with the Mamanatowick's cast doubt on Strachey's hegemonic characterization, leading some researchers to read the authority of Chief Powhatan and Algonquin *weroances* as "incomplete" (Rountree 1993). Indeed, the individual Powhatan's authority appears in the historical record to be far-reaching but rooted in cultural categories that linked power to the ability to act rightly (i.e., morally) (Gleach 1997:37). In Gleach's innovative structural analysis of Powhatan categories of power, politics, and privilege, the authority of Powhatan and the *weroances* of the Chesapeake region ultimately flowed from their connections to the sacred, a connection that manifested itself in culturally appropriate behavior. At the time of the colonial encounter, Powhatan possessed an overwhelming authority due to its basis in the sacred realm and in its inherited status. Powhatan drew spiritual power from a shamanic status as the "one who dreams," while his inherited political status as a *weroance* gave him authority over districts in the core region of his chiefdom (Gleach 1997:32).

Leadership among the Virginia Algonquins differed somewhat from the authority of European rulers, not only in paralleling a cosmology in which the sacred and the political formed a seamless realm. Authority structures among the Powhatan also reflected a social order in which communities shared decision making collectively. Coastal *weroances* and, indeed, Powhatan himself ruled only after consulting and receiving the consent of councils comprised of men who had undergone the *huskanaw* rite of passage, a term translated as "he has a new body" (Gerard 1907). The Powhatans considered such men to be *quioccosuks*, who embodied a divine status (Smith 1986d:125). Powhatan reportedly had a hunting house or a "court" where councilors and priests met with the Mamanatowick and advised him, and "when they intend any wars, the *weroances* usually advise with their priests or conjurers, their allies and best trusted councilors and friends" (Strachey 1953:104).

Priests, men in possession of considerable spiritual power, tended temples outside of villages and thus existed on the periphery of the Powhatan social order. Colonial accounts suggest that *weroances* mediated between priests and commoners in Powhatan society (Williamson 1979). Priests lived outside of villages, tending the bodies of dead ancestors in temples, which only priests and *weroances* could enter. Though associated closely with *weroances*, Powhatan priests dominated an alternative field of sacred authority. Conceptually, *weroances* appear to have shared characteristics of priests, who were socially dead to the Powhatans, and commoners, who participated in life-giving pursuits (Williamson 1979:404–405). It is their mediation between the structural categories of Powhatan society that may have allowed these men to appear, somewhat misleadingly, as "kings" to the English colonists. Their mediation involved a culturally sanctioned role that required the establishment of social relationships that ranged beyond the village context, an often dangerous realm from which the Tassantasses originated.

The Powhatans shared political authority in other ways as well. Several references in the colonial record indicate that the Powhatans had a political system comprised of dual chiefs: an external chief who presided in matters of war and a more powerful internal or peace chief (Gallivan and Hantman 1996; Gleach 1997:35; Kupperman 2000:102). Though in many ways Powhatan acted as the internal chief of the Powhatans while his aggressive brother, Opechancanough, served as war chief, Powhatan at times dominated both authority structures. By placing himself as an intermediary between the English colonists and Powhatan communities, the Mamanatowick mediated the colonial divide just as he mediated structural divisions between priests and commoners within Powhatan society. Such mediation depended in part on the unique historical circumstances of the sixteenth-century Protohistoric period during which Powhatan arose as a political power and the subsequent colonial era when his strategic ties to the English enhanced his status.

Solidarity and Factionalism in the Coastal Plain

A careful reading of the colonial ethnohistory indicates that a blend of solidarity and factionalism was central to the political dynamics of the early-seventeenth-century Coastal Plain. When Captain Christopher Newport first headed up the James to explore the river on which the English had settled, he and his men made it as far as the falls, visiting Powatah, *weroance* of Powhatan village and son of the Mamanatowick. Gabriel Archer (1998a:106–107), one of Newport's men, reported that "in discoursing with him we found that all kingdoms from the Chessipians were friends with him, and to use his own word, *cheisc*, which is 'all one with him' or 'under him.'. . . Hereupon he very well understood by the words and signs we made the signification of our meaning moved of his own accord a league of friendship with us, which our captain kindly embraced." Later Powhatan himself sought to establish relations of alliance with the English, pleading with Smith to put aside his weapons since the English and Indians were all "friends and forever Powhatans" (Smith 1986d:195). Among the Powhatans, the *huskanaw* ritual fostered relations of solidarity that brought young men from the Coastal Plain together for a yearly rite of passage that joined residents from many villages (Strachey 1953:98).

Despite such institutions and the Mamanatowick's efforts to exercise a unifying authority, the Virginia Coastal Plain of the early colonial era was, in fact, a social landscape fraught with divisive factionalism. Numerous Virginia Algonquins disobeyed Powhatan's dictums with regard to interaction with colonists and rarely reflected the sense of solidarity as Powhatans that Chief Powhatan sought to foment. In the heart of Powhatan's domain, the Chickahominies continued to remain an independent group led by a council rather than a *weroance*. As noted earlier, the English frequently encountered the political maneuvers of *weroances* who sought to leverage ties to the Tassantasses for their own ends. The English eventually complained to Powhatan about attacks from his fractious "subjects" that ran counter to Powhatan's professed "love" of the colonists: "upon our complaint to him it is laid upon some of his worst and unruly people, of which he tells us that even King James (commanding so many divers men) must have some irregular and unruly people; or ells upon some petty *weroances*, whome peradventure [i.e., perhaps] we have attempted [i.e., tempted] (saith he) with offenses of the like nature, then that is any act of his, or done by his command, or according to his will" (Strachey 1953:58). Though Powhatan hinted at his suspicions that the English provoked the ire of "his people," he also laid the blame for the hostilities in the hands of insubordinate *weroances* acting on their own. Strachey questioned Powhatan's veracity here, though other events suggest Powhatan was likely telling the truth. The repeated efforts of *weroances* to co-opt the English into exchange relations that circumvented the Mamanatowick speaks to the competitive nature of the political economy during John Smith's two voyages around the Bay and its tributaries. Several years later, when Powhatan's younger brother, Opechancanough, planned his first coordinated attack on the colonists in 1621, he reportedly sought poison to use against the English from a *weroance* on the Eastern Shore but was refused (Gleach 1997:146). Even the most powerful figure in Powhatan society was incapable of quelling the divisive Native political dynamics of the early seventeenth century.

The Powhatans as a Complex Chiefdom

Given the concurrence of the Powhatan paramountcy's emergence during the late sixteenth century and the acceleration of hostile Algonquin-European encounters, ethnohistorians understandably assign culture contact an important role in the emergence of political complexity among Virginia Indians (e.g., Gleach 1997:22; Fausz 1985:235; Feest 1966, 1978:254; Axtell 1988:181; Kupperman 2000:36–37). Historians and ethnohistorians generally place sporadic European contacts alongside internal factors as critical in the consolidation of political authority and the emergence of political hierarchies in Virginia. Lacking written or archaeological evidence of this process, some researchers have suggested that trade monopolies among Virginia Algonquins interacting with Piedmont groups resulted in wealth accumulation and social inequality (e.g., Feest 1966:78–79; cf. Potter 1993). Under this scenario, intergroup hostilities encouraged military alliances and the development of a socially integrative ritual conducive to the formation of ethnic confederacies. One researcher has proposed that European-introduced epidemics of the sixteenth century caused a rapid depopulation of coastal Virginia and that this depopulation triggered the formation of the Powhatan paramountcy (Barker 1992). With curtailed tribute available for exploitation from a smaller population, Algonquin chiefs, including Powhatan, expanded their domains militarily to establish control over communities that could supply additional tribute payments. How a chiefly political economy first emerged is left unaddressed in this scenario, and archaeological evidence provides no support for the proposed demographic sequence. The consensus view among ethnohistorians involves multiple causes for the emergence of the Powhatan paramountcy, with the hostile threat posed first by the Monacans and later by Europeans playing leading roles (e.g., Rountree 1989:149–151).

Generally, then, the Powhatan Indians of the early-seventeenth-century Virginia coastal region comprised a complex chiefdom marked by social stratification, political hierarchy, and a political economy dominated by elites. When the English established Jamestown in 1607 they settled amid what researchers have characterized as one of the most complex polities in North America (e.g., Potter 1993:1; Feinman and Neitzel 1984). However, Powhatan social organization remains enigmatic given the shallow temporal depth of its chiefly political system and ambiguity regarding the role of European contacts in the consolidation of the Mamanatowick's position. Colonial accounts suggest that political dynamics included Powhatan's efforts to establish a hegemonic solidarity while *weroances* pursued political strategies independent of the Mamanatowick's. In the process, *weroances* placed themselves at the center of networks of power, networks that ensnared the English colonists. Concurrently, collective events, including the *huskanaw* and council sessions, reflected institutions through which the Powhatans shared power and decision making across the society.

Late Precontact Coastal Plain Archaeology

From the rather equivocal sense of Native American life in the early colonial Coastal Plain left by the documentary record, archaeologists have drawn concepts for interpreting the late precontact archaeological record. Unlike most ethnohistorians, archaeologists' interpretations of the sociopolitical developments among coastal Virginia Indians generally invoke a long-term process whereby acceleration of population growth and the intensification of subsistence production spurred the formation of complex polities. Much of this research draws upon a combination of regional settlement pattern studies and ethnohistorical analysis, quite different sources of historical knowledge whose linkage poses epistemological challenges.

Regional archaeological survey in several areas suggests to archaeologists that the Chesapeake's chiefly societies emerged out of a social transition whereby Middle Woodland (500 B.C.–A.D. 900) "harvesters of the Chesapeake" became Late Woodland (A.D. 900–1500) village agriculturalists (Potter 1993:139; Binford 1964; Turner 1976; Dent 1995). Prior to this transformation, a focus on estuarine resources and intensive settlement along major waterways in the Coastal Plain began during the Late Archaic (3000–1000 B.C.) and Early Woodland (1000–500 B.C.) periods throughout the Atlantic coast region, likely driven by a subsistence emphasis on shellfish and anadromous fish. Paralleling this trend, an Early Woodland shift to lowland, estuarine areas is apparent in regional settlement patterns (e.g., Steponaitis 1987). Detailed analysis of shell midden formation has produced similar evidence of increasing exploitation of oysters during the Late Archaic and Early Woodland periods in the Potomac River basin (Waselkov 1982:207). Archaeological evidence of intensive shellfish exploitation is contemporaneous with a stabilization of the Chesapeake region's shorelines, making it difficult to separate the possible cultural transition from natural processes that heighten the visibility of post–Middle Archaic shoreline sites and submerged or destroyed earlier ones (Klein and Klatka 1991:165). Regardless of the timing of its commencement, extensive use of estuarine environments was in place in the Virginia Coastal Plain by the later centuries of the Middle Woodland period.

Survey data from the south shore of the Potomac River record late precontact settlement patterns that oscillated between population concentration and dispersal through the late precontact era (Potter 1993). During the early Late Woodland centuries, large sites disappeared as newly agricultural populations dispersed in intermediate-sized settlements along the floodplains and neck lands of the Coan River. For the period between A.D. 1300 and 1500, a settlement pattern matching that described in colonial accounts emerged, with a large and internally dispersed village along the Coan River. The villages of the terminal Late Woodland contained a diversity and abundance of artifacts in the context of midden deposits, suggesting settlements occupied for a substantial portion of the year and favored locations that drew populations for multiple reoccupations. The survey data also suggest that population growth accelerated with the establishment of relatively sedentary communities during the final precontact centuries.

Interpretations of such regional settlement patterns generally envision the development of complex polities from the interplay between high population densities, social circumscription, hostilities across the fall line, and control of important resources and communication arteries by inner Coastal Plain groups (Potter 1993:168; Binford 1964; Turner 1976). This control may indeed have conveyed a selective advantage upon groups like the Powhatans on the James and the Patawomekes on the Potomac in the sixteenth century's competitive social climate. Some researchers have suggested that chiefdom polities ultimately arose as a solution to social and ecological problems posed by the sixteenth-century cultural landscape in the Chesapeake (e.g., Potter 1993:149). In the Potomac River Valley, the palisaded Potomac Creek (44ST2) and Accokeek Creek (18PR8) sites appear as fortified settlements of Piedmont emigrants in a hostile inner Coastal Plain (Potter 1993:120–121; Blanton 1999). The lack of subsurface storage at these locations raises the possibility that chiefs were present who controlled surplus maize production in aboveground cribs (Potter 1993:120–121). In some Eastern Woodlands settings, the appearance of a political economy in which chiefs dominated household production resulted in the absence of subsurface storage pits (DeBoer 1988; Ward 1985).

The inner Coastal Plain may indeed represent the primary ecological setting for chiefdom emergence in the Chesapeake with its evidence of dense population concentrations amid the overall demographic increases of the late precontact Coastal Plain (Turner 1976:68, 205). Due to the high agricultural productivity of floodplain soils and the increased numbers of Late Woodland settlements adjacent to rivers, competition for fertile land may have induced warfare, as indicated by the presence of fortified floodplain sites in the final centuries of the Late Woodland period. The demographically large inner Coastal Plain groups who controlled Piedmont/Coastal Plain exchange appear to have prevailed in this hostile context, which spurred the formation of complex societies (Turner 1976:267). The increasingly limited spatial distribution of Late Woodland ceramic wares compared to Middle Woodland patterns likely paralleled increased territoriality critical to the late precontact emergence of regionally distinct Native polities (Turner 1993).

Recent excavations have produced information regarding Coastal Plain burial practices that complement this settlement pattern research. However, where ethnohistorical accounts clearly distinguish between ritual practices associated with the burials of Powhatan commoners and chiefs, Coastal Plain mortuary archaeology generally does not record the clear expression of social differentiation until the Contact period. Ossuary burial, which often comprises the final stage of a complex, two-stage ritual process, forms the most common mortuary practice of the Late Woodland (Boyd and Boyd 1992:261–263; Curry 1999; Jirikowic 1990). While colonial accounts mention both primary interments and secondary burial ritual, it is not entirely clear whether either practice conferred a higher status. Disarticulated bone bundles, articulated burials, and cremated remains have all been identified in Coastal Plain ossuaries, which usually date to the final Late Woodland centuries and the early colonial era. Individuals from all age groups and both sexes appear within ossuaries, providing no evidence of the exclusion of social categories from this institution. Protohistoric and Contact era sites contain a greater diversity of burial forms, including primary interments and ossuaries, a development that may signal heightened social differentiation.

Grave goods rarely accompany precontact ossuary burial, though the Contact era Paspahegh site (44JC308) located near Jamestown did include ossuary burials associated with European-produced copper artifacts (Lucketti et al. 1994:164). Amateur archaeologists uncovered a clearly high-status burial containing copper and shell grave goods in the Potomac drainage, again dating to the early colonial era (Potter 1989). The increased occurrence of copper in ossuary burial on the Potomac Neck after A.D. 1630 may signal widespread access to this symbolically potent material and the end of chiefs' monopolization of prestige-goods trade (Potter 1989). Early colonial accounts emphasize the placement of shell beads and copper objects with the high-status burials in the Coastal Plain. The paucity of precontact evidence of high-status burials may be a product of the Powhatans' practice of placing chiefs in aboveground temples that have escaped archaeological detection or the limited sample of excavated precontact burials. In support of the latter possibility, a Late Woodland component at the Great Neck site (44VB7) exhibits a notable exception to the pattern in which precontact burials lack clear evidence of status differences. Excavators identified three forms of Great Neck burial associated with a fifteenth-century palisaded village, one of which incorporated copper grave goods (Hodges 1993).

Generally, then, archaeological studies of late precontact sites record a social transformation in the Coastal Plain from a foraging and hunting economy drawing upon the rich and diverse Chesapeake estuary to a subsistence economy that complemented these resources with maize-bean-squash horticulture concentrated in floodplain locations. By the final precontact centuries relatively large communities dotted the riverbanks of the Coastal Plain, with palisaded settlements near the fall line. Ethnohistorical accounts likewise indicate the presence of fortified settlements on the James, including at Powhatan village, where the man who would become paramount chief was born. An overall pattern of late precontact increase in population density is evident, with an acceleration of population growth in the final precontact centuries. Political complexity most likely arose near the fall line where rich and diverse resources, high population densities, and a proximity to the trading and raiding Piedmont Indians made complex political organization a particularly attractive solution to social and ecological problems.

Archaeological studies generally accord with this reconstruction by providing evidence of a focusing of settlement in large, relatively permanent settlements and an intensification of subsistence production, sedentariness, and population increase. The social dynamics whereby Virginia Algonquins translated this focusing of settlement and increased production of food and children into institutionalized inequality and political hierarchy, though, have been described in vague terms that are weakly corroborated by archaeological evidence. Outside of the seventeenth-century context, patterns related to sedentariness, settlement population, and the organization of households and communities remain poorly understood in the Coastal Plain and the surrounding Chesapeake region.

Monacan Ethnohistory
As the review of Powhatan ethnohistory and archaeology suggests, the Monacans of the Virginia Piedmont played a critical role during the Protohistoric and early colonial eras. Nonetheless, Jamestown colonists only briefly mention the Monacans, and then rather cryptically. John Smith, the principal recorder of Powhatan cultural patterns, never traveled to the Piedmont and recorded information regarding the Monacans that he had learned "by relation only." The archaeological record of the Monacans' Piedmont region has, until quite recently, suffered from a lack of systematic survey and excavation.

On his *Map of Virginia* John Smith recorded the location of 12 Monacan and Mannahoac villages in the central Virginia Piedmont. "Upon the head of the Powhatans," wrote Smith of the James River Piedmont, "are the Monacans, whose chiefe habitation is at Rasauwmeake, unto whom the Mouhemenchughes, the Massinacacks, the Monahassanuggs, the Monasicka-panoughs, and other nations pay tributs" (Smith 1986b:165). Smith's map depicts the James River Monacans and the Mannahoacs of the Rappahannock River Piedmont as having the same settlement hierarchy of "Kings' Howses" and "Ordinary Howses" that marked the Powhatan political landscape. The Mannahoacs are "all confederates with the Monacans, though many different in language" (Strachey 1953:107). While the linguistic diversity of the Piedmont Indians and the Siouan linguistic classification first proposed by Mooney (1907) remain controversial, it is clear from the Jamestown colonial texts that the Piedmont Indians formed a coherent social entity known collectively as the Monacans in their dealings with the Powhatans (Hantman 1993:98; Mouer 1983:23). The Monacans' settlement hierarchy and references to the Monacans' own *weroances* (e.g., Smith 1986c:238) and tribute paid to the village of Rassawek suggest that the Monacans possessed a centralized political economy and some form of complex sociopolitical organization characterized by relations of inequality during the early seventeenth century.

Several of the colonists' written references to the Monacans emphasize the Powhatans' perceptions that "the Monanacah was his enemy, and that he came down at the fall of the leaf and invaded his country" (Archer 1998a:109). Others (e.g., Strachey 1953:34–35) wrote of chronic warfare between the Monacans and Powhatans that made them deadly enemies. The relationship between these groups probably involved intergroup hostilities prior to 1607, though colonists reported no such warfare in the early years of the Jamestown colony. In the context of specific events, the ambivalence of the Algonquins regarding Powhatan/Monacan tensions suggests a relationship in considerable flux (Hantman 1993:103). Prior to the arrival of Jamestown colonists, who brought large amounts of copper for trading, the Monacans probably served as a source of this symbolically potent material for the Indians of the Coastal Plain (Hantman 1990). Regardless of the precise nature of Monacan political organization and their relationship with the Powhatans, the Monacans kept their distance from the English throughout the colonial era.

Hantman's (1990:680–682) lexical and contextual analysis of three written references to the Monacans suggests that the Monacans were "diverse" and "barbarous" only in the sense of being numerous and different than the English. Macrobotanical (Mouer 1983; Gallivan and Hantman 1998) and bioarchaeological (Gold 1998; Trimble 1996) evidence indicates that late precontact Indians of the Piedmont subsisted on a mixed horticultural economy similar to the Powhatans'. Analysis of Late Woodland skeletal remains recovered in the Piedmont and in the Ridge and Valley identified patterning in dental caries, tooth wear, and enamel hypoplasia indicating that horticultural resources played an important role in a mixed subsistence regime that combined cultivated and noncultivated foods (Gold 1998). Similarly, stable isotope analysis of teeth and bones has demonstrated that cultigens contributed substantially to the diet throughout Virginia (Trimble 1996). Piedmont consumption of c4 plants (i.e., maize) comprised somewhat less than 50 percent of the diet. The minority status of maize in Piedmont diets may explain the infrequent occurrence of macrobotanical evidence of cultigens at Late Woodland sites in the Piedmont, a paucity echoed in Late Woodland excavations on the Coastal Plain.

In 1670, roughly two generations after the Monacans first encountered Jamestown colonists, John Lederer traveled in the Virginia and North Carolina Piedmont among the Monacans and culturally related Siouan-speaking groups to the south (Lederer 1958). Lederer wrote that some of these groups were governed by an absolute monarch who controlled a great store of pearls, while others made decisions collectively under the collective influence of old men and oracles (1958:24, 27). Two chiefs led another group, with each presiding over a different social realm (Lederer 1958:25). Similar to earlier accounts from eastern Virginia, these characterizations of Native political systems in the interior reflect social dynamics involving both powerful chiefs and political structures with a collective orientation. Apparently, societies throughout the larger Chesapeake region adopted a range of political structures that incorporated a blend of centralized authority and collective decision making.

Late Precontact Piedmont Archaeology

The riverine-centered settlement system reflected in John Smith's *Map of Virginia* has a long history in the James River Piedmont. Survey data from the central Virginia Piedmont for the Middle and Late Archaic periods record a roughly balanced division of sites between those associated with major rivers (i.e., on floodplains or adjacent bluffs) and those located in upland areas (Klein and Klatka 1991; Hantman 1985; Klatka 1988; Klatka et al. 1986; Klein 1987), implying a broad-based settlement pattern involving an even distribution of sites on the landscape prior to the Early Woodland period. With the commencement of the Woodland period, a greater focus on floodplain locations at the expense of upland sites accompanied settlement patterns entailing increased sedentariness and population density.

Late Archaic through Early Woodland sites in the eastern Piedmont exhibit spatially associated artifact concentrations, midden deposits, and large, deep features (Mouer 1990; Mouer et al. 1981). Rock clusters and platform hearths common to Late Archaic and Early Woodland sites throughout Virginia (McLearan 1991:115) are complemented by more substantial pit features at sites in the vicinity of Elk Island, a focus of eastern Piedmont settlement. In general, these sites suggest the emergence of a more spatially concentrated, functionally variable, and temporally enduring floodplain presence in the Piedmont during the final Late Archaic centuries and the Early Woodland period.

Archaeological survey indicates an even greater intensity of floodplain settlement after A.D. 900, with a general withdrawal from interfluvial and upland locations and a concentration of settlement along the major rivers (Hantman 1985; Klatka et al. 1986; Klatka 1988). This temporal pattern and the overall density of Late Woodland sites in the Piedmont closely parallel the results of settlement studies in the Coastal Plain. Survey and ethnohistorical studies suggest that as many as 15,000 Monacans may have resided in the Piedmont circa 1607 (Hantman 1993:100), although colonial texts fail to provide the same documentary basis for estimating Piedmont demography that researchers have used in inferring Powhatan population.

The appearance of a fall-line boundary in the distribution of ceramic types circa A.D. 200 likely parallels a distinction between coastal Algonquins and interior Siouan-speakers (Egloff 1985). Prior to this period a shared ceramic tradition spanned both of these areas. Typological approaches to the classification of Virginia ceramics have relied primarily on differences of temper to distinguish between wares (e.g., Evans 1955; Egloff and Potter 1982). By A.D. 200 a distinction between the shell-tempered Mockley ceramics of the coastal areas and the lithic and sand–tempered wares of the interior suggests social boundary formation. This distinction between shell-tempered ceramics of the Coastal Plain and lithic and sand–tempered ceramics of the Piedmont continued into the Late Woodland period with the contrast between Townsend ware of the coastal region and the Albemarle series in the Piedmont. By the terminal Late Woodland, ceramic types with more restricted distributions proliferated in Virginia (e.g., Turner 1993:84–87). Shell-tempered Roanoke simple-stamped ceramics dominated the lower James, while sand and crushed quartz–tempered Gaston simple-stamped appeared in the inner Coastal Plain of the James and York river drainages. Townsend fabric-impressed occurred throughout the lower York, Rappahannock, and Potomac drainages. Sand and crushed quartz–tempered Potomac Creek pottery, a ware with distinctive rim decorations, occurred in the Potomac's inner Coastal Plain. West of the Blue Ridge, Ridge and Valley groups of the Middle Woodland and early Late Woodland centuries produced quartz-tempered Albemarle ceramics similar to those found in the Piedmont (Gardner 1986). By the latter half of the Late Woodland the predominance of ceramics in the Ridge and Valley tempered with limestone and gastropod shells indicates a contrast with Piedmont ceramics, where finely crushed lithic temper replaced the coarsely crushed quartz that tempered Albemarle series pottery.

Aside from differences of temper, Native potters shared stylistic attributes and technological trends across the fall line and the Blue Ridge. By the end of the Late Woodland period, some see in ceramic ware distributions distinct "spheres of cultural interaction" (Egloff 1985). However, placing boundaries on these spheres remains difficult due to the sharing of nontemper attributes across wide areas of the Middle Atlantic. Attribute-based analysis of ceramics has indicated that late precontact ceramic styles varied "clinally," a pattern in which gradations of subtly differing ceramic styles occur across geographic space (Klein 1994).

Archaeologists characterize Late Woodland Piedmont settlement forms on the floodplain as either linear arrangements of features or compact clusters of artifacts and associated midden deposits (e.g., Mouer 1983). Mouer's (1983:27) James River Piedmont survey identified several circular middens containing material diagnostic of the final Late Woodland or Protohistoric centuries, suggesting a possible trend toward the nucleation of settlement on the floodplain. The diversity and abundance of debris recovered in surface collections at these locations and the presence of midden deposits suggest the possibility of increases in sedentariness and in settlement population.

The unity of Monacan society as inferred from written references is matched archaeologically by evidence of burial mounds that are seen as physical evidence of a shared Monacan ideology (Hantman 1990:684; Holland 1978:31; cf. MacCord 1986:3). The Monacans constructed mounds of earth that contained mass burial features in some ways similar to Coastal Plain ossuaries. Thirteen accretional mounds containing thousands of skeletal remains appeared in the Piedmont and the Ridge and Valley during the Late Woodland period (Dunham 1994). These mounds include human "bone beds" deposited during discrete burial events. The precise chronology of the Piedmont burial mounds is unclear, yet radiocarbon-dated contexts from the Rapidan Mound site (44OR1) suggest that the most intensive use of the mound occurred during the latter portion of the Late Woodland (Gold 1998; Holland et al. 1983). Radiocarbon dates from similar mounds located west of the Blue Ridge have a somewhat longer sequence that begins at the opening of the Late Woodland (MacCord 1986:4; Gold 1998). These dates suggest the diffusion of mound-building practices eastward from the Ridge and Valley, with mound construction in the Piedmont taking hold during the thirteenth through fifteenth centuries.

As in Coastal Plain ossuaries, these collective burial features generally involved a multistage ritual process. The archaeological record offers a glimpse of only the final stage (Dunham 1999). Since the institution represented by burial mounds spans the Blue Ridge, groups in the Piedmont and the Ridge and Valley appear to be linked during the Late Woodland period through shared ritual practices (Hantman 1998). Estimates of the number of individuals interred within various mounds vary widely due to mound deflation from cultivation practices and overbank river flooding (MacCord 1986; Dunham 1994; Gold 1998). Intensive investigations at the Rapidan Mound in the Rappahannock River Piedmont indicate that the mound originally contained the remains of 1,000 to 2,000 individuals (Dunham 1994; Gold 1998). Paralleling late precontact ossuary burial of the Coastal Plain, Piedmont mounds resulted from communal burial events during which Native communities interred disarticulated bones in bundles or layers, generally without accompanying grave goods.

Burial mounds of the Piedmont and Ridge and Valley may in fact have embodied a Late Woodland institution through which social power was linked to historical associations between ancestors and territory (Hantman 1990). Mounds, with their mass burials and lack of distinguishing marks of social status, may have masked social inequality behind ceremony that emphasized shared community equality in the afterlife. Indeed, symbolic analysis of burial mounds as products of such ritual practices suggests that mound burial reproduced and transformed social relations as a "common ground" for the embodiment of contradictory social impulses (Dunham 1994:18). As the product of newly sedentary horticulturalists, these burial mounds may be read as landscape features symbolically unifying riverine territories, ancestors, and multicommunal labor (Dunham 1999:127).

Interpretation of the Monacans as representing the temporary confederacy of a segmentary lineage society (Mouer 1981) or a complex chiefdom (Hantman 1990), as well as other labels applied to this group (e.g., Custer 1986:157), reflects different ways of reading an ambiguous ethnohistorical record and a modest archaeological database. These data limit definitive statements that may be made regarding Monacan social organization (Klein 1986:54). Nonetheless, ethnohistorical accounts do paint the Monacans as a coherent polity with the power to threaten the Powhatan chiefdom militarily during the early colonial era. The Monacans' access to copper probably gave them leverage in the regional political economy, at least before Jamestown colonists became the source of copper objects in the Chesapeake region. Ethnohistorical references to *weroances*, the villages of kings, and tributary relations linking a multicommunity political organization suggest a society that incorporated some measure of social inequality and political hierarchy. Archaeological data indicate patterning in Piedmont subsistence, settlement, and demography corresponding closely with that of the Coastal Plain. Although Amoroleck counted the Powhatans and Monacans as two of the three "worlds" he described to his English captors (Smith 1986d:175–176), these worlds appear to have shared important elements and a long history of interaction.

Ridge and Valley Late Precontact Archaeology
Since Europeans did not encounter the Indians of the province and knew little about the early colonial Ridge and Valley, the direct historic approach cannot be applied to the late precontact era in the Ridge and Valley. However, systematic surveys and large-scale excavations of sites spanning the Late Woodland centuries have elucidated aspects of the Ridge and Valley's late precontact era more sharply than the eastern provinces of the Chesapeake region. While this research reflects settlement and subsistence practices that parallel Piedmont and Coastal Plain patterns, Ridge and Valley archaeology has also yielded some of the clearest evidence of specialized architecture, prestige-good exchange, differential mortuary treatment, and palisaded villages. These are precisely the archaeological attributes associated with a centralized political economy and social inequality that archaeologists have had difficulty identifying in the Coastal Plain and in the Piedmont.

Paradoxically, though, most researchers view Ridge and Valley archaeology as indicative of either an egalitarian tribal level of sociopolitical organization (Whyte and Thompson 1989:291), cognatic tribes (Custer 1986:158), or a situational alliance (Gardner 1986:90). In the absence of a written record of social inequality and political hierarchy, archaeologists favoring neo-evolutionary typological classification have hesitated to "read" these from the archaeological record. Archaeological evidence undoubtedly provides a less precise means of inferring social organization than does ethnohistory, yet colonial records (which incorporate their own biases) arguably carry an undue influence in the interpretation of Virginia's late precontact era. Late Woodland archaeology of the Ridge and Valley offers evidence of social dynamics driven by tensions inherent in many middle range societies, tensions involving social differentiation, inequality, and intergroup hostilities.

By the early eighteenth century colonists reported the presence of few Indians in the Ridge and Valley. In 1671 explorers Robert Fallam and Thomas Batts encountered a small group of Indians west of the Blue Ridge and on the Roanoke River who were most likely Siouan-speakers culturally related to the Monacans (Alvord and Bidgood 1912; Gardner 1986:92). As noted above, shared cultural traditions tied to burial mound ritual and ceramic style hint that central Virginia Ridge and Valley groups shared a long-standing cultural affiliation with Piedmont groups.

However, the Ridge and Valley province's cultural geography ensured that groups residing along the headwater streams of the James experienced a variety of social influences during the late precontact era, when river basins channeled much of the social interaction. Rivers flowing to the distant northeast, southeast, northwest, and southwest were accessible from the James River basin portion of the Ridge and Valley province. Late Woodland pottery in the central Ridge and Valley remained similar to Albemarle series ceramics of the Piedmont until after A.D. 1200, when quartz-tempered Albemarle ceramics gave way to a changing mix of ceramic series, including those tempered with limestone (Page and Radford), sand (Dan River), or freshwater shell (New River and Keyser). Rim decoration of ceramic vessels became increasingly common and varied by the latter half of the Late Woodland, adding to indications that ceramic style assumed a heightened social prominence. The Ridge and Valley has appropriately been characterized as a "mosaic of blended cultures" in which pottery traditions do not correspond neatly to spatially bounded societies, linguistic units, or polities (Egloff 1992:203). Generally, late precontact ceramic patterns in the Ridge and Valley suggest dynamic social interaction amid periodically shifting populations more clearly than demonstrating the presence of spatially bounded groups trackable through ceramic wares.

Subsistence and settlement in the Ridge and Valley offer a familiar set of patterns. As mentioned previously, the region's bioarchaeology indicates that Late Woodland Ridge and Valley populations participated in an agricultural subsistence economy (Gold 1998; Trimble 1996), with Trimble's research recording a slightly higher consumption of maize in the Ridge and Valley than in the Piedmont. The paucity of macrobotanical evidence for the presence of maize and the overall health of mound-interred populations (Gold 1998) suggests that Ridge and Valley groups, like their neighbors in the Piedmont and Coastal Plain, continued to rely on a mixed subsistence repertoire throughout the late precontact era.

Survey data reflect a Late Woodland settlement transition in favor of floodplain locations paralleled elsewhere in the region. Archaeological surveys record a general late precontact withdrawal from upland areas with a more subtle movement between the Middle Woodland and Late Woodland periods from the swampy backwater segments of riverine environments to floodplain levees immediately adjacent to major drainages (Walker and Miller 1992:166–167). These shifts likely parallel the use of well-drained and easily tillable floodplain soils for horticulture. Surveys in several areas of the Ridge and Valley have identified significant differences between combined Late Archaic/Early Woodland settlement patterns and those of the Late Woodland, with a familiar shift from an even distribution of sites to a focus on river floodplains (Custer 1980, 1984, 1987:147). Prior to the Woodland period, survey data indicate greater settlement mobility, though large floodplain "base camps" associated with the annual harvesting of wild plants suggest that a seasonal focusing of social life on floodplains has a substantial history (Custer 1980:18).

Given the differences in survey methodologies, it is difficult to generate comparable demographic data for the Ridge and Valley and the more easterly provinces. However, similar patterns of population growth that accelerated during the Woodland period are apparent in all areas of the James River basin (e.g., Walker and Miller 1992:166). Surveys of Late Woodland sites indicate that Ridge and Valley groups increasingly tethered themselves to floodplain settlements (Dunham 1994:37–44), a pattern matched in the Coastal Plain and Piedmont. Floodplain sites suggest a spatial and temporal concentration of settlement that was novel to the Late Woodland period.

Late Woodland mortuary patterns in the central Ridge and Valley reflect similarities with the Piedmont, along with evidence largely absent from the Piedmont that burial rituals expressed a measure of social differentiation. Late Woodland accretional burial mounds in the Ridge and Valley also contrast with the Middle Woodland "stone cairns" of northwest Virginia (Boyd and Boyd 1992:259). The earlier forms appear to represent single-event tumuli with one to four interments, some of which included artifacts reflecting an Adena or Hopewell influence (Fowke 1894). Though poorly understood, these mounds may mark the emergence of "big man" political systems and an early example of the cycles of centralization that characterized the late prehistoric Middle Atlantic (Hantman and Gold 2000). Where the Middle Woodland mounds imply the symbolic validation of powerful individual men, Late Woodland accretional mounds contain mass interments similar to those in Piedmont mounds and Coastal Plain ossuaries. Radiocarbon dates between A.D. 900 and 1500 bracket the use of accretional mounds in the Ridge and Valley (MacCord 1986:26; Gold 1998). As in the Piedmont, several different burial forms appear in mounds, and burials outside of mounds appeared throughout the Late Woodland period. Ridge and Valley mounds generally have fewer multiple interments than those in the Piedmont. Fowke (1894:43–44) described bone beds containing disarticulated remains but lacking accompanying grave goods, while other features within mounds contained the articulated remains of one or two individuals in primary interments accompanied by various "relics." Nonutilitarian grave goods accompanied approximately 16 percent of Ridge and Valley mound burials, including shell, bone, and (rarely) copper beads, while utilitarian items such as projectile points, pipes, and bone awls appeared alongside 12 percent of the burials (Boyd and Boyd 1992:258; Walker and Miller 1992:175).

Grave items do not provide an easily decoded map of social structure (Huntington and Metcalf 1979), and grave offerings need not be reflexive of social status differences in any direct manner (Shanks and Tilley 1982). Yet varying mortuary treatment does point toward the expression of intragroup distinctions, or what some (McGuire 1983; Dunham 1994:132) have referred to as "social heterogeneity." In comparing Ridge and Valley mounds to those in the Piedmont, Gold (2000) notes that the frequent inclusion of burial offerings in Ridge and Valley mounds, including those that may signify differences in status, stands in marked contrast to Piedmont mounds, which lack such items. Piedmont mounds also appear to contain a greater number of bodies than do mounds west of Blue Ridge. Gold (2000) argues persuasively that Piedmont mounds and Coastal Plain ossuaries served to emphasize group collectivity over individual identity, in contrast with the mortuary practices of the Ridge and Valley. Ridge and Valley communities apparently did not share the same constraints on expressions of personal status that marked Piedmont practices.

Community organizational evidence from the Ridge and Valley consists of a rich data set that includes house patterns and associated features from several large-scale excavations conducted in conjunction with cultural resource management projects (e.g., Whyte and Geier 1982; Snyder and Fehr 1984). Although no regional analysis of house and pit feature organization exists for the Ridge and Valley, several authors have made a typological distinction between hamlet settlements of the early Late Woodland and palisaded villages common after A.D. 1400 (Gardner 1986; Walker and Miller 1992). Such hamlets included a small number of circular houses with associated storage and cooking features clustered on the floodplain (e.g., Snyder and Fehr 1984). Villages, by contrast, represented larger, nucleated settlements. Unusual "longhouse" architecture appeared within villages by the fourteenth century and continued to appear sporadically through Protohistoric settlements of the sixteenth century. Unlike the generally circular floor plans of domestic architecture in the Ridge and Valley, longhouse structures appear elliptical in plan, with dimensions of approximately 15 by 6 meters at the Bessemer (44BO26) (Thompson 1989) and Perkins Point sites (44BA3) (Whyte and Geier 1982). Interpreted as either council houses or elite residences, such structures dwarf other identified house patterns at these settlements.

In sum, Late Woodland Ridge and Valley archaeology generally parallels Piedmont and Coastal Plain trends in settlement and subsistence, though evidence of social differentiation that is difficult to infer from Coastal Plain and Piedmont archaeology does appear in the Ridge and Valley. The Late Woodland shift from hamlets to nucleated, palisaded settlements hinted at in the Piedmont and Coastal Plain is more completely documented in the Ridge and Valley. Unusual longhouse architecture, also not unknown in the Coastal Plain (Hodges 1993:137), appears at several Ridge and Valley sites beginning circa A.D. 1300. Surveys suggest increasing population throughout the Woodland period, with a Late Woodland acceleration of population growth. Mortuary practices reflect elements of communal burial shared with Piedmont and Coastal Plain groups. Yet the inclusion with some burials of items obtained through long-distance exchange implies an expression of differential status largely suppressed in Piedmont mounds and Coastal Plain ossuaries, at least before the colonial era.

During the early colonial era, Ridge and Valley sites south of the Po-

tomac generally lack European trade goods, while Powhatan villagers near
the Chesapeake Bay buried considerable amounts of European copper with
their dead. With the arrival of Europeans in the Chesapeake, Virginia Indians
incorporated exotic prestige items as they had in the precontact era. However, the distribution of prestige goods appears to signal a balance of power
in the James River basin that shifted with the European presence in Virginia.
Where some Late Woodland burials in the western portion of the James River
drainage incorporated shell beads and, occasionally, copper objects, precolonial Coastal Plain and Piedmont burials generally lacked exotic grave goods.
With Jamestown's settlement, coastal villages such as Paspahegh on the eastern edge of the river basin amassed substantial quantities of copper (Lucketti
et al. 1994:244). Coastal Algonquin societies had incorporated the English
colonists into Native cultural categories and practices, including those related
to prestige-good exchange. In doing so, these groups effected an eastward
shift in the concentration of wealth items within mortuary contexts, altering
the fundamental dynamics of the political economy in the process.

Ridge and Valley archaeology manifests evidence of social differentiation
largely neglected by researchers captivated by documentary accounts of the
colonial encounter to the east. Ridge and Valley archaeological evidence
is by no means unequivocal regarding the nature of social differentiation.
Longhouse structures may have been public architecture or chiefs' quar-
ters. Palisaded villages may have housed elites or may have served to defend
populations against external foes in the societal crossroads of western Virginia. Prestige-good relations are memorialized in burial features containing
exotics, yet shell beads appear most often with the remains of infants and
children, complicating efforts to read evidence of a ranked social structure
from mortuary ritual (Gardner 1986:87).

Such efforts may be misguided even in less equivocal contexts if, as some
have suggested (McGuire 1992; Dunham 1994:774–776), interpretive frames
that view ritual symbols as "referential" of social organization fail to grasp the
rather complex manner in which such burial practices conveyed meaning.
Rather than a mirror of social relations, mound burial likely functioned as a
symbolic reservoir of conflicting values involving social integration, differentiation, and inequality. Elements of burial ritual that established relations of
equivalence appear to have complemented those expressing social inequality.
In contrast to Middle Woodland stone cairns containing a small number of
individuals interred with platform pipes, mica sheets, and gorgets originating
in the Adena or Hopewell world of the North American interior, Late Wood-

land mounds incorporated hundreds, even thousands, of individuals alongside ancestors. Late Woodland dynamics in the Ridge and Valley appear to reflect yet another iteration of a social cycle driven by those striving to centralize social relations involving power and prestige alongside those seeking to avoid such a concentration of power, as occurred during the Middle Woodland period (Hantman 1998; Hantman and Gold 2000). Review of Ridge and Valley archaeology indicates that the mortuary patterns' ambiguity is repeated in a number of other social domains, implying that Late Woodland social relations in the Ridge and Valley incorporated a contradictory amalgamation of egalitarian and nonegalitarian elements.

Chapter 3

Archaeological Approaches to the Establishment of Village Life

During the early seventeenth century, the Powhatans and Monacans engaged in expressions of alliance and enmity, hierarchy and egalitarianism, solidarity and factionalism. Political authority oscillated between individual *weroances* and collective decision-making bodies as Native political structures incorporated the newly arrived Tassantasses. The historical record of these social practices raises the question: What cultural transformations and long-term historical developments prompted the origin and development of hierarchical polities in the Chesapeake?

During the centuries immediately following the circa A.D. 900 introduction of maize in the James River Valley, settlement and subsistence patterns reflected a continuation of long-term trends involving population growth and a settlement focus on riverine locations. By the end of the Late Woodland period, though, community organization had changed fundamentally across the region. Archaeological sites reflect residential settlements on floodplains and adjacent bluffs that differed from those of earlier periods in size and complexity. Abundant evidence of pit features used for food preparation and storage accompanied substantial house patterns that were largely absent from the archaeological record of earlier periods. Communal features, including palisades and burial grounds, reflected new priorities in defense and collective expressions of the sacred. Regionally, the geographic scope of pottery styles diminished, as smaller style zones appeared in the Chesapeake. In short, the daily practices and cultural institutions of Native societies in the Chesapeake changed considerably during the Late Woodland centuries.

An understanding of the colonial encounter in the Chesapeake must begin by considering the implications of this Late Woodland reorganization of social life, a reorganization centered in the residential communities lining the region's major rivers. This chapter outlines an approach to these issues intended to address the emergence of social inequality and political hierarchy in the James River Valley. My approach emphasizes changes in practices tied to the domestic, communal, and regional scales associated with the settlement of village communities and political strategies that exploited the funds of power generated by these changes.

Social Inequality

Recent archaeological research into the evolution of middle range societies similar to those of the late prehistoric Chesapeake has turned the focus of inquiry to the origins of social inequality (e.g., Price and Feinman 1995). From at least the time of the Enlightenment (e.g., Rousseau 1968), researchers have viewed the introduction of pervasive inequality into social life as one of the most fundamental transformations in the history of humanity. Social inequality entails the degree to which a society is marked by differential access to material and ideal resources, including wealth and power.

Previously, archaeological approaches to the origins of inequality generally emphasized a stark divide between egalitarian and hierarchical societies. Members of hunter-gatherer groups and egalitarian horticultural societies were assumed to have essentially equivalent access to roles, rights, and privileges (e.g., Fried 1967). Since there was little or no competition for positions of status, egalitarian groups were thought to have as many positions of status as there were individuals to fill them. Nonegalitarian societies, by contrast, were conceived of as larger, hierarchical, and organized by ranking or stratification that assigned each individual's social status by birth.

Weaknesses in this rigid dichotomy have led anthropologists to seek alternative models for understanding hierarchy and egalitarianism (e.g., Ehrenreich et al. 1995; McGuire and Saitta 1996). The recognition of hierarchy in "egalitarian" contexts (e.g., Flanagan 1989) has complicated the study of egalitarian social relations. Indeed, ethnographies of supposedly egalitarian hunter-gatherer (e.g., Lee 1981) and peasant communities (e.g., McGuire and Netting 1982) demonstrate that true equality may be a social impossibility (McGuire 1983:100). Given the ubiquity of social inequality, relatively egalitarian societies can no longer be conceived as self-organizing or the "natural" state of humanity (cf. Rousseau 1968) but are actively constituted by a society's members as nonhierarchical. Sometimes this lack of inequality results from what has been termed the collective "domination" of leaders by their followers (Boehm 1993). Egalitarian societies may be arrayed "against the state" (Clastres 1989) by enforcing a social power to limit the ambitions of leaders through the influence of corporate institutions or alternative sources of authority.

Indeed, middle range societies, including those variously classified as tribes and chiefdoms, harbor considerably more variation than can be accommodated by social categories such as "chiefdom" (Feinman and Neitzel 1984). Relations of inequality, power, and wealth vary along continua lacking sharp modalities, while the political, economic, and ideological dimensions of hierarchical societies frequently are not correlated. The manner in which societies are hierarchical varies considerably as well.

One suggestive line of research has explored the ways in which information processing, decision making, and "scalar thresholds" play critical roles in the hierarchical relations of middle range societies (Johnson 1978, 1982, 1983). Johnson (1983:175) has argued on both theoretical and empirical grounds that the ability to process information related to decision making constrains the size of relatively egalitarian communities. "Information processing overload" (Johnson 1983:196) creates stress points that constrain the size of communities dependent upon consensual decision making. Small-scale societies often reorganize once they surpass a certain scalar threshold, often above the number of six interacting social entities such as households, lineages, or communities, in order to make decisions responsive to the range of available information sources (Johnson 1982). The social reorganization may entail group dissolution or the development of decision-making hierarchies. Such hierarchies may be "simultaneous," implying the conventional notion of hierarchy in which social elements are ranked in terms of their influence, or they may be "sequential," which involves consensual decision making that passes among different social groups.

The recognition that societies are constituted in varying degrees both by egalitarian relations and by relations of inequality and hierarchy is critical to understanding the archaeological and historical record of the Powhatans and Monacans. Indeed, this recognition raises questions central to understanding precontact and Contact era societies in the Chesapeake: How did the social inequality that pervaded Native societies during the colonial era come to be institutionalized? In what ways did the Powhatans and Monacans accept or avoid efforts to impose systems of inequity? The institutionalization of social inequality involved the historical processes through which such relations were culturally legitimized, socially inherited, and reproduced over multiple generations so that they became inherent and socially accepted (Paynter 1989:387). Through this process sequential hierarchies become simultaneous ones. In the Chesapeake and elsewhere, the institutionalization of social inequality and the appearance of simultaneous hierarchy serve as a critical element in the foundation of complex polities (Price and Feinman 1995:4).

Transitions to Sedentary Village Life

As in a wide range of cultural and historical contexts, the transition to sedentary village life appears to have played a pivotal role in the development of the social inequality that marked Native societies of the Contact-era Chesapeake. Archaeological studies have demonstrated that transitions to sedentary village life often entail changes in the nature of household production, communal integration, and regional interaction fundamental to the institutionalization of inequality and political hierarchy.

The Organization of Production

Prior to the Late Woodland period in the Chesapeake, archaeological evidence suggests that hunter–gatherers in the region supplied themselves with resources through specially organized task groups operating from a residential base camp that moved frequently (e.g., Blanton 1992). Ethnographers suggest that such mobile foraging societies often share a common socioeconomic mode of production that structures relations of production, distribution, exchange, and consumption (e.g., Lee 1979, 1990; Leacock and Lee 1982; Southall 1988; Wills 1992:160; Woodburn 1982). Foragers generally exhibit core features, including collective ownership of the means of production and access by all to the forces of production. A band or a camp of foragers often share local land and its resources under the communal mode of production, with individual ownership limited to personal items such as tools. Knowledge required for the creation of tools critical to production is accessible to all, though an engendered division of labor frequently distinguishes men's and women's labor (Lee 1982).

A right of reciprocal access to important resources also marks the communal mode, or "primitive communism" (Lee 1990), with access gained through marriage ties, visiting, and shared production. Little emphasis on accumulation is apparent in most mobile foraging societies, and close to total sharing or generalized reciprocity links those residing in a camp with the obligation to give without expecting anything in return. These groups' mobility and use of the land as a larder make accumulation impractical and unnecessary, while the obligation to share food among all members of a local residence group is complete and unaccompanied by the reckoning of outstanding debts (Leacock and Lee 1982:8). Since mobile foraging families have little economic autonomy, there is no great incentive for individuals to increase their labor input through a longer workday, their labor supply through biological repro-duction, or their surplus through storage technology (Gardner 1991; Wills 1992). Territorial and social boundaries tend to be loosely defined among foragers, as an obligation to share resources often extends beyond the local camp to include other neighboring groups, and local group composition may be small and fluid. Though situational leadership plays an important role in foraging societies, foragers generally make decisions collectively and by consent (e.g., Silberbauer 1982).

This characterization of social relations within foraging societies conforms in general terms with much of the Chesapeake's archaeological record prior to the Late Woodland period. However, the economic relations of horticul-tural villagers in the Chesapeake differed quite markedly from this character-ization of a foraging mode of production. Colonial accounts emphasize that, among the Powhatans at least, economic relations hinged on the complemen-tary production of engendered labor that came together in the household, the fundamental unit of economic production. While the local settlement group is central to production and consumption among foragers (Woodburn 1982), individual households generally serve as the principal production and consumption unit among food producers (Netting 1990; Wilk 1984). The labor needs associated with food production often may be supplied most effectively by the independent family household, which derives much of its subsistence from its agricultural production.

Households served well as the primary production unit among the Pow-hatans and do so in other agricultural economies due to the ease with which domestic groups transmit critical knowledge, coordinate production activi-ties, and adjust labor force composition in a food-producing economy (Net-ting 1990:40). Drawing on the role of households as primary production units in many small-scale agricultural communities, Sahlins (1972; cf. Chayanov 1966) has suggested that a "domestic mode of production" that entails under-productive economic relations characterizes these groups. Households hang in the balance created by production practices oriented to domestic group needs and the outward obligations of kinship and reciprocity. The "political negation" of the domestic production mode may occur in the context of interhousehold relations. Production intensifies with a shift to production for a political economy powered by those vying for elite status.

Multiscalar Social Change and the Establishment of Villages

Not only were the production relations of the Powhatans distinct from those of foraging societies, but community organization and regional interaction differed as well. Native societies throughout the Chesapeake region during the Contact era lived in sizable "towns" or villages, which are absent from the archaeological record prior to the Late Woodland period. During the colonial era and the Late Woodland period, palisades surrounded some settlements, and several settlements featured public architecture associated with elites and the sacred realm. Jamestown colonists described expressions of group identity among the Powhatans and Monacans and intensive relations of trade and alliance that linked communities across the region in a complex and shifting web. In fact, the Chesapeake region's ethnohistorical and archaeological records hint at a Late Woodland rearrangement of social relations within the domestic, communal, and regional scales associated with food production and sedentary village life.

Flannery's (1972) classic discussion of the origins of the village as a settlement type offers a model of this transition that may prove useful in understanding the culture history of Native societies in the Chesapeake. The distinction between economic relations idealized in the foraging production mode and those centered on households in food-producing societies lies at the crux of Flannery's ideas. Flannery suggests that the origins of sedentary life in Mesoamerica and Southwest Asia resulted not from agriculture per se but from changes in the physical and social environments associated with the construction of permanent facilities and the establishment of hereditary ownership of areas with high resource potential. Whether agriculture preceded sedentism (as in Mesoamerica) or followed the establishment of permanent settlements (as in Southwest Asia), social changes implicated in the shift to sedentism included a reorganization of domestic production, community structure, and regional social organization.

Flannery (1972:29–32, 38–40) illustrated the transformation by contrasting two ideal settlement types, the "circular hut compound" and the "true village." Circular hut compounds maintain the social and economic organization of mobile hunter-gatherers idealized in the communal mode of production. Food storage is communal and public, and thus food is relatively accessible to all. The entire compound forms the basic production and consumption group. In true villages, by contrast, each domestic structure includes an associated storage facility located within the house. Households serve as the primary social institution that structure relations of production and consumption and the distribution of surplus. The earliest villages in these regions often included public architecture heralding the appearance of new, communal-scale institutions. At the regional scale, Flannery (1992) pointed to evidence that early village societies embraced changes in group ideology from one of weak territoriality to notions of a territorial core to be defended and legitimized through concepts of descent and ties to ancestors.

Flannery (1992) suggested that the success of village settlements, which hinged upon these changes in production relations, community organization, and regional identity, became essential for further political evolution. Production intensification occurred in village societies and generally not in compounds (or among foragers with a communal mode of production) due largely to alterations in the ways in which production was shared. Where compound dwellers and foragers share surplus (literally) in the open, there is little incentive to increase production. In villages, sharing becomes more selective, and the ability of a household head to benefit from increased labor inputs follows from the reduced scope of generalized reciprocity. The basis for the financing of leadership with considerable authority emerges with village life, authority far more coercive than the persuasive power of leaders among foragers.

These changes in production relations and social organization are paralleled in a number of North American contexts that saw increased residential permanence, notably in the American Southwest (Plog 1990a). In drawing on similar contrasts between mobile foragers and sedentary village agriculturalists in the American Southwest, Plog (1989, 1990a) has pointed to social and environmental obstacles blocking the transition to sedentism, obstacles that may be overcome through a rearrangement of social life in a number of realms. Sedentism, particularly when coupled with agriculture, poses social risks that differ in important ways from those foragers face. Sedentary agricultural villagers confront risks of subsistence shortfall and risks of group conflict and dissolution that foragers largely avoid through their mobility and fluid group membership. The time lag in the Southwest between the first appearance of productive cultigens and significant dependence on agriculture and sedentism may be explained by the need to develop the technological mechanisms and social institutions critical for reducing these risks (Plog 1990a:182).

Though Flannery's model focuses on the domestic and communal scales associated with the shift to village settlement, the establishment of village

communities has been tied to recurrent changes in the regional archaeological record as well. A transition from distributions of artifact style over
large areas to geographically smaller style zones accompanied the advent of
sedentary villages in several areas of North America (e.g., Plog 1990a:187).
These developments reflect the emergence of spatially diminished yet more
intensive social networks of sedentary agriculturalists (Braun and Plog 1982).
Prior to the appearance of sedentary villages, low-density, mobile foragers
participated in relatively open, undifferentiated interaction spheres that trans-
mitted material and information in an unbounded manner (Hantman and
Plog 1982:250). With the transition to sedentary village life, though, food
producers altered their primary means of buffering environmental variation
from spatial averaging mechanisms (e.g., mobility) to temporal averaging
mechanisms (e.g., storage) (Hantman and Plog 1982:252). Accompanying
this shift, the geographically widespread social ties characteristic of mobile
foragers declined in importance as interaction and exchange became more
localized and boundaries between networks emerged. Once spatially more
compact social networks appeared, stylistic patterns over large geographic
areas often became increasingly diverse (Braun and Plog 1982:512).

Similar changes at the domestic, communal, and regional scales appeared
with the transition to village life within the Eastern Woodlands (e.g., Kelly
1990; Peregrine 1992; Mehrer 1995). In the North American midcontinent,
a trend toward more autonomous family units (Peregrine 1992) and the
formalization of village plans around communal facilities (Kelly 1990) accompanied the Late Woodland to Emergent Mississippian transition. In the
first stage of this transition to sedentary agricultural villages in the American
Bottom, the Mississippi River floodplain below the mouths of the Missouri
and Illinois rivers, the sequence of community forms suggests a rapid cycle
of settlement fusion and fission, perhaps reflecting communities that lacked
institutions capable of alleviating the potentially fragmentary consequences
of sedentism. The internal spatial organization of settlements suggests that
households formed the basic subsistence unit, a pattern extending through
the Mississippian period (Kelly 1990:108). Within Emergent Mississippian
villages, houses were tightly nucleated around central features that included
a specialized, nondomestic structure and an open plaza containing several
large pits or a large post. Members of these communities apparently added
public architecture in a central plaza tied to new expressions of communal
integration (Kelly 1990:109).

Sedentary village settlement in North America often had important implications for social heterogeneity as well. In several regions, ceramic vessels visible in the communal setting exhibited greater stylistic diversity with the shift to village life, possibly paralleling the signaling of more diverse social identities within villages (Braun 1991; Hegmon 1986). As Braun (1991:367) has demonstrated in the context of a similar transformation in the central riverine Midwest and Hegmon (1986) has documented for parts of the Colorado Plateau, greater stylistic diversity within a settlement frequently accompanied the emergence of villages characterized by increased population density, a wider range of social groups, and intracommunity tensions less resolvable through mobility.

Generally, then, archaeological patterning first identified by Flannery and subsequently by others (e.g., Plog 1990a; Byrd 1994) implies that a similar set of social changes often accompanied the shift to sedentary village life. These changes occurred within Native North American contexts with parallels in other regions. While all historical settings undergoing transitions to sedentary village life entail culturally specific developments, social changes implicit in the reorganization of production, community organization, and regional interaction appear to have occurred in a range of locations and eras as mobile foragers became sedentary, village-dwelling agriculturalists. Where foragers often organize production around the entire residential group and practice generalized reciprocity within a local community, households frequently serve as the principal production unit among sedentary, food-producing villagers, and sharing is more restricted. Little incentive to intensify production appears in the communal mode of production, and the accumulation of surplus plays a minor role in the political life of most foraging societies. The household-based economies of sedentary village societies, by contrast, entail the coordination of labor and surplus production in ways that make intensification possible and, indeed, advantageous.

Political Strategies within Middle Range Societies

With these changes in a number of cultural and historical contexts, societies crossed a threshold beyond which a greater range of political dynamics became possible. The reorganized production relations, integrative communal institutions, and regional interaction that appear with village life contributed to "funds of power" (Sahlins 1963) upon which actors in the political realm could draw. Intensified production, sanctified communal institutions, and formalized exchange networks each offer material or ideational resources that could be leveraged through novel political strategies.

In the Chesapeake region, household-centered economic units, communal facilities with a sacred or defensive tenor, and regional interaction involving bounded social groups were all apparent to English colonists during the colonial encounter. Throughout the Chesapeake, Native political strategies drew from multifaceted funds of power that produced authoritarian *weroances*, powerful priests, and collective decision-making institutions. During John Smith's travels along the Chesapeake, it was the *weroances*, rather than collective bodies of *quioccosuks*, who commanded the fractious political landscape, in part through their the influence that flowed from access to English goods. Though the Mamanatowick sought to build a Powhatan solidarity across much of the Virginia Coastal Plain, the Jamestown ethnohistory documents a political field dominated by factional competition between *weroances* seeking to build networks of wealth and power.

Feinman (1995) and Blanton et al. (1996) have developed a "dual processual" theory of political strategies that seeks to explain the oscillation of political institutions between individualized and collective authority structures similar to those witnessed in the early colonial Chesapeake. These authors contrast "exclusionary" and "corporate" power strategies that are present to some degree in all polities. Political actors pursuing the exclusionary power strategy strive to create a factional following and a political system designed around their monopoly control of sources of power. The corporate political strategy involves the sharing of power across different groups and sectors of society so as to inhibit the development of divisive factions and exclusionary strategies.

Political actors pursuing the exclusionary approach to faction building often operate on a large spatial scale by manipulating distant social connections through the exchange of exotic goods or marriage partners, hence Feinman's (1995:264–266) and Blanton et al.'s (1996:4–5) application of the term "network" to the strategy. Network tactics entail efforts to attract followers and to divert followers from political rivals through feasting, warfare, and the accumulation of prestige goods.[1] Where a network strategy is the basis of the political economy, any individual or household theoretically may establish a network of social connections, making the political field highly competitive and volatile. Since a network strategy's success rests on individual trading, warfare, and social skills, networks frequently endure for a generation in length.

The corporate strategy entails symbols of authority that emphasize collective representations and accompanying ritual highlighting the solidarity of a society (Feinman 1995:264–266; Blanton et al. 1996:5–7). Broad themes that recur in corporate polities invoke fertility and renewal in society and the cosmos and appear alongside an ecumenical code that stresses the integrated wholeness of a group (Blanton et al. 1996:6). In this way, corporate strategies may be tied to a knowledge-based political economy (Lindstrom 1984) in which leadership stems from the manipulation of ideational systems and communal institutions to orchestrate a local consensus (e.g., Strathern 1969:49).[2] Corporate polities generally place a greater emphasis on egalitarian relations, although political structures endorsed by the corporate code and enacted in communal ritual may incorporate high-status offices and a complex social structure. With the inward focus of political life, prestige-good exchanges appear to be less important to corporate coalition building, while staple finance (D'Altroy and Earle 1985) plays a more prominent role.[3]

Feinman (1995:264) and Blanton et al. (1996:5–6) suggest that elements of both the corporate and network strategies may appear in any given context, though structural antagonisms between these orientations mean that one or the other will dominate the political arena at any given moment (e.g., Strathern 1969:42–47). As a heuristic typology, this network/corporate contrast is suggestive. Considered as coexisting strategies in leadership negotiation, the model offers particularly useful language for framing political dynamics. Although not without weaknesses, the contrast that these authors draw has distinct implications that illuminate social dynamics poorly contextualized in stage-based models of political systems (e.g., Fried 1967; Service 1975). Like such approaches, the corporate/network contrast combines suites of social attributes related to production, political organization, and ideological systems, which may or may not be linked in a given setting. As Leach (1973) pointed out, an almost infinite number of social patterns could have produced the archaeological patterning associated with a particular time and place. Unlike stage-based approaches to political organization, though, the corporate/network contrast emphasizes political competition and the strategies of political agents attempting to build factions or collective coalitions. As such, it provides a useful heuristic that may throw light on the disjunctions and ambiguities of the Chesapeake region's Native American past.

A Model of Late Prehistoric James River Social Dynamics

The previous discussion suggests that a critical issue, perhaps the central one, concerning social change in middle range societies involves the historical circumstances surrounding the institutionalization of social inequality. The historical conditions critical to this process in parts of North America and Southwest Asia occurred in the context of newly sedentary, agricultural villages. A reorganization of social relations within the household, community, and regional scales allowed villagers in these regions to cross a threshold beyond which a different set of social and political practices became accessible. With the shift to a social landscape composed of villages, households gained control of production, communities incorporated novel institutions for orchestrating interhousehold relations, and regional social organization involved more intensive, bounded interaction networks. The technological, ideational, and social organizational changes associated with the transition to sedentary village life created new funds of power upon which elites could draw. Whether such political agents elected to intensify the domestic production of agricultural surplus, manipulate symbols or events of community integration, or control the movement of prestige items or marriage partners depended on internal cultural constraints and on historical events.

Colonial accounts indicate that similar developments in the late precontact and early colonial Chesapeake likely played a role in transitions to sedentary village life and in the implementation of political strategies. Accordingly, the social elements highlighted in table 3-1 and evaluated in the following chapters include those related to floodplain settlement structure, the domestic economy, community organization, and regional interaction. In order to arrive at a determination of a settlement's status as a "village" or whether trends in settlement structure moved in the direction of larger and more permanent communities, methods for measuring relative sedentariness and population size in Chesapeake-region archaeological contexts become important. Variables related to the domestic economy that may be inferred archaeologically include domestic group size, production intensity, the spatial association of storage facilities, and interhousehold differentiation. Attributes of community organization important in late prehistoric social dynamics include the nucleation of floodplain settlements, patterning related to public facilities, and social heterogeneity within a community. Regional interaction may be gauged according to the boundedness of social networks and the spatial organization and intensity of exchange relations.

Judging from the colonial accounts and the archaeological record, these variables may be closely linked in the transition to sedentary villages during the Late Woodland period in the James River Valley, as modeled in figure 3-1. Archaeological survey data indicate that large, intensively occupied communities appeared during this period. Ethnohistorical accounts imply the

**Table 3-1. Social variables critical to
James River Valley social dynamics**

Settlement Structure:	Sedentariness
	Settlement population size
Domestic Economy:	Domestic group size
	Production intensity
	Spatial organization of storage
	Interhousehold differentiation
Community Organization:	Stylistic diversity within a community
	Nucleation of floodplain settlements
	Presence of public facilities
Regional Interaction:	Boundedness of social interaction
	Intensity of exchange relations

importance of the village context in subsequent colonial era social dynamics. However, no systematic means of gauging sedentariness or settlement population size exist for the region. The first step in the analysis interprets the relative sedentariness and community sizes of riverine settlements.

The settlement of relatively large and sedentary villages of horticulturalists during the Late Woodland likely triggered changes related to the organization of production. Households may benefit more exclusively from production and (biological) reproduction with the more restricted sharing of surpluses that characterizes a domestic mode of production. A shift to a domestically oriented mode of production also generates surpluses that are periodically distributed across households inequitably. Such differences may constitute a basis for the development of social inequality. To evaluate these possibilities, I will consider archaeological patterning related to domestic architectural floor plans, associated storage pits, and the spatial organization of household features.

As ethnographers have emphasized (e.g., Kent 1989; Hitchcock 1987), increased residential permanence raises serious technological and social challenges relevant to the communal social scale. Along with the settlement of higher numbers of households within a village and households possessing a greater degree of economic autonomy, social distinctions are likely to proliferate and become more consequential in the negotiation of social tensions within a community. This negotiation may be reflected in the increased intensity of nonverbal communication or "social symboling" within residential

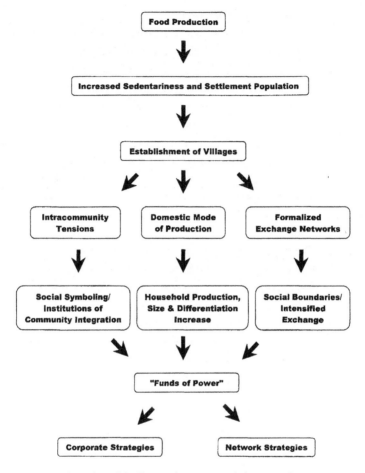

Figure 3-1. Hypothetical model of late prehistoric social change in the James River Valley

settlements, symboling that may be evaluated through the diversity of ceramic stylistic motifs.

Archaeologists have suggested that Late Woodland mound and ossuary burial practices reflect the introduction of novel institutions spawned by increased social heterogeneity and intracommunal tensions during late prehistory. Additional evidence related to communal institutions may be apparent through detailed analysis of the residential setting. Such evidence may take the form of nondomestic architecture or facilities associated with communal events. As with mortuary rituals, these events likely drew households separated as economic units into large, nucleated communities characterized by greater social heterogeneity. While potentially integrative, collective burial and other communal institutions may convey a range of historically variable meanings through dynamic symbols. With regard to these developments, I will evaluate archaeological patterning related to feature construction, non-domestic architecture, and the nucleation of floodplain settlements.

Regional social organizational changes linked to alterations in the domestic and communal spheres include those related to the spatial scale and intensity of intergroup interaction. The emergence of a regional landscape of relatively permanent communities in other contexts meant that villagers faced other villagers across more formalized, intensive, and spatially diminished interaction networks (e.g., Hantman and Plog 1982). In the Chesapeake, archaeologists have identified evidence pointing to the late prehistoric development of social boundaries amid indications that at least some forms of exchange across physiographic boundaries increased during the Late Woodland. Archaeological evidence of social interaction within the late prehistoric James River Valley allows these proposals to be evaluated in the context of changes in the domestic and communal spheres. In order to understand such regional-scale developments, I will evaluate the geographic distribution of ceramic attributes and architectural stylistic patterns for evidence of social boundaries. Consideration of the intensity and spatial scale of exchange relations will draw from distributions of nonlocal artifacts in feature contexts.

Changing practices within the domestic, communal, and regional scales provided a potential basis for the enactment of new political strategies. Strategies tied to the corporate model emphasize the communal institutions and symbols of social solidarity that become prominent in the village setting. Network strategists manipulate intercommunity movement of wealth items that may become more intensive in the social landscape of village communities. In these ways, the village context offered funds of power exploitable by political agents in accordance with the internal constraints imposed by cultural traditions. Oscillation between these political orientations may explain some of the puzzling discrepancies and ambiguities present in the ethnohistorical and archaeological records.

Methodological Framework

Multiscalar analysis of Native culture history in the James River Valley requires methods of interpreting the chronology and function of archaeological features and of classifying the region's material culture (table 3-2). Evidence of substantial residential settlements in the Chesapeake region commences

Table 3-2. Chronological divisions, James River Valley

Middle Woodland I	500 B.C.–A.D. 200
Middle Woodland II	A.D. 200–900
Late Woodland I	A.D. 900–1200
Late Woodland II	A.D. 1200–1500
Protohistoric	A.D. 1500–1607
Contact	A.D. 1607–1646

with the Late Archaic period and intensifies thereafter. It is not until the Middle Woodland period, though, when a substantial number of riverine sites bearing domestic architecture and pit features datable using radiocarbon assays appear throughout the area. Archaeologists in the Chesapeake region generally divide the Middle Woodland into two phases distinguished by changes in coastal pottery. The 500 B.C.–A.D. 200 predominance of Pope's Creek ceramics marks the Middle Woodland I, a phase when small Coastal Plain sites containing shell middens and pit features appeared for the first time. A break in ceramic design in favor of shell-tempered Mockley ceramics ushered in the A.D. 200–900 Middle Woodland II phase.

The circa A.D. 900 appearance of domesticates throughout the Chesapeake region divides the Late Woodland from the Middle Woodland. For the first three Late Woodland centuries, survey data from the Potomac River Coastal Plain (Potter 1993) and the James River Piedmont (Gallivan 1994) record a dispersal of small to medium-sized settlements along the floodplain. The appearance of large, nucleated, and sometimes palisaded communities during the thirteenth through fifteenth centuries in parts of the Chesapeake region provides the justification for distinguishing a Late Woodland II phase of A.D. 1200–1500.

Segregating the sixteenth century as the Protohistoric period acknowledges the potential impact of European exploration, trading, missionary settlement, and colonization in the Chesapeake during the century prior to Jamestown's settlement. After the 1607 establishment of the Jamestown colony, contact between Europeans and Native Americans in Tidewater Virginia had a decisive role in shaping the region's history. The loss of Powhatan autonomy following the signing of the Treaty of 1646 provides an ending date for the Contact period (Hodges 1993:14).

As an ordinal scale of measurement, this phase-based chronological framework may disguise aspects of social change. An emphasis on modal patterns associated with a phase frequently masks temporal and spatial variation. To

Table 3–3. Sites included in the study

COASTAL PLAIN			
Phase	*Site*	*Number*	*Reference(s)*
Middle Woodland I	Powhatan Creek	44JC26	Reinhart 1976
	Hampton Univ. #1	44HT36	Edwards et al. 1989
	Hampton Univ. #2	44HT37	Edwards et al. 1989
Middle Woodland II	Great Neck	44VB7	Hodges 1993
	Hampton Univ. #2	44HT37	Edwards et al. 1989
	Irwin	44PG4	MacCord 1964;
			Johnson et al. 1989
	Reynolds–Alvis	44HE470	Gleach 1986; Gleach 1987
Late Woodland I	Irwin	44PG4	MacCord 1964;
			Johnson et al. 1989
Late Woodland II	Great Neck	44VB7	Hodges 1993
	Newington	44KQ6	Winfree 1969
	Carter's Grove	44JC118	Muraca 1989
Protohistoric	Jordan's Point sites	44PG302	Mouer et al. 1992
		44PG307	McLearan and Mouer 1994
		44PG300	Morgan et al. 1995
Contact	Paspahegh	44JC308	Lucketti et al. 1994

PIEDMONT			
Phase	*Site*	*Number*	*Reference(s)*
Middle Woodland II	Wood	44NE143	Gallivan 1999
	Spessard	44FV134	Gallivan and Hantman 1998
Late Woodland I	Wingina	44NE4	MacCord 1974
	Partridge Creek	44AH193	Tourtellotte 1990;
			Gallivan 2003
	Spessard	44FV134	Gallivan and Hantman 1998
	Wood	44NE143	Gallivan 1999
Late Woodland II	Partridge Creek	44AH193	Tourtellotte 1990;
			Gallivan 2003
	Little River	44GO30b	Gallivan 1999
	Leatherwood Creek	44HR1	Gravely 1983; Gallivan 1997a
Protohistoric	Wright	44GO30	Gallivan 1999
Contact	Lickinghole Creek	44AB416	Hantman et al. 1993

RIDGE AND VALLEY			
Phase	*Site*	*Number*	*Reference(s)*
Middle Woodland II	Cement Plant	44AU51	Valliere and Harter 1986
Late Woodland I	Huffman	44BA5	Geier and Warren 1982a;
			MacCord 1982
	Cement Plant	44AU41	Valliere and Harter 1986

continued

RIDGE AND VALLEY			
Phase	*Site*	*Number*	*Reference(s)*
Late Woodland II	Areas 2/3	44WR300	Snyder and Fehr 1984
	Noah's Ark	44BA15	Geier and Warren 1982b
	Bessemer	44BO26	Whyte and Thompson 1989;
			Geier and Moldenhauer 1977
Protohistoric	Perkins Point	44BA3	Whyte and Geier 1982
	Beaver Pond	44BA39	Geier and Dutt 1978

minimize this problem, I will place the features and site components in the data set on an interval-level scale of calendrical years when sample sizes permit. An absolute (i.e., interval) scale of calendrical years allows consideration of the timing and tempo of cultural change that phase-based approaches frequently camouflage. Phase-based dating becomes necessary for analysis that benefits from comparison of groups of cases. Radiocarbon dates used to order these archaeological data in time were adjusted in accordance with the radiocarbon calibration curve (Stuiver and Reimer 1993).

Site Selection

Due to the role of river systems in channeling the dynamic and loosely bounded interaction of late prehistoric and early historic societies, this study focuses on an archaeological record centered on the James River Valley. Although I sought to include data from all floodplain settlements located in the James River Valley that entail some combination of pit features or postmold patterns, I prioritized those sites with radiocarbon dates and substantial areal exposures excavated systematically. Data meeting these criteria were drawn from sites excavated in conjunction with the University of Virginia's Monacan Archaeology Program (Hantman 1990) as well as from excavations in the Coastal Plain and Ridge and Valley that have been reported thoroughly. Twenty-seven sites are included in the sample: 12 in the Coastal Plain, 8 in the Piedmont, and 7 in the Ridge and Valley province (table 3-3; figure 3-2). These provide the best available database for understanding late precontact changes in the organization of floodplain settlements.

Included in the study are several sites located in adjacent river systems. Four of the 27 sites—Newington (44KQ6) along the Mattaponi River, Leatherwood Creek (44HR1) near the Dan River, Cement Plant (44AU51) near the headwaters of the Shenandoah River, and 44WR300 on the Shenandoah River—fill voids in the James River Valley's archaeological record. Given the broad regional cultural trends and loosely bounded social networks

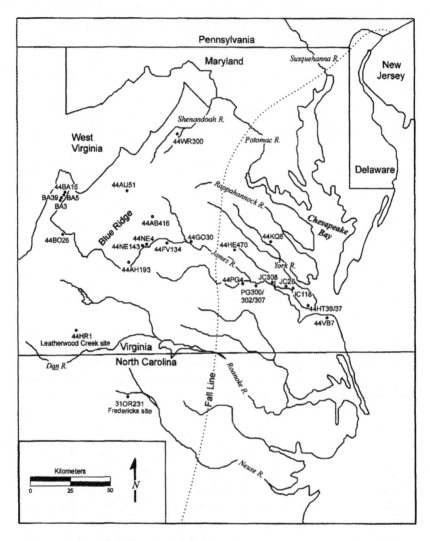

Figure 3-2. Sites included in the analysis

of late prehistory and the early historic era, the study retains its James River focus even with the inclusion of these sites. Newington and Cement Plant lie immediately outside the James River basin, while Leatherwood Creek and 44wr300 bolster the evidence of domestic and community organization during centuries with limited James River data.

This set of archaeological sites provides an unbroken sequence of change in all three provinces in the form of 616 pit features and 142 house patterns. The earliest portion of the sequence entails the least detail. Beyond the Coastal Plain, evidence from the Middle Woodland period is limited to two Piedmont sites and one in the Ridge and Valley. Piedmont sites contribute a disproportionately large part of the Late Woodland I phase's data due to the intensive research on this context by University of Virginia archaeologists and an absence of similar fieldwork elsewhere in the region. Finally, the most complete data sets from the Protohistoric and Contact periods derive from the eastern and western portions of the drainage.

Dating Features and Site Components

The construction of a chronology for the features and site components in the James River sample relied primarily on 74 radiocarbon dates from sites in the sample and on an application of Klein's (1994) absolute seriation. Appendix 1 describes the sites and provides an interpretation of their chronological placement. Radiocarbon dates are best conceived of not as representing a single point in time but rather as a normally distributed probability with a mean and standard deviation. In order to facilitate comparison of the 758 features in the sample, however, I assigned a single date to each context considered here. Radiocarbon-dated features received the date of the calibration curve intercept or the median intercept when multiple intercepts occurred.

An absolute seriation of Chesapeake ceramics (Klein 1994) supplied a second means of dating features in the sample. In a study that has revolutionized chronology construction in the region, Klein developed regression equations from changes in the attributes of ceramics recovered from radiocarbon-dated features in the James, Potomac, and Roanoke river drainages. These equations allow ceramic assemblages to be assigned an absolute calendrical date with an error factor. Dates generated using the Klein absolute seriation from features in the sample closely matched the results of radiocarbon assays. I drew from the radiocarbon assay results when present, though, due to the smaller error factor produced by this dating method.

The absolute dates generated by radiocarbon assays and absolute seriation served as the basis of a settlement chronology for the James River sites.[4] These dating methods provided evidence of 35 separate settlements in the sample ranging from A.D. 1 to 1610. When statistical comparison of absolute dates from a site suggested the likelihood of distinct occupations, I assigned features to an occupation based on comparison of diagnostic artifacts and spatial contexts. Postmold patterns were dated through radiocarbon assays, diagnostic artifacts recovered from postmold fill when this information was available, or according to the dating of spatially associated pit features when neither of the other dating methods was possible.

This approach to chronology construction allowed the creation of a basal unit of analysis consisting of the archaeological feature and a second data set of temporally discrete site components entailing the contemporaneous features within a site. Together, these chronologies permit archaeological patterning to be evaluated within two different frames of reference: an event-driven perspective related to feature usage and artifact deposition, and a occupation-level perspective that combines the suite of features and deposits associated with a temporally limited settlement.

Pit Features: Assigning Meaning to Garbage-Filled Depressions

Beyond artifacts and postmold patterns, subsurface features are the principal vestiges of behavior within prehistoric Eastern Woodlands settlements. Pits may be conceived of as nonportable containers, and the increasing Woodland period pit use contributed to the Eastern Woodlands's "container revolution" (B. Smith 1986). Eastern Woodlands Indians generally excavated pits to create subsurface receptacles for storage, food processing, fire, or burial. Pit features offer a particularly informative archaeological context as they are sealed containers of material generated by routine behavior—that is, the cultural practices that shaped life in a residential community.

Understanding pit features in the James River Valley may begin with ethnohistorical analogy. Accounts of the Powhatans' feature use frequently involve fire. References to house hearths (e.g., Smith 1986b:162) suggest that residents dug pits to enclose fires and to prevent sparks from igniting nearby house walls or other flammable material. Feasts entailing the consumption of enormous amounts of food prepared in unusually large cooking facilities were mandatory as displays of hospitality for visitors and during the *huskanaw* rite of passage. In one reference Strachey (1953:122) writes of the Powhatans' preparation of tuckahoe bread, which required large cooking facilities used for special food preparation: "They use to rake up a great number of them in old leaves and ferne, and then cover all with earth and sand, in the manner of a coale-pitte; on each side they continue a great fier a daie and a night." Fires burned within mortuary temples (Beverley 1947) and served as a focus of dancing and the "sacrifice" of boys in the *huskanaw* (Purchas 1617:953). A hearth served as the focal point during a "conjuration" ritual involving John Smith (1986b:170–171). Clearly, fire played a central yet varied role in Powhatan life—for practical and solemn purposes and within sacred and profane spaces and times. The Powhatans also used subsurface features for storing food and for hiding important items (Strachey 1953:78–79), and pits served as receptacles for Powhatan dead (Smith 1986b:169).

Deducing Pits' Original Functions

Archaeologists generally agree that the contents of a pit identified archaeologically provide only an indirect reflection of its original purpose. As a result, interpretations of feature function must also rely on morphological attributes including feature diameters, depths, and profile shapes. Ordinarily, burial pits may be defined by the human remains entombed within. Hearths and food preparation facilities also may be identified partly through their contents. Classification of such pits may rely on the presence of fire-cracked rock, burned soil, or other heat-altered materials.

Moving beyond such associations, systematic interpretations of pit feature function (e.g., Ritchie and Funk 1973) generally define feature categories based on a combination of ethnohistorical references and logical inferences concerning the most appropriate morphological attributes. In an innovative effort to test such feature classifications, Dickens (1985) combined evidence of feature morphologies and spatial associations with ethnobotanical evidence of seasonality (table 3-4). Dickens estimated the time of year in which feature types would most likely be abandoned and examined the seasonality profiles of botanical remains recovered from each category. This analysis largely supported the hypothesized pit feature types.

A useful refinement to this typology drew on ethnohistorical and archaeological evidence suggesting that roasting pits served as facilities for large-scale food preparation frequently related to communal feasting (Ward 1993). Ward identified an association between large features, variously referred to as earth ovens, food preparation facilities, or roasting pits, and the feasting ceremonies of Siouan communities in North Carolina. Archaeological examples of these features measure 1 to 2 meters in diameter with relatively shallow depths, a basin-shaped profile, and evidence of fire in the form of fire-cracked rock, ash, and wood charcoal. Judging from the single soil horizon, ceramic refits, and lack of wall slumping that characterize these features archaeologically, Piedmont groups filled the roasting pits rapidly after use. Based on their dimensions and contents, these unusual features apparently mark large-scale food preparation and consumption events that were distinct from the day-to-day activities of a single household. Strachey's description of roasting pits entailing "a great fier a daie and a night" supports this interpretation of roast-

Table 3-4. Pit feature classification (modified from Dickens 1985)

Type	Orifice Shape	Diameter (cm)	Profile	Depth (cm)	Contents/ Association
Storage	Circular	60–140	Straight sided or bell shaped	60–130	Rock slab covering
Borrow pit	Circular	160–280	Basin shaped	20–60	—
Structure floor	Elliptical or rectangular	500–1000	Basin or dish shaped	10–40	Packed floor, associated posts and pits
Hearth	Circular	40–100	Basin shaped	5–15	Lined with rocks or burned clay; associated with structure floor
Roasting pit	Circular	100–200	Straight sided or basin shaped	10–60	Burned areas or concentrations of fire-cracked rock
Palisade ditch	Linear	120–180	Shallow sloping sides	30–80	Adjacent post mold alignment
Post hole	Circular	5–30	Straight sides and round to pointed bottom	10–120	May occur individually, in an aligned pattern, or within a narrow trench
Burial pits	Elliptical or rectangular	80–160	Straight sided or undercut	50–120	Human remains

ing pits and provides evidence of their existence in the James River Valley. With this refined understanding of roasting pits, Dickens's typology served as the basis of my feature classification in the James River Valley.

Artifacts from Sealed Contexts: Pottery and Lithic Analysis
While features may reflect a temporally limited depositional event, the association of pit contents with spatially proximate features, such as domestic structures, appears to be more problematic. An artifact's abandonment location does not necessarily reflect the immediate spatial context in which it was used (Kent 1984:169; Schiffer 1976:67–69). Garbage deposited in an abandoned storage pit adjacent to a domestic structure does not necessarily correspond with material used by the domestic group that resided in the house. In comparing features between sites, pit contents appear to be a poor gauge of the deposition of specific social units, such as households, due to

the impact of site formation processes (e.g., Hayden and Cannon 1983:117, 160; Schiffer 1987). Rather, pit features represent a sealed context and a temporally limited period of deposition that may be associated most securely with a settlement and the community at large rather than with an individual household.

As such, artifacts recovered from pits in the James River sample provide comparable evidence of the nature and intensity of the activities carried out in floodplain settlements. My analysis of pottery emphasized attribute-level data (as opposed to typological classification). Lithic artifact analysis focused on general functional categories. The heavy use of quartz and quartzite in Coastal Plain and Piedmont tool production, combined with the ubiquity of expedient tools, limits the number of identifiable formal tools in most assemblages, making detailed tool classification difficult. For this study, I classified lithic artifacts according to their raw materials and as either fire-cracked rocks, ground-stone tools, chipped-stone tools, debitage, or projectile points.

Identifying Post-in-Ground Architecture

Post-in-ground architecture is a category of material culture tied to a range of issues including demography, the organization of production, kinship, residence rules, gender relations, and the communication of social status (e.g., Blanton 1994; Kent 1990; McGuire and Schiffer 1983; Wilk and Rathje 1982; Rapoport 1982; Bourdieu 1973). Before considering any of these issues, though, architectural remains must be recognized as such. In the James River Valley, postmold patterns produced by house construction exist alongside those reflecting drying racks, maize cribs, palisades, sweat lodges, menstrual huts, and other structures. Determining the purpose of architecture reflected in postmold patterns represents a challenge similar to the interpretation of pit function, although one more easily met with references to ethnohistorical accounts. Due to the sporadic occurrence of Native American architectural data in the region, until recently (Klein and Gallivan 1996), no effort had been made to synthesize regional house patterns or to address the social implications of these data.

John Smith (1986b:161–162) wrote of Powhatan houses, "Their Buildings and habitations are for the most part by the rivers or not farre distant from some fresh spring. Their houses are built like Arbors of small young [saplings] bowed and tyed, and so close covered with mats, or barkes of trees very handsomely, that notwithstanding either winde, raine or weather, they are as warme as stooves, but very smoky, yet at the toppe of the house there is a hole made for the smoake to goe into right over the fire." The Powhatans buried the bases of these sapling-framed structures in the ground, sometimes producing patterns of postmold stains recognizable in the archaeological record. Postmolds are small (5–15 centimeters diameter in plan), circular stains generally produced when the buried ends of sapling-framed structures were removed from the ground, leaving shallow depressions that filled with dark, organic-rich soil from a living surface. Some postmold stains formed after sapling posts rotted in place or burned to the ground. Whatever the case, the resulting set of postmolds may be interpreted as an architectural footprint that includes information regarding the size and shape of a structure.

Smith reported that domestic structures in the Coastal Plain slept from 6 to 20 Powhatans (1986b:162). Also writing of the Powhatans, Spelman (1998:487) noted that *weroances'* houses were both broader and longer than the rest and incorporated partitions that created dark, inner compartments. Strachey (1953:78) emphasized the substantial labor investment necessary for the construction of Powhatan houses, commenting, "but then those be principall howeses, for soe many barkes which goe to the making up of a howse, are long tyme of purchasing."

These observations support the notion that differences in house construction reflect variable access to resources such as wood suitable for frames, reed matting for wall coverings and the roof, and the labor to gather and process these materials. Not surprisingly, the homes of Powhatan elites were larger and more complex than those of others. Additional documentary references to the social significance of house size and decorative elaboration imply that postmold patterns reflect aspects of style and social status. John Smith (1986b:173–174) described one of Chief Powhatan's buildings, a structure in the woods outside of Orapax that stored Powhatan's wealth items: "At the 4 corners of this house stand 4 Images as Sentinels, one of a Dragon, another a Beare, the 3 like a Leopard, and the fourth like a giantlike man, all made evillfavorably, according to their best workmanship."

Evidently, the Powhatans incorporated stylistic elements in their architecture to express powerful messages to the culturally initiated that may have conveyed something of their intended significance to English colonists. Colonial accounts also indicate that domestic residences lacked the highly adorned character of Powhatan's storehouse. Much of the original stylistic variation of architecture that did exist cannot be accessed archaeologically due to the ephemeral nature of post-in-ground architecture. Nonetheless, the archaeological record suggests that the James River Valley data do indeed reflect elements of stylistic variation, notably in the layout of domestic architectural floor plans.

Powhatan ethnohistory also raises a cautionary flag in its reference to storehouses, temples, mortuary platforms, and other nondomestic structures that left behind postmold stains. Although domestic structures were the most ubiquitous portion of the Powhatan built environment described in Powhatan ethnohistory, methods for distinguishing such structures are necessary. Hariot (1972:24) estimated house lengths at 12 to 24 yards (11–22 meters), although few archaeologically identified postmold patterns in the James River Valley (excluding palisades) have lengths greater than 10 meters (11 yards). For this study, I included circular, elliptical, or rectangular postmold patterns from 2 to 20 meters (2–22 yards) in length within the sample of domestic architectural patterns. This convention, widely adopted by archaeologists in the region, resulted in the identification of 142 structures for sites in the sample.

Household Clusters

I designated pit feature and domestic architectural associations on a site-by-site basis, generally linking the features from the same occupation located inside a postmold pattern or within 5 meters of a house wall. The goal in associating pit features with architecture is to evaluate the usefulness of the "household cluster" concept (Winter 1976) in the James River Valley. If domestic structures may be linked accurately with contemporaneous pit features constructed or used by the occupants of a house, the daily practices of domestic groups become more accessible.

The household cluster, defined as domestic architecture and associated pit features, may be conceived of as the archaeological unit of analysis linked to the household, a social institution. Following others (e.g., Netting et al. 1984), households are considered here as task-oriented residence units. This definition emphasizes the practices of domestic group members rather than kinship or residence rules. As social entities structured by symbolic systems that are difficult or impossible to access archaeologically, Native American households of the past obviously cannot be studied in the same manner as an ethnographer would approach this institution in a contemporary village setting. Nonetheless, the household cluster concept provides an archaeological unit of analysis through which patterning closely related to household-based practices may be evaluated through 17 centuries and across 340 miles (550 kilometers) of river drainage. As noted above, the contents of pit features cannot be linked easily to households due to the variable manner in which garbage found its way into such receptacles. However, the primary function of a pit feature may be associated less problematically with a spatially proximate domestic structure and its resident domestic group.

Geomorphological Context: Alluvial Dynamics and Archaeological Site Formation

All of the sites considered in this analysis occur in alluvial environments dominated by running water that are subject to a complex and dynamic range of geomorphological forces. Before evaluating patterning in James River feature use, the natural transformations that have affected the sites in the sample bear consideration. Archaeological sites in a riverine context cannot be divorced from the history of deposition, erosion, and stream migration that shapes site formation in alluvial environments. The following briefly addresses the principal concepts of alluvial geoarchaeology before considering late prehistoric James River floodplain geomorphology and the potential impact of changing floodplain conditions on riverine sites.

Floodplains, the landforms upon which most of the sites included in this study rest, are the flat lowlands next to rivers susceptible to flooding (Brown 1997:17). Whether a floodplain receives sedimentary deposition, surrenders deposits to erosion, or remains stable greatly affects the archaeological record. These processes depend upon factors driven by climate change, extreme weather events (such as hurricanes), and altered drainage basin conditions (including deforestation). Floodplain aggradation, the gradual accumulation of land by deposition of water-borne sediment, generally results from intervals of more frequent and higher magnitude flooding, which transports and drops sediments along with overbank water flow. Such flooding deposits fine-grained sediments, which play a role in the creation and augmentation of elevated floodplain features, including levees and point bars, that often served as ideal locations for Native settlements (Waters 1992:132).

As an alternative to floodplain aggradation, scouring and erosion of floodplain sediments may result when overbank flooding is particularly powerful. Erosion also occurs on the concave side of river meanders with sloughing and slumping of the channel bank. Relatively stable floodplains, where sediments neither accumulate nor erode, expose surface deposits for longer intervals. In this setting, soil formation occurs when sediments are weathered and transformed into organic-laden deposits through a combination of chemical and biological activity. Soil, unlike sediment, consists of a mixture of lithic and organic material capable of supporting plant growth (Herz and Garrison 1998:37).

As this discussion illustrates, the same floodplains upon which Native Americans resided may aggrade (i.e., become higher through sedimentary deposition), erode, or remain stable. Relatively undisturbed archaeological sites occur more often in aggrading floodplains than in the other two floodplain modes. Features along the lowlands adjacent to a river may become inundated during a flood and buried as fine-grained sediments settle on the floodplain. A vertical sequence of settlement (i.e., a stratified site) results from repeated occupation of an aggrading floodplain. Alternatively, scouring of archaeological deposits may accompany overbank flooding once the flooding reaches a high enough velocity. Sites near the floodplain surface may be completely destroyed by such flooding, or differential erosion may leave features pedestaled above the scoured floodplain surface (e.g., Gallivan 2003). Relatively stable floodplains that are subject to minimal aggradation or erosion are the most conducive to long-term settlement. As a result, stable floodplains frequently host the thickest, most artifact-rich (and easily recognized) archaeological deposits.

Hayes and Monaghan's (1998) model of the relationship between environmental change and archaeological site formation in alluvial settings in the James and Potomac river drainages provides a means of evaluating the impact of such floodplain dynamics on the James River sample. These geoarchaeologists have traced a floodplain history that oscillates between aggradation and stability linked to changing climate (figure 3-3). During periods in which flood frequency increased, the curving line in the graph moves to the right. At this stage in the cycle, sediment rapidly accumulates on the floodplain surface, generally burying and preserving archaeological sites (Hayes and Monaghan 1998:4). As flood frequency decreases, depicted in figure 3-3 by the curving line moving to the left side of the graph, floodplains become more stable and soils develop. This latter process fosters archaeological site formation once middenlike deposits develop where repeated settlement produces artifact- and organic-rich strata.

According to this reconstruction of alluvial dynamics in the Late Archaic through early historic Chesapeake, floodplain aggradation tied to overbank flooding peaked during the Middle Woodland period, circa A.D. 1. During this high flood interval, floodplain surfaces rapidly aggraded along the James, burying archaeological evidence of settlements and preventing the formation of midden deposits and organic-rich soils. With the subsequent decline in

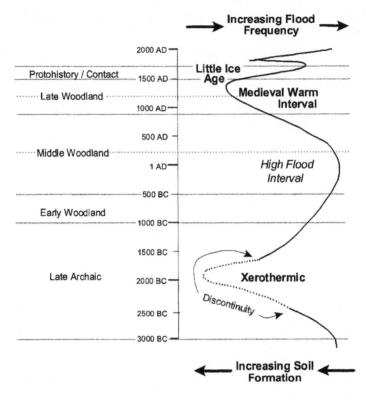

Figure 3-3. Model of James River floodplain geomorphology (modified from Hayes and Monaghan 1998)

floodplain aggradation and the increased soil formation of the Middle Wood-land II, burial of floodplain settlements by alluvium occurred less often. This trend correlates with the earliest stage at which substantial numbers of features have been excavated in all portions of the James River Valley. More intensive sedimentation may preserve archaeological deposits and limit disturbance by repeated human occupation, but finding such sites has proven to be difficult without the use of heavy equipment and deep trenching of floodplains.

Declining flood frequency and lower sedimentation rates during the A.D. 1000–1300 Medieval Warm Interval allowed organic- and artifact-rich deposits to form. Such conditions peaked in A.D. 1300 and produced more stable landforms suitable for long-term settlement. Floodplain soil formation during this interval offered ideal conditions for the low-input horticultural practices of Indians in the Chesapeake region.

With the onset of the cool and moist Little Ice Age between the fourteenth and nineteenth centuries, the system reversed itself once again, and flooding and sedimentation increased. Levees and some alluvial terraces became less desirable locations for settlement as floodwaters inundated the floodplain, burying and concealing older Late Woodland deposits with sediments in some locations. Periodic inundation affected floodplain settlements of the terminal Late Woodland, Protohistoric, and Contact periods. The difficulty in identifying James River Piedmont sites dating to this era may be tied to site formation processes and settlement pattern changes associated with this increased inundation. Geoarchaeological patterns suggest that Piedmont floodplains experienced an unequal share of high magnitude flooding due to the Piedmont's high stream flows (relative to the Ridge and Valley) and minimal wetlands (relative to the Coastal Plain).

The improved understanding of James River geoarchaeology provided by this sequence of floodplain dynamics allows the late prehistoric archaeology to be considered from a new dimension. The lack of substantial numbers of archaeological features that predate the Middle Woodland period does not imply that Indians in the Chesapeake region failed to build substantial houses or dig pit features. Rather, floodplains offered a less suitable living surface during the high flood interval of the Early and Middle Woodland periods. Buried floodplain sites dating to the Early and Middle Woodland are also difficult to detect with current survey methods. Nevertheless, stratified deposits from these periods may reflect a high level of integrity.

Late Woodland floodplain dynamics favored the development of archaeo-logical sites detectable using the site discovery techniques favored in Middle Atlantic archaeological surveys (i.e., shovel test pits and surface reconnaissance of plowed fields). In addition to cultural and historical factors, the prolifer-ation of pit features and architectural patterns within Late Woodland living surfaces resulted from the extended "residence times" of these deposits. The subsequent burial of these deposits in conjunction with increased flooding and sedimentation after A.D. 1300 favors the preservation of features dating to the four centuries between A.D. 900 and 1300.

In order to understand James River culture history, Late Woodland flood-plain archaeology must be weighed against the period's geomorphology. Longer mean residence times for floodplain surfaces during the early Late Woodland undoubtedly generated an archaeological record with temporally mixed deposits in some locations. Such deposits may be misconstrued as reflecting a single floodplain occupation. For post–A.D. 1300 settlements, flooding and aggradation of floodplain surfaces frequently resulted in buried sites (Hantman et al. 1993) and single occupation sites (Lucketti et al. 1994). With the termination of floodplain stability that marked the early part of the Late Woodland, Virginia Indians likely altered settlement practices in response to the more frequent floodplain inundation.

A neo-environmental determinism in which cultural developments responded solely to floodplain dynamics is obviously not warranted in the James River Valley. However, an understanding of alluvial geoarchaeology does allow the changes initiated by Indian communities along the James to be framed in a more complete context. The natural environment clearly presented constraints and opportunities that shaped the region's culture history. Late Woodland conditions marked by stable floodplain surfaces and organically rich floodplain soils must be seen as important factors as communities embraced horticulture and increased residential permanence. Similar conditions that existed two to three millennia prior to the Late Woodland probably played a role in the floodplain-focused (though nonhorticultural) economies of the "Transitional" period (Mouer 1990). Heightened flooding during the Protohistoric and early Contact periods makes the persistence of floodplain settlement a somewhat unexpected pattern demanding a cultural explanation.

Chapter 4

Sedentariness, Community Size, and Village Settlement

Understanding the cultural dynamics of James River societies may begin with a consideration of settlement mobility and demography. The following draws principles from archaeological methods that link evidence of feature construction and artifact discard behavior to residential permanence and settlement populations. Such "accumulations research" (e.g., Varien and Mills 1997) offers tools for building middle range links between the archaeology of residential settlements and behavioral patterns fundamental to late prehistoric and early colonial social life.

Characterizations of prehistoric mobility and settlement size in the James River Valley, as in many other regions, currently rely on typological or qualitative distinctions that fall short of the precision needed to evaluate competing models of the behavioral and cultural changes that produced the social inequality and political hierarchy documented during the colonial encounter. The frequent reoccupation of favored riverine locations complicates analysis of sedentariness and settlement population in the James River Valley and the Middle Atlantic generally. Archaeologists' overwhelming reliance on phase-based dating in the region adds to the difficulty of characterizing such variables. As outlined below and detailed elsewhere (Gallivan 2002), I have attempted to alleviate these problems in three ways: reliance on the absolute dating methods described in the previous chapter, modification and application of Lightfoot's (1984) multivariate approach to interpreting sedentariness, and analysis of pottery accumulation patterns as indicators of settlement population within residential settlements.

Measuring Sedentariness in the James River Valley

Researchers working in the Middle Atlantic region struggle to distinguish the archaeological signatures of relatively sedentary communities from short-term, repeated site occupations. Especially in floodplain settings, a location may contain archaeological deposits that, on the basis of their abundance, appear to reflect a single, long-term occupation. These patterns may instead reflect the frequency with which a place has been used over many different

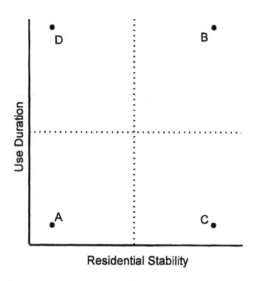

Figure 4-1. Orthogonal model of sedentariness (from Lightfoot 1984).

occupations, a common occurrence in the James River Valley. A form of accumulations research useful for characterizing the archaeological record of such locations distinguishes between a settlement's "residential stability" and its "use duration" (Sullivan 1980; Lightfoot 1984; Lightfoot and Jewett 1986). As developed by Lightfoot (1984), "residential stability" refers to the span of time spent at a location during the annual cycle. Residential stability may range from less than a single day to an entire year. The concept of "use duration" accounts for the overlapping effect of multiple-occupation sites. The use duration of an archaeological place refers to the cumulative time over which the site has been used. As such, use duration gauges the total length of time that a location is either continuously or discontinuously occupied.

Use duration and residential stability may be plotted on two axes as a means of clarifying the sedentariness patterns of four archaeological site types (figure 4-1). Point A on the graph suggests a site with low use duration and low residential stability that is occupied briefly and only once. Point B depicts a high use-duration/high residential-stability settlement that may be characterized as a long-term settlement occupied continuously for many years. Point C reflects a long-term settlement occupied once. Point D depicts a briefly occupied location whose inhabitants return many times.

As a simple heuristic that accounts for both the use and the reuse of important places in a settlement system, the chart offers a means of characterizing sedentariness in a wide array of settings. Analysis of the settlements in the James River sample may begin with a consideration of residential stability and use duration as these concepts apply to the region. Jamestown colonists' accounts of Powhatan mobility patterns indicate that during the fall and winter some domestic groups left floodplain villages for periodic forays away from the riverine setting. In fact, the Powhatans' yearly round incorporated a diverse range of subsistence strategies throughout which riverine villages served as a central locus of activities. By late November at least some households departed from their villages for fall and winter hunting grounds located in the uplands. In 1608 Smith (1986d:178) noted upon visiting the Piankatanks' village that "most were a-hunting, save a few old men, women, and children," suggesting that villages were rarely completely abandoned by all of their residents.

Residential Stability Index

Given the ethnohistorical indications that households served as important social and economic units during the seventeenth century and that domestic groups periodically departed from village settings, analysis of sedentariness may begin with a focus on household mobility. The range of tasks performed by household members offers a means of considering such mobility, which has predictable implications for the archaeological record. The range of features present in a settlement likely parallels the range of tasks accomplished by a domestic group. Native communities undoubtedly performed a greater diversity of activities with a residential presence that incorporated a longer portion of the domestic cycle and settlement round.

Feature diversity, measured here in terms of the number of feature categories present in a settlement (i.e., richness), provides a point of departure for constructing an index of residential stability in the James River Valley. Since the preservation of postmolds, pit features, and house patterns at the sites in the sample is uneven, a measurement tool comprised of several archaeological variables is needed to limit the impact of any one attribute on the index and to incorporate all relevant information. Accordingly, I combined feature richness measures with six other variables tied to occupation duration that correlate positively and significantly with feature richness. These include lithic tool assemblage diversity (evenness), house floor area, post diameter, frequency of structure wall posts, number of interior house features, and pit volume.

Each of these variables measures a distinct archaeological pattern tied to behavior closely associated with settlement permanence. Accordingly, the variables were incorporated into a single residential stability index as a means of limiting the impact of any single variable on the analysis. The composite residential stability index is effectively a mean of the values for these seven variables.[1]

Measured in this way, residential stability increased through time for James River settlements in the sample (appendix 2).[2] Dividing the data set into Coastal Plain, Piedmont, and Ridge and Valley settlements produces similar results—residential stability increases through time in all three provinces of the James River Valley.[3] A pattern of longer residential permanence through time is clearly apparent throughout the valley.

Use-Duration Index

The use-duration index used to measure the cumulative length of settlement occupation duration also combined the average of several archaeological variables. Archaeological attributes reflecting a location's use duration are predominantly those related to the density of artifacts, structures, burials, and facilities. Locations occupied for a substantial portion of the year (i.e., a site with high residential stability) produce a diverse array of feature and artifact classes. By contrast, a favored location that mobile groups revisited briefly and often would not manifest the same high diversity of material culture but would nonetheless exhibit a high density of artifacts and features. For this analysis, use duration combined feature density, postmold density, burial density, artifact density, and burial-to-house ratios.

The resulting values (appendix 3) indicate that households in the James River Valley used floodplain locations for increasingly longer durations through the sequence considered.[4] Positive relationships between these variables are apparent in the Piedmont and in the Coastal Plain, though the small sample of sites from the Ridge and Valley lacks a clear pattern through time.[5] Nonetheless, trends toward longer residential stability and use duration are reflected in the late precontact archaeology of residential sites throughout much of the James River Valley.

The use duration and residential stability of settlements in the sample are plotted on two axes in figure 4-2 to compare patterning in the James River sample with Lightfoot's (1984) ideal settlement types modeled in figure 4-1. The chart depicts relative measures of sedentariness. Dashed lines at the 50 percent level divide the scatterplot into quadrants. Points below the horizontal dashed line mark sites with use-duration values in the lower half

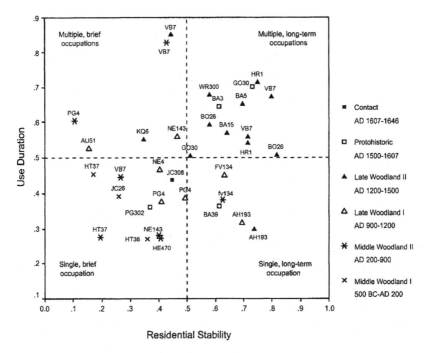

Figure 4-2. Scatterplot of use duration against residential stability, James River Valley settlements

of the sample; points to the left of the vertical dashed line have residential-stability values in the lower half of the sample.

As indicated in the chart, the sedentariness of James River Valley communities changed in a patterned manner over the sequence considered. The upper right quadrant marking relatively permanent settlements is dominated by occupations dating to between A.D. 1200 and 1607. The lower left quadrant, with settlements bearing the sedentariness values of a single, brief occupation, is dominated by Middle Woodland (500 B.C.–A.D. 900) cases. Once these patterns are combined with evidence of changes in settlement demography considered below, the history of residential settlement during the late precontact and early colonial eras in the James River Valley becomes clearer.

Settlement Population: Modeling Pottery
Discard Behavior in the James River Valley

Colonial accounts of the Powhatans provide a rough sense of group size in the seventeenth-century Coastal Plain, though it is unclear how these ranges relate to precontact community sizes throughout the river valley. According to Smith (1986b:162), Powhatan settlements consisted of anywhere from 2 to 100 houses, a range he later revised to between 2 to 50 houses (1986d:116). In what appears to be a reflection of typical settlement size as recorded ethnohistorically, Gabriel Archer (1998b:123) wrote that Powhatan towns housed some 40 to 50 residents, including households arrayed along the river front "not past a mile or half a mile asunder in most places." Despite the wide range of population sizes implied by Smith's account, other colonists reported that even the principal towns of early-seventeenth-century eastern Virginia were rather modest affairs, and much of the population lived in even smaller hamlets. As Archer indicates, some residential settlements in the Chesapeake were dispersed along the floodplain, complicating colonists' and archaeologists' estimates of settlement population.

General population estimates for the groups that comprised the Powhatan paramountcy have been inferred from Smith's (1986b:146–148) and Strachey's (1953:45–47, 63–69) census of "warriors" per village. Researchers have used various ratios to convert these counts to population estimates, arriving at figures ranging from approximately 100 to 1,000 individuals for the named Powhatan "petty chiefdoms" (e.g., Feest 1978:67; Ubelaker 1974; Turner 1982:50–59). These numbers report not the size of individual settlements but the population of groups that were definable through relations of alliance and kinship that drew together warriors during hostilities.

As with these ethnohistorical references, archaeological data do not provide a straightforward indication of population size in the precontact settlements of the James River Valley. Few sites have enough excavated and well-dated house patterns from which to infer overall population using ratios of house floor area per resident frequently employed by archaeologists. The sizes of artifact scatters identified on survey serve as a poor proxy for habitation area due to the palimpsest effect of multiple occupations, rendering equations for computing population size from this variable inaccurate.

As in other contexts, though, settlement size may be estimated through evidence of pottery discard behavior. Another variant of accumulations research, analysis of pottery discard behavior emphasizes pottery use and breakage combined with a mathematical "discard equation" (e.g., Nelson 1909; Nelson et al. 1994; Pauketat 1989; Schiffer 1975, 1976, 1987; Varien 1999; Varien and Mills 1997). Such equations derive demographic estimates from the accumulation of ceramic debris in a location. The discard equation may be modified to estimate the number of households in a settlement (H) from the total discarded ceramics (T_D) in an occupation, ceramic vessel use life (L), the size of a typical household pottery assemblage (S), and a settlement's occupation span (t), such that:

$$H = \frac{T_D \times L}{S \times t}$$

As a "strong" archaeological case containing sealed house floor deposits, the Leatherwood Creek site (44HR1) provides useful guidelines for estimating the size of a typical household pottery assemblage in the region. The Leatherwood Creek site, located in the Roanoke River drainage, included two distinct Late Woodland occupations. The site contained several house floor features dated to the thirteenth century that were remarkably undisturbed by historic plowing (Gallivan 1997a). The houses appear to have burned in place, filling the floor features with charcoal and several large vessel sections. The associated deposits appear to represent items in use by a household when the structure burned (Gravely 1983:121).

To the extent that vessels recovered from house floors at Leatherwood Creek can be considered representative of household pottery in the region, a typical late precontact domestic group used one large jar and two to three small bowls. Given the variety of media used in fabricating household containers documented ethnohistorically (i.e., shell, leather, textiles, and especially wood), pottery vessels likely formed a subset of the containers used in the domestic context.

Breakage rates of domestic pottery, necessary to compute ceramic vessel use life (the variable L in the discard equation), were drawn from values recorded by ethnographers from five Native societies (Deal 1983:157; Foster 1960; DeBoer 1974:340; DeBoer and Lathrap 1979). Using an average of these values, a typical domestic group with a household assemblage of 1 jar and 2.5 bowls contributes approximately 0.58 jar and 2.56 bowls to the archaeological record through breakage in a typical year. Translating these values to sherd counts using a sample of reconstructed vessels from the James River Valley, I estimate that a typical household in the region contributed approximately 370 sherds per household per year.

Time (t) remains a variable in the equation. The opportunity for a vessel to break at a settlement rises with increasing sedentariness and the accumulated length of multiple occupation spans. In other words, the opportunity for vessel breakage increases with both use duration and residential stability. As a result, the sedentariness values calculated earlier become useful in estimating settlement population size. However, there is little basis from which to convert the relative sedentariness measures generated above to absolute values. Fortunately, a second strong archaeological case exists in the region that may be used to calibrate the temporal portion of the discard equation (t). The Fredricks site (31OR231), located in the Eno River drainage in the North Carolina Piedmont, represents the principal Occaneechi settlement at the close of the seventeenth century (Ward and Davis 1993, 1988). A palisade surrounded the settlement at Fredricks, nearly all of which has been excavated. The site contained few overlapping features, limiting the likelihood of a complicated history of multiple reoccupations. Just as the Leatherwood Creek site provides a strong archaeological case in the form of rapidly sealed house floor assemblages, which is highly unusual in the Middle Atlantic, the Fredricks site offers a rare archaeological glimpse of an entire village community occupied over a relatively brief span of time.

The Fredricks site excavation plan reveals the remains of 12 or 13 houses and presumably the accumulated pottery debris of 12 or 13 households. For this portion of the analysis, I calculated use-duration and sedentariness measures for Fredricks using the same approach applied to the James River data. The product of these values served as a measurement of occupation span, or t in the equation. Inserting the Fredricks site data into the equation permits the variable for time to be calibrated with a constant, so that

$$H = \frac{T_D \times L}{370t \times 4.297}$$

The calibrated equation estimates the number of households for the settlements in the James River Valley sample. The equation produces estimates of households per settlement that generally rise through time, accelerating after A.D. 1200. A scatterplot of the number of households against occupation date suggests a nonlinear relationship between settlement population and time (figure 4-3), with settlement population size increasing at a rate that increases during the Late Woodland centuries.[6]

The results of the calculations, summarized in appendix 3, and the regression line drawn on figure 4-3 suggest the presence of two to four households within Middle Woodland settlements in the riverine setting. Little change in the Late Woodland I mean is followed by substantially higher (and more variable) numbers of households residing in settlements after A.D. 1200. These results show that remarkably low numbers of households resided in floodplain settlements prior to A.D. 1200. During the following centuries, the num-

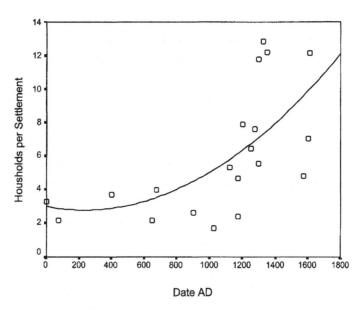

Figure 4-3. Scatterplot of households per settlement against occupation date

ber increases to a mean of approximately eight households per settlement. Assuming six persons per household, the minimum of the range recorded by Jamestown colonists (Smith 1986b:162; Strachey 1953:79), the equation produces a minimal estimate of 29 to 73 residents for Protohistoric and Contact period settlements. Though somewhat wider, this range is comparable to Jamestown colonist Gabriel Archer's (1998b:123) estimate of 40 to 50 Powhatans per village. Generally, the model of pottery discard behavior produces credible estimates of settlement population. More important, the analysis records relative change in settlement population over seventeen centuries in the James River Valley.

The Establishment of Village Communities in the James River Valley

The patterns identified in this analysis substantially increase understanding of Native settlement history in the Chesapeake. As indicated in figure 4-2, Middle Woodland occupations generally fall within the lower left quadrant that approximates the ideal site type labeled as "single, brief occupation," while two of the Middle Woodland occupations approximate the site type idealized as "multiple, brief occupations," that is, a location occupied temporarily but repeatedly over many years. Middle Woodland settlements clearly reflect floodplain occupations with low sedentariness relative to later periods. Populations in Middle Woodland settlements also proved to be remarkably low. The Middle Woodland data accord well with models of small-scale, mobile foragers, with some riverine locations that were used over multiple settlement rounds exhibiting a particularly dense array of archaeological deposits.

Late Woodland I (A.D. 900–1200) sites in the sample, the earliest containing evidence of agriculture, have slightly higher sedentariness values. Use-duration and residential-stability values for Late Woodland I phase cases generally fall in the lower half of the sample, though, reflecting occupation spans that differed only modestly from preceding centuries. The absence of Late Woodland I settlements with high residential-stability and use-duration values points to settlements that were not reoccupied often and lacked facilities designed for long-term, multiyear use, an important attribute of village settlement (Rafferty 1985). Likewise, Late Woodland I settlement sizes diverged little from the Middle Woodland period, with an average of fewer than four households per settlement.

Late Woodland II (A.D. 1200–1500) cases dominate figure 4-2's upper right quadrant modeled as comprising "multiple, long-term occupations." Cases from all physiographic provinces dating to this phase fall into this category. These sites approach the ideal of a year-round residential village occupied for multiple years. Between A.D. 1200 and 1500 floodplain settlements entailed a substantial and measurable increase in relative sedentariness, while residential settlement population jumped appreciably for the first time in 12 centuries. These results suggest that the fundamental nature of floodplain settlements changed in the James River Valley after A.D. 1200. Sedentariness measures indicate that domestic groups in the James River Valley occupied settlements for a substantially greater portion of the year and returned to these settlements with a greater frequency than previously during the Late Woodland II phase. Concurrently, relatively large settlements of eight or more households first appeared.

Taken together, the trends in sedentariness and demography signal the emergence of floodplain settlements different enough from preceding periods to merit use of the label "village" for the first time. Settlement populations in the sample appear to have been uniformly small prior to A.D. 1200, while after that date community sizes were larger and more variable. The histograms in figure 4-4 depict the range of settlement sizes for the periods before and after A.D. 1200 and the number cases that fall within each size range. Figure 4-4 raises the possibility that a trend from a unimodal to a bimodal distribution of site sizes occurs in the region, with the post–A.D. 1200 period offering evidence of a settlement hierarchy in the James River Valley.

Not all sites of the Protohistoric (A.D. 1500–1607) and Contact (A.D. 1607–1646) periods continue the sedentariness pattern exhibited by Late Woodland II sites. Two of the five cases fall into figure 4-2's lower left quadrant otherwise dominated by Middle Woodland sites, while another case falls within the "single, long-term occupation" quadrant. In contrast, Protohistoric cases from the Piedmont and the Ridge and Valley produce residential stability values that place them within the quadrant approximating a year-round residential village. The presence of interior settlements that maintained precontact trends raises the possibility that proximity to a European presence near the coast played a role in the observed pattern. As noted previously, recent research into the Chesapeake region's climatological variation indicates that severe droughts in the coastal area accompanied the colonial presence at Roanoke and Jamestown (Blanton 2000). The emergence of the militant Powhatan paramountcy also may have altered group mobility patterns subsequent to its development during the sixteenth century. Settlements in the coastal region that witnessed the most intensive European contact, unusually dry climatic episodes, and encompassment by a tributary chiefdom produced the lowest sedentariness values of the sixteenth and seventeenth centuries, suggesting that historical and environmental factors had already altered fundamental aspects of the social context described by Jamestown colonists.

Sedentariness and Settlement Demography: Summary of Trends

This analysis of sedentariness and settlement patterns has identified rather dramatic changes in the nature of settlement on the James River floodplain during the Late Woodland Period. The previous consideration of floodplain dynamics over the same interval suggests that the external constraints of the riverine environment played a role in the sedentariness and settlement size patterns detected above. Declining flood frequency and lower sedimentation rates peaked circa A.D. 1300, offering relatively stable floodplain landforms with organic-rich soils—ideal conditions for the settlement of long-term residential villages on the floodplain. The continued settlement of relatively large and permanent villages during subsequent centuries when flood frequency increased offers evidence of persisting cultural patterns in the face of environmental change.

The demographic patterns that emerge from this application of accumulations research indicate that fewer than six households resided in most

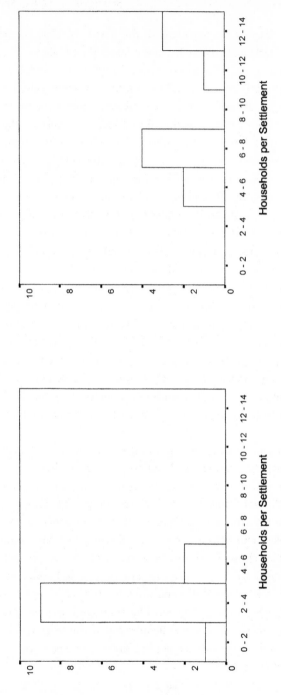

Figure 4-4. Households per settlement, A.D. 1–1200 (left) and A.D. 1200–1610 (right)

floodplain settlements prior to A.D. 1200, while after that date communities became more variable in size but rarely incorporated fewer than six households. On the basis of community size, it appears that Powhatan and Monacan communities in the James River drainage crossed a quantitative threshold, and likely a social threshold as well, during the Late Woodland II phase.

As discussed earlier, Gregory Johnson (1982) demonstrated that information processing and decision making by groups of social units (such as households) that rise above five or six units can no longer easily accommodate consensus-based decision making requiring the gathering of information and equal weighing of opinions from all participants. Some Native American groups, such as the Iroquois (Trigger 1990), developed extraordinary social and political institutions to limit the "scalar stress" produced by large village communities and multicommunity polities. The colonial accounts of the Powhatans and Monacans during the sixteenth and seventeenth centuries indicate that Native societies in the Chesapeake region followed a different historical trajectory marked by social inequality and political hierarchy.

It is also apparent from the analysis that a cultural landscape of village communities lagged several centuries behind the introduction of maize horticulture in the James River Valley. Sedentariness and settlement demography during the two-to-three-century "time lag" following the adoption of horticulture differed only modestly from the preceding Middle Woodland period. Evidently food production was initially added to the subsistence regime of relatively mobile James River communities without resulting in a considerably altered settlement system. Key elements of a settlement pattern in which relatively small-scale, mobile groups focused seasonally on the riverine environment remained fundamentally unchanged from the end of the Late Archaic period, circa 1000 B.C.–A.D. 1200. Following the adoption of food production, transitions to sedentary village communities throughout North America were apparently neither automatic nor immediate but frequently followed a time delay of considerable length (e.g., Plog 1990a).

In fact, James River villagers after A.D. 1200 did not alter their subsistence practices or embrace technical innovations that set them apart from communities of earlier centuries. Rather, in creating a novel cultural landscape of village communities during the final prehistoric centuries, Native Americans in the Chesapeake region reorganized their social relations in fundamental ways, as outlined in the following chapters.

Chapter 5

The Domestic Economy

Archaeological evidence from the James River floodplain indicates that 300 years after the introduction of maize horticulture into the region, village communities appeared for the first time. By the late sixteenth and early seventeenth centuries many of these villages had been subsumed within the Powhatan paramountcy and a hierarchical Monacan polity. In the interim, daily practices keyed to social arrangements at the domestic, communal, and regional scales underwent an interrelated set of changes. I begin my analysis of these developments by examining ethnohistorical and archaeological evidence related to the domestic scale in the James River Valley.

The domestic group, or the household (terms used interchangeably here), has been labeled "the next bigger thing on the social map to the individual" (Hart 1995). While studies often focus on the domestic context as it relates to the cultural construction of gender and practices surrounding food preparation and child rearing, domestic relationships are often so intertwined with relationships of power that to separate the domestic from the political would be misleading (Yanagisako 1979:191). Especially since household archaeology has been defined as a distinct field of inquiry (Wilk and Rathje 1982), archaeologists have focused on this microscale of social action.

In this chapter I argue that changes in domestic groups' economic practices and social reproduction played a central role in the James River's late prehistoric social dynamics. Archaeological evidence considered here indicates that after the establishment of village communities, domestic group size increased and household members organized practices related to production, consumption, and the control of surplus to an unprecedented extent. Patterning in domestic architecture and household storage also suggests a marked increase in social differentiation during the Late Woodland II phase. For the first time, the funds of power necessary for the institutionalization of social inequality became available in the domestic sphere with the establishment of village communities.

Household Archaeology

The architectural and pit feature data compiled for this study provide unprecedented access to the practices of late precontact and early colonial do-

mestic groups in the Chesapeake region. My consideration of households
as residence units whose members share daily tasks follows other archaeological studies of this social scale (e.g., Kent 1990; Rogers and Smith 1995;
Mehrer 1995;Wattenmaker 1998). This approach emphasizes spatial patterning related to domestic activities rather than kinship norms and residence
rules (Hendon 1996:45–46; cf. Longacre 1964; Hill 1970). As feminist and
economic anthropologists have emphasized (e.g., Moore 1992; Wilk 1989;
Yanagisako 1979), households are culturally variable social institutions defined
by complex symbolic structures. Nonetheless, households have become the
focus of archaeological inquiry due to their links to discrete dwellings and
spatially associated features that provide a bounded, nonarbitrary context
comparable across sites.

Utilitarian, Indexical, and Canonical Implications of Domestic Architecture
Domestic architecture places boundaries on and organizes the use of space
(Kent 1990). The social use of space and the construction of the built environment relate to one another in a reflexive manner, with structures erected
to conform to social needs and architecture constraining and ordering social interaction in turn (e.g., Blanton 1994). The relatively impermanent
and vernacular architecture of societies such as those of the late prehistoric
James River Valley may be more responsive to alterations in social practices
than the built environment requiring specialized labor for raising structures
that endure for multiple generations. Building technology and construction
materials place some restrictions on the possible configurations of the built
environment, yet the relatively small-scale domestic structures of the precontact Eastern Woodlands have proven to be remarkably malleable to culture
change (e.g., Kapches 1990; Braun 1991; Snow 1989).

Considered as products of pragmatic considerations relating to the need for
shelter, on the one hand, and as a central part of a society's system of nonverbal
communication, on the other, houses reflect a social design process involving
an amalgamation of potentially conflicting goals. The most prominent utilitarian variables relevant to North American middle range societies are the
size and the residential mobility of domestic groups (McGuire and Schiffer
1983:280–289). These variables are closely intertwined and are frequently
influenced by the organization of economic production. Small households
may serve best under conditions of relatively high group mobility and are
often found where production within a society is uniform among members.
Larger households may respond best to circumstances in which production

is diversified and a need to perform multiple tasks at the same time arises (i.e., "task simultaneity") (Wilk and Rathje 1982:625, 631). As production intensifies and becomes more spatially and temporally variable, something that occurs with food production, larger households frequently provide a solution to the demands for task simultaneity.

As a channel of nonverbal communication, houses also operate in an "indexical" mode that conveys aspects of a household's social status (Blanton 1994:10). Domestic architecture's indexical information relates to the social identity of a domestic group and status-related variables such as a household's wealth and its stage in the domestic cycle. Domestic architecture often parallels heightened social inequality, with increasing variability in the dimensions, construction techniques, and house forms of a community (McGuire and Schiffer 1983:282).

The domestic built environment may also relay information in a "canonical" form that involves messages related to enduring features of social relations (Blanton 1994:11; Rappaport 1979). Symbolic studies in this vein point to the role played by houses, sometimes including small and simple structures, as media for expressing and inculcating sacred propositions and ideas of central cultural importance (e.g., Cunningham 1964; Bourdieu 1973). Even while embodying such ideas, domestic architectural design also responds to changes in the daily practices of the domestic sphere. Unraveling the canonical meanings communicated by domestic architectural style during prehistory poses serious challenges (cf. Hodder 1990). Houses have no fixed symbolic connotations outside everyday practices that respond to and modify the ideologies of historically situated actors (Bourdieu 1977).

Due to the remoteness of such practices from the archaeological record, the following analysis does not attempt to decode the canonical principles or "spatial texts" (Moore 1986) imparted by the architecture of James River Valley groups. Rather, I focus on archaeological data keyed to "utilitarian" elements, especially domestic group size, and indexical aspects such as the variability of house forms and associated storage.

Ethnohistory: Powhatan Domestic Groups
Before tackling these issues, some basic principles behind the organization of Virginia Indians' domestic groups at the end of the historical sequence considered in this study may be drawn from Powhatan ethnohistory. The seventeenth-century descriptions provided by Jamestown colonists, including John Smith, William Strachey, and Henry Spelman, indicate that the

Powhatans formed coresidential households that served as units of subsistence production and consumption. Strachey informs us that Powhatan men sought to create large families so that their wives and children would feed and maintain them well into old age (Strachey 1953:116). The Mamanatowick Powhatan was uniquely successful in his efforts to expand the size of his household, keeping many wives in his principal village and others in villages throughout the region. Smith (1986b:160) noted that "each household knoweth their owne lands and gardens, and most live of their own labors." Though the English at Jamestown understood Powhatan notions of land tenure in only a vague way, this passage and others suggest that seventeenth-century Powhatan households played a defining role in the organization of production. During the spring and summer, Powhatan groups lived in villages and raised maize, beans, squash, and tobacco. Smith's (1986b:156–157) description of Powhatan seasons suggests that village life extended from an April planting to a mid-November harvest, the season of the "chief feasts and sacrifice." After celebrating the fall harvest, some domestic groups dispersed to hunt and forage in the uplands away from the village setting.

Smith's account of engendered Powhatan labor categories captures fundamental domestic relationships: "The men bestowe their times in fishing, hunting, wars and such man-like exercises, scorning to be seene in any woman-like exercise. . . . The women and children do the rest of the worke. They make mats, baskets, pots, morters, pound their corne, make their bread, prepare their victuals, plant their corne, [and] gather their corne" (1986b:162). William Strachey's account describes Powhatan marriages: "[Powhatan men] expresse their loves to such women . . . by presenting them with the fructs of their labors by fowle, fish, or wild beasts, which by their huntings . . . they bring unto the young woman. . . . [T]he Parents must allow of the Sutor, and for their good wills, the [man] promise[s] that the daughter shall not want of such provisions nor of deares skins. . . . [A]s soon as he hath provided her with a howse . . . he takes her home" (1953:112).

These passages from Smith and Strachey indicate that Powhatan men and women, combined with their children, formed domestic groups whose members exchanged the horticultural products of women (and children) for male products of hunting—meat and animal skins. Powhatan domestic groups stored maize destined for consumption by the members of a household within their houses or immediately outside domestic structures (Spelman 1998:492–493). Spelman (1998:493) describes the annual harvesting of the "king's corn" as an event that provided a crucial linkage between households and the political economy. The harvesting of the king's corn occurred on a day in the fall when all the local men and women gathered for this purpose. Upon completion of this annual event, the *weroance* reciprocated with handfuls of beads.

During the Powhatans' annual planting rite, men's participation alongside women transformed the typical division of labor between men and women. In most circumstances men did not participate in planting, weeding, or harvesting (Smith 1986b:157). During these annual rituals, commoner men worked alongside women, an occurrence that appears to have enacted the structural analogy "as a wife to her husband, so a commoner to the *weroance*" (Williamson 1979:406). The events may in fact have symbolized the *weroance's* unequal status with regard to other villagers. This status appears to have been conceived of through the metaphor of engendered labor that defined the domestic realm. During the planting ritual, the *weroance* reoriented labor that generally remained within the household sphere toward the political economy.

Once mobilized from "commoner" households, Powhatan chiefs' corn was stored in one of the few nondomestic structures described by the English. Powhatan's treasury housed skins, beads, pearls, and copper (Smith 1986b:173). Within this structure, corn, divine images, copper, and beads rested amid the bones of Powhatan ancestors (Spelman 1998:486). In this way, Powhatan chiefs' aboveground storage of corn occurred in the context of symbolically important items.

Although ethnohistorical accounts mention the Powhatan household context only briefly, the spatial correlates of household activities may still be inferred. Strachey (1953:78–79) describes the domestic area as the context for a variety of activities, including food preparation and storage, though he also notes that some storage occurred in pits concealed in the woods to shelter valuables. Based on English reports of the considerable burden entailed in tribute payments of subsistence products and horticultural labor given to paramount chief Powhatan (Smith 1986b:174), the Powhatans' concealment of corn and other valuables in storage pits may have reflected, in some contexts, silent defiance of the tribute demands of chiefs (cf. DeBoer 1988:9). Whether storage occurs underground or aboveground, within domestic structures or in a chief's treasury, storage facilities reflected important aspects of the role of surplus in the Powhatan political economy.

With the benefit of these written accounts, several statements about the Powhatans may be made. Following marriage, the Powhatans formed coresidential households that shared in a number of food production activities. Within the mixed horticultural, hunting, and foraging practices of the Powhatans, horticultural products, principally maize, provided a critical link between domestic production and political relationships. The concealment of maize and other products in subsurface pits also provided a mechanism for retaining surplus production within the household. Storage facilities cannot be imagined as commensurate with social relationships or equivalent to surplus, but storage does reflect practices intimately linked with the Powhatans' domestic production and the political realm. Stored food appeared in several different physical spaces: inside houses, in subsurface storage pits, and in aboveground granaries. Storage practices correspond with several social institutions—the domestic group, the village *weroance*, and the paramount chief—each of which had fundamentally different roles in the political economy.

Social Dynamics within the Domestic Sphere

The colonial accounts indicate that the architecture and storage practices of Powhatan households may be linked to important domestic social practices. The model of James River Valley social dynamics presented earlier directs attention to several of these practices.

First, household members likely altered domestic group size and surplus production during the late precontact era with the transition to a horticultural economy that saw the end of a foraging mode of production. The evidence reviewed in the preceding chapter demonstrates that sedentariness and community size increased during late prehistory, with an acceleration of these trends circa A.D. 1200–1500. The adoption of horticulture and declining mobility during the Late Woodland introduced incentives for domestic groups to generate larger surpluses and higher birth rates that may have altered the social reproduction process in the James River Valley. Studies indicate that the availability of maize impacts fertility levels by providing a suitable food for weaning children, thus reducing lactation time (Lee 1979:329–30; Binford and Chasko 1976:138). Children may contribute to a domestic group's labor force in a horticultural economy and increase the productive potential substantially (Ford 1974; Wiessner 1977:376–377). As a result, household members may increase the size of the domestic group in order to increase the labor available for surplus production, something noted by Strachey (1953) in his reference to Powhatan household size. With the mixed subsistence economy of the Late Woodland period, households also engaged in production practices requiring a greater degree of task simultaneity and a more complex scheduling of production activities than during preceding centuries, both of which benefited from increases in domestic group size.

Second, the organization of economic practices likely changed with the emergence of the village as a settlement form. As outlined earlier, ethnological studies of small-scale agricultural societies (e.g., Sahlins 1972; Netting 1990:38) and archaeological studies of North American communities undergoing a transition to sedentism and horticulture (e.g., Kelly 1990:108; Plog 1990a) demonstrate that households frequently became predominant economic units with the transition to village life. Related changes in resource distribution accompanied this development in several contexts, with the shift from a socially sanctioned emphasis on collective sharing to more circumscribed notions of ownership centered on the household unit or a limited number of households (e.g., Plog 1990a:185; Hegmon 1989). With the "collective" to "domestic" transition suggested by these trends, a more restricted social network for sharing production and consumption activities emerged.

Once combined, these two trends likely produced precontact social dynamics whereby households became larger and more variable in terms of their sizes and surplus production, while at the community level economic activities such as production and consumption incorporated a more limited social sphere focused on the domestic group. This scenario does not propose the emergence of autonomous households in the James River Valley, but that households became more prominent institutions for the organization of economic relations during late prehistory.

Floor Area of Domestic Structures

Analysis of household archaeology in the James River Valley may begin with "utilitarian" aspects tied to domestic group size and storage practices. While the colonial written accounts of Powhatan households provide compelling evidence of domestic organization and the importance of storage and surplus production, an understanding of long-term trends in domestic organization requires archaeological evidence. Smith's (1986b:162) estimate of 6 to 20 Powhatans per household offers only a vague statement regarding domestic group size and a rather high range for the modestly sized floor areas of late precontact architecture in the James River Valley.

Postmold patterns reflecting the footprint of domestic architecture provide archaeologically accessible evidence of household size. Cultural differences

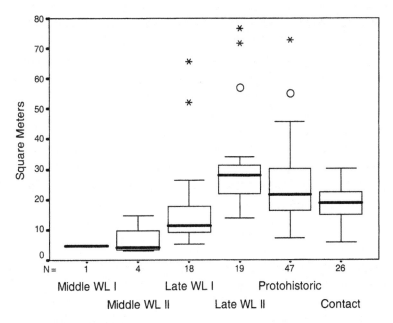

Figure 5-1. Floor area boxplots

obviously result in a variable relationship between house size and the absolute size of the domestic group (e.g., Naroll 1962; Kramer 1979:153; Wiessner 1974), yet domestic structures' floor areas generally provide a reliable relative indicator of household size within a given social context. Ethnological research into small-scale agricultural societies also suggests that a close correlation exists between the wealth of domestic groups and the number of household members, such that intracommunity variation in household size is best explained by wealth differences (Netting 1982).

Figure 5-1 depicts house floor area in the James River through time in a boxplot format.[1] As indicated in the boxplot, house floor areas generally increased through the Late Woodland II phase and declined thereafter, a pattern repeated in the mean values of the three physiographic provinces. The pattern indicates that a Late Woodland II increase in mean house floor area occurred across the drainage.[2]

Prior to A.D. 1500 floor area correlates positively with occupation date, suggesting a precontact increase in house size.[3] This pattern occurs throughout the James River Valley, including a statistically significant increase in floor area during the Late Woodland II phase.

The Protohistoric decrease in mean house floor area resists concise explanation.[4] The post–A.D. 1500 data do not provide statistically significant evidence of an overall decline in house floor area, nor do they indicate a continuation of the clear pattern of precontact increase. An interruption in the social dynamics influencing domestic group size appears to have occurred circa A.D. 1500. Concurrent with this interruption, communities throughout the James River Valley largely ceased their use of storage pits spatially associated with domestic architecture, as addressed below. The relatively brief period between A.D. 1500 and the social collapse of the Powhatan and Monacan polities during the seventeenth century apparently saw the emergence of a different set of factors influencing house construction and, inferentially, household composition.

Associated Features of the Household Cluster

The model of social dynamics introduced earlier raises the possibility that economic relations, including production and consumption, shifted in orientation from the collective settlement to the household during late prehistory. In archaeological terms, the most secure evidence concerning the production practices of the domestic group comes from features located within domestic structures. Establishing the association of pit features and domestic architecture on Eastern Woodlands archaeological sites can be difficult, but the idea that domestic groups used the pits within their houses is a fairly defensible proposition.

The number of interior pits is considered here as an indicator of the degree to which production tasks occurred within the interior of the domestic structure. The spatial organization of such activities offers an indication of the extent to which households dominated production and consumption, with a shift from economic practices structured around the collective settlement to those centered on domestic groups. The number of interior features also relates to sedentariness. A household present on the floodplain in colder months is more likely to use interior features, especially hearths.

Figure 5-2 displays the average number of features located within domestic structures throughout the James River Valley. Houses dating to the thirteenth through fifteenth centuries stand out as having a substantially greater number of interior features than those of preceding and subsequent periods.[5] A clear trend toward high numbers of Late Woodland II interior features is apparent in the James River Valley.

Assuming that the number of interior features reflects elements of household production and consumption, an overall precontact increase in the asso-

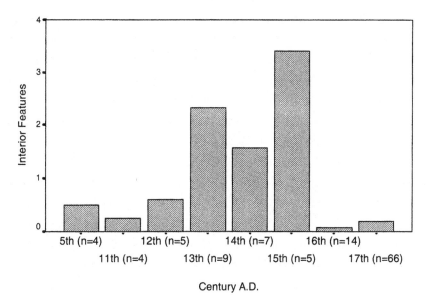

Figure 5-2. Mean number of house interior features

ciation of these tasks with domestic space can be seen in the data. The peak during the Late Woodland II phase suggests that households played a defining role in production relations at that time. As occurred in relation to house size, a Protohistoric interruption of the precontact pattern of increasing numbers of interior features ensued. Production tasks associated spatially with houses and tied to the domestic group no longer occurred in the high frequencies of preceding centuries.

The household cluster concept, originally applied to early Mesoamerican villages (Winter 1976), has rarely been considered in relation to the precontact archaeology of Virginia or the Middle Atlantic region. If the notion of a household cluster that combines domestic architecture, internal features, and external features is appropriate for the region, the patterning of interior features should correspond closely to patterning related to exterior features designated as part of the same cluster. Interior features may be associated with domestic architecture less problematically than exterior features. On the other hand, changes in sedentariness may have had less of an effect on the frequency of exterior features than on the construction of interior features. A floodplain occupation during colder months might encourage the use of pit features located inside a house but would not necessarily lead to increased numbers of features located immediately exterior to house walls. Accordingly,

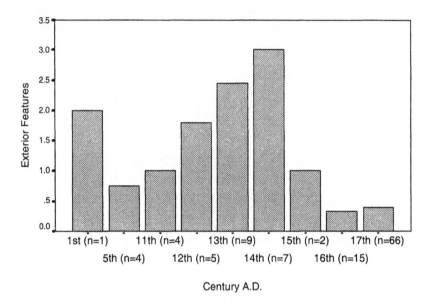

Figure 5-3. Mean number of exterior features per household cluster, James River Valley

patterning in exterior pit feature frequency allows the household cluster
concept to be evaluated and provides a way of examining the spatial proximity
of production tasks to domestic architecture that is less sensitive to changes
in sedentariness.

Figure 5-3 demonstrates that exterior feature patterning largely matches
the trends recorded in interior feature construction.[6] These data support the
inference that the household cluster concept fits the James River Valley context well, especially during the Late Woodland II phase when features were
associated in high numbers with domestic architecture. With the exception
of the anomalous data from one first-century A.D. site, the mean number of
external features associated with a household cluster (figure 5-3) increases
gradually until an abrupt fifteenth-century drop that continued in subsequent centuries. These data support the notion that Powhatan and Monacan
communities came to center their production practices on the household
unit during the final Late Woodland centuries.

Ceramic Vessel Diameter

Ceramic vessel diameter is an aspect of material culture substantially different
than those feature-related variables considered in this chapter but one that
may be tied to the consumption practices of domestic groups. The most

prominent changes in the ceramic vessel shape in the late prehistoric Eastern Woodlands correspond with functional differences in pottery use associated with the transition to agriculture (e.g., Braun 1983; Klein 1994:133). A shift from straight-walled to globular vessels provided increased thermal conductivity for vessels in the Midwest as well as in the Middle Atlantic.

Beyond this transformation, ethnographic observation indicates that a vessel's size and shape generally reflect aspects of its use as a cooking jar, a storage jar, a serving bowl, or some other function (Braun 1980). Vessel capacity also reflects elements of consumption practices, since the size of large cooking jars used to prepare meals often corresponds with the volume of prepared food and the size of the group consuming meals. Changes in the pit features associated with household clusters considered above suggest that economic activities shifted in scope from a larger corporate group to the domestic sphere during the Late Woodland period in the James River Valley. If the typical consumption unit similarly shifted from a community at large to the single household, the vessels used to prepare food would likely decrease in size through time as well.

In order to evaluate this possibility, I compared sherds recovered from feature contexts in the James River Piedmont to determine whether trends in vessel size are apparent. Overall vessel morphology and size proved to be difficult to determine based on the fragmentary nature of the recovered assemblages. However, a sample of cooking jar sherds large enough to estimate vessel diameter was present in the assemblage (n = 226), allowing this attribute to serve as a coarse estimate for vessel size.[7] As figure 5-4 indicates, median vessel diameter increased through the eleventh century A.D. and generally declined thereafter. For sherds postdating A.D. 1000, body diameter correlates negatively with occupation date.[8]

Mean vessel diameter declined after the beginning of the Late Woodland period. Since the trend in body diameter changes in a different direction through time than do changes in house size, it appears likely that this attribute relates more closely to vessel usage than to domestic group size or any other social organizational variable. The declining vessel capacities suggest the scope of individuals sharing in consumption decreased with the shift to village settlement in the James River Valley.

Domestic Architecture and Storage Features

Subsurface storage features reflect aspects of domestic production and the distribution of surplus. "Surplus" considered as a quantitative measure can-

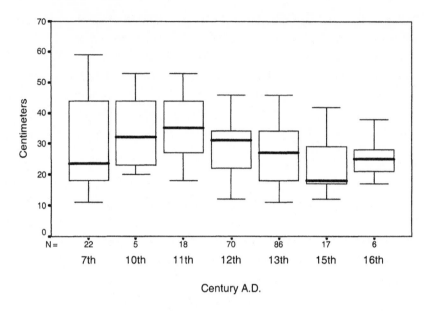

Figure 5-4. Estimated vessel diameters, James River Piedmont

not be defined easily and depends largely on cultural context (Hantman 1989:422). The mobilization of surplus production appears as a key component in most theories of political economy (e.g., Marx 1977; Johnson 1989; Saitta and Keene 1990; Welch 1991). Although there is no absolute surplus that can be defined universally in terms of excess above biological needs, a relative surplus designated as such in an institutional context becomes a meaningful concept. Production above producers' consumption needs and the technical prerequisites of production becomes surplus when it is directed to nonproducers. The existence of stores of sufficient quantity to outlast the "insurance" needs of a group creates the institutional conditions in which the transformation of stored food into surplus can occur (Testart 1982:527–528).

With this understanding of surplus, it is difficult to demonstrate that any storage facility on an archaeological site held surplus production, since this designation cannot be abstracted in any simple way from the flow of the subsistence economy. Regardless, subsurface features excavated to store food for future consumption do provide an indirect link to surplus production practices. Assuming that subsurface pits serve as important facilities for storage, their sizes and spatial configurations parallel important elements of surplus production practices.

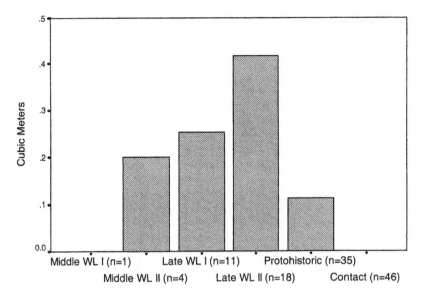

Figure 5-5. Associated storage volume per household cluster

Understanding domestic storage practices in the Chesapeake region requires consideration of the features combined within a household cluster. In
the James River Valley the volume of associated storage pits per household
cluster mimics trends in several other related variables: a precontact increase
peaked in Late Woodland II followed by Protohistoric and Contact period
decreases (figure 5-5).[9]

These developments in storage practices had a spatial dimension as well.
Household clusters in the region may be divided into those lacking associated
storage pits, those with storage pits located inside of domestic architecture,
and those with storage pits placed outside of domestic architecture and within
the spatial zone used to define the household cluster. Prior to the Late Woodland period the spatial relationship between houses and storage pits remains
unclear, in part due to the paucity of identified house patterns predating
A.D. 900. Archaeological evidence from the Coastal Plain and the Ridge and
Valley provinces records an abandonment of the pit as a means of food storage
during the Protohistoric period. This Protohistoric and Contact period shift
to aboveground storage likely relates to increasing sedentariness (Ward 1985;
DeBoer 1988) and reliance on central food stores (Potter 1993:170–173),
developments with important implications for the political economy, which
I will return to later.

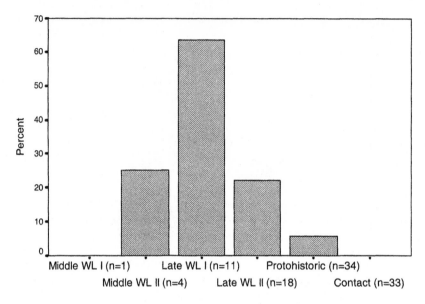

Figure 5-6. Percentage of household clusters with external storage pits

During the intervening Late Woodland period, Powhatan and Monacan communities in the James River Valley shifted their storage facilities from locations immediately outside their dwellings to interior locations. As indicated in figure 5-6, the percentages of household clusters with external storage pits peaked during the Late Woodland I phase. Most Late Woodland I household clusters in the James River Valley include external storage pits. External storage pits dominate Late Woodland I household clusters, a dominance absent from preceding and subsequent periods.[10]

Storage pits located within house interiors date to the Late Woodland through Protohistoric periods (figure 5-7). Domestic groups in the James River Valley clearly made the most use of internal storage during the Late Woodland II phase, when houses with such storage features occur in all three physiographic provinces.[11]

These patterns indicate that the placement of storage pits immediately outside of houses marks the Late Woodland I practices, followed by a shift toward placing storage pits inside houses during the Late Woodland II phase. Subsequently, household clusters generally lack subsurface storage altogether. During the precontact centuries, storage volumes associated with household clusters increased significantly. Taken together, these developments suggest

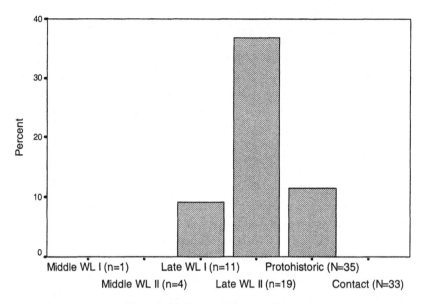

Figure 5-7. Percentage of household clusters with internal storage pits

an increased precontact association of surplus storage with domestic groups. First, this association occurred in the "public" space outside of houses. Later, storage within houses suggests a shift toward "private," or at least domestic, control of surplus production (cf. Byrd 1994). These patterns support the inference that households produced larger surpluses and controlled surpluses more closely with the shift to village settlements.

Production and Domestic Spatiality: Summary of Trends
Household archaeology in the James River Valley provides evidence of important changes in the domestic sphere tied closely to the settlement of large, sedentary villages. Household size apparently increased throughout the region during late prehistory, while production tasks requiring pit features were increasingly associated with domestic spaces. Powhatan and Monacan households made use of ever larger storage volumes during late prehistory, shifting their sizeable storage facilities from house exteriors to house interiors during the Late Woodland II phase. These developments support the notion that surplus production grew during the Late Woodland, while control of surplus shifted to the domestic group. During the same centuries, changes in ceramic vessel diameters imply that food preparation and consumption involved fewer individuals. Overall, these trends provide evidence that economic funds of

power became particularly accessible to domestic groups during the Late Woodland II phase.

Protohistoric and Contact period sites in the sample indicate that these late precontact patterns ended after A.D. 1500. Mean house size ceased to increase as it had for the previous thousand years and in fact declined. The increasingly close precontact association between pit features and houses ended once Protohistoric and Contact era households largely abandoned the use of associated storage. With the exception of the Perkins Point site (44BA3), Protohistoric and Contact era sites in all three physiographic provinces generally lacked subsurface storage facilities altogether. Beyond the James River Valley, Native communities continued to use storage pits on early colonial era sites along the Roanoke River to the south and to the west in the Tennessee River drainage, raising the possibility that changes in settlement structure unique to the Chesapeake region developed during protohistory.

Social Differentiation in the Domestic Sphere

The archaeological patterning considered above raises the possibility that social reproduction changed throughout the James River Valley with the transition to village life, as household sizes abruptly increased. With this development larger households could mobilize a greater labor force and produce larger surpluses. Along with the increased size of domestic groups and associated storage volumes in the James River Valley arose the potential for household leaders to manipulate these factors in order to finance positions of wealth and authority. Control over surplus food storage and the labor needed to produce it eventually served as important funds of power in the early colonial James River Valley.

The following section considers the variability of house sizes and household storage volumes, archaeological data related to indexical elements of domestic groups. Cross-cultural studies of small-scale agricultural societies indicate that house size generally corresponds with household size and wealth (e.g., Netting 1982). Storage pit volumes are associated, albeit indirectly, with surplus production strategies (e.g., DeBoer 1988). The focus on architecture and storage pits is not meant to imply that social differentiation manifested itself solely in house construction and storage patterns. Rather, these features are both archaeologically accessible and may be linked with some confidence to the practices of domestic groups and core elements of the political economy.

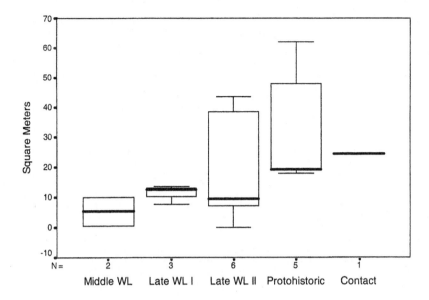

Figure 5-8. Structure floor area range values per occupation

Intrasettlement House Floor Area Variation

One way of considering social differentiation in the James River Valley is to evaluate whether domestic architecture became more variable during the late precontact through early colonial sequence. Several measures of variability may be applied to house floor areas, including range and coefficient of variation. The most meaningful range values with regard to the James River's archaeological record come from contemporaneous houses within a single settlement.

To compare house differentiation through time, I measured range as the difference between the smallest and the largest excavated structure floor areas within a settlement containing at least two architectural patterns. As depicted in figure 5-8, the range values generally increase through time, reflecting a diversity of house sizes that increased from the Middle Woodland period through the colonial era.[12]

House floor range increases through time, correlating positively with occupation date.[13] Figure 5-9 depicts floor area range against time. Although few cases predate A.D. 1200, the scatterplot does suggest a nonlinear relationship between floor area range and time, with house size range increasing more dramatically after A.D. 1200.[14] House pattern data generate a consistent pattern through the drainage basin of increasing floor area range through

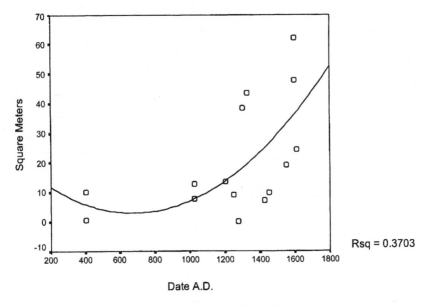

Figure 5-9. Floor area range values versus time with nonlinear regression line

time. The range values provide clear evidence of increased differentiation of domestic architecture through time. It appears that large and small houses within James River settlements became increasingly divergent in floor area through time, especially after A.D. 1200.

In terms of the social context of a residential settlement, the range indicates the extent to which particularly large houses occurred, an important statistic given the questions raised in this study. As a measure of dispersion, though, the range may be misleading in ways that the coefficient of variation is not.[15] Figure 5-10 depicts coefficient of variation values in a boxplot format. With the exception of the Middle Woodland II boxplot, the graph reflects patterning similar to that observed in the range values. Two widely different Middle Woodland II values occur, including a coefficient of variation measuring 74 percent for structures at the Great Neck site (44vB7). This high value results from the difference between a small postmold pattern that may or may not represent an entire structure and a more clearly defined structure (Hodges 1993:248–249). Once this potentially misleading case is removed from the sample, the coefficient of variation correlates positively with occupation date.[16] These results reflect an increase in the variability of architectural dimensions through protohistory.

The increased variability reflected in the precontact house floor coeffi-

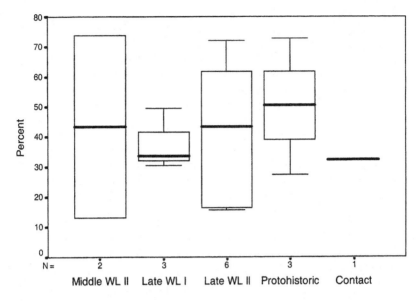

Figure 5-10. Coefficient of variation for structure floor area

cients of variation corresponds well with the floor area range data. The wide
range of values for the coefficient of variation during the Late Woodland
II phase reflects a highly variable context and a diverse range of settlement
forms, some with widely dispersed house sizes and others lacking such dispersion. Comparative Contact period data on house floor areas comes from
only one site, Paspahegh (44jc308). The relatively low coefficient of variation values is unexpected, especially since this site likely represents the core
village of a component chiefdom in the Powhatan paramountcy. With 46
house patterns, the coefficient of variation at Paspahegh may be dampened
by the unusually large sample of architectural evidence relative to the other
sites in the occupation database.

The Association between Large Structures and High Storage Volumes
The archaeological data considered above indicate that domestic architecture
became larger and more diverse during late prehistory and that storage volumes associated with this architecture increased through time. By the Late
Woodland II phase the spatial arrangement of storage pit features also suggests
that households served as primary units of production. These developments
point to a social environment by the end of the precontact era in which
domestic groups of diverse sizes controlled increasingly large surpluses. The

following discussion examines whether particularly large domestic structures were associated with high storage volumes during late prehistory and the early colonial era. The analysis considers the archaeology of large domestic groups who increased funds of power available to them by expanding their surplus stores.

In an effort to identify large houses in the data set, I converted house floor areas from all periods in the James River sample to z scores. Z scores standardize a set of values by comparing an individual value to the mean and standard deviation of a distribution.[17] Standardized in this way, the house floor areas correlate positively with household cluster storage volumes— an expected pattern since households have food storage needs that increase relative to the size of the domestic group.[18]

In order to evaluate whether the storage volume of household clusters in the sample rose above the nutritional needs linked to domestic group size, I calculated an index of storage volume per house floor area for each occupation in the sample (cf. Lightfoot and Feinman 1982:73). Household clusters whose associated storage volume per house floor area was greater than the mean ratio for a particular occupation were designated as having a "high" storage volume. This designation implies that the amount of storage associated with a domestic structure was greater than the average storage volume per household member, with household size inferred from house floor area.

The data indicate that large houses in the James River Valley were indeed associated with larger storage volumes than expected based on house floor area.[19] Sixty percent of the largest houses (n = 10) were associated with a high ratio of storage-to-floor area. Conversely, small or average-sized houses were associated with low storage volumes more often than expected. Seventy-three percent of the small to average-sized houses (n = 34) were associated with storage volumes equal to or less than the mean ratio of storage-to-floor area.

These results support the inference that large households were associated with unusually high storage volumes in the James River Valley. In order to accumulate a large sample of occupations with completely excavated household clusters, I included data from the entire set of James River sites in this analysis. These data ranged from the Middle Woodland II through the Protohistoric period. Breaking down this sample for each phase reveals that more than expected large houses with high storage volumes occur during every period except for the Protohistoric period. A trend toward the use of aboveground storage likely explains this Protohistoric development. Indications that large households controlled particularly high storage volumes is apparent from the Middle Woodland II through the Late Woodland II phases or throughout the late precontact era.

Domestic Foundations of Social Inequality in the James River Valley

Analysis of archaeological data associated with the household sphere implies a basis for the foundations of social inequality in the domestic economy. Household size and domestically controlled surpluses expanded through time, providing growing funds of power for domestic groups. Household control of production and surplus also increased through late prehistory, peaking during the Late Woodland II phase. Large households with control of high storage volumes existed throughout late prehistory, but the Late Woodland II phase, when Native communities established village settlements, likely provided the social landscape within which such funds of power could be leveraged best in the political economy.

During the Protohistoric and Contact periods, patterning in several variables tied to domestic groups indicates a change in the domestic economy. Pit features were no longer associated spatially with domestic architecture in the same high frequencies that marked the preceding centuries, and the average house's floor area ceased to increase. Concurrently, the variability of house floor areas and associated storage volumes grew larger.

Perhaps relevant to the early colonial alteration of domestic social dynamics is the overall scarcity of subsurface storage during this era. In a convincing argument, Potter (1993:170–173) suggests that the absence of subsurface storage within the Potomac Creek site (44ST2) in the Potomac River Coastal Plain may have resulted from the presence of a chief who controlled surplus food in aboveground corncribs. Whereas storage pits disguise surplus through concealment, corncribs may misrepresent surplus through ostentation (De-Boer 1988:1). In the early colonial James River Valley, the lack of Coastal Plain storage pits and the paucity of Ridge and Valley storage features suggest the possibility of similar misrepresentation. Although neither the excavation of the Protohistoric Wright site (44GO30) nor the excavation of the Contact period Lickinghole Creek site (44AB416) exposed a large area, the excavators identified no storage features within these Piedmont settlements.

A shift toward the use of aboveground storage likely occurred throughout the James River Valley, as indicated by the overall scarcity of storage pits dating after A.D. 1500. Whether this shift responded to the presence of chiefs who monopolized control of storage and moved it to central stores aboveground represents an important question for the region's culture history. Increased sedentariness (rather than the politicization of storage practices) may similarly result in the absence of subsurface storage. Villagers who remained in floodplain settlements for much of the year lacked the same motivation for concealing surpluses belowground that characterized earlier, more mobile groups who were frequently absent from a residential settlement. Distinguishing between the impact of these two processes—sedentarization and the political mobilization of surplus—on storage practices in the James River Valley becomes important given the patterns identified in the archaeological record. Chapter 4's analysis of sedentariness demonstrated that Late Woodland II phase settlements represent village communities with occupation spans as lengthy as—and in some cases lengthier than—those of the subsequent Protohistoric and Contact periods. Nonetheless, Late Woodland II villages contained the highest percentage of household clusters with interior storage pits, indicating that sedentarization cannot be the primary factor leading to the curtailed use of the storage pit in the James River Valley after A.D. 1500. The fact that early colonial households no longer concealed storage within and beneath their houses as they had during Late Woodland II reflects an increased opportunity for the political mobilization of surpluses by village leaders with powerful economic funds upon which to draw.

During the Protohistoric and Contact periods, such a political strategy may have affected the domestic orientation of economic relations in the James River Valley. Sahlins (1972:101) maintains that a completely domestic mode of production never truly happens since households cannot exist in a social vacuum free of obligations and social relations that incorporate social networks, reciprocal obligations, and ritual duties operative at several scales. A shift from the predominance of household-oriented economic practices to those driven, at least in part, by political relations and chiefly authority such as is manifested in Powhatan ethnohistory apparently occurred in the James River Valley during the sixteenth century. Protohistoric and Contact period changes in storage practices and domestic architecture construction appear to reflect this development.

Chapter 6

Community Organization

As they reorganized their production, consumption, and surplus distribution, Powhatan and Monacan villagers living on the James River also embraced practices that reconfigured the communal social scale. Ethnographers have defined community as the maximal group of people who live together and experience face-to-face association such that all members are bound together by a network of interpersonal relationships (Murdock 1949:79, 82). A community entails "a subjective but self sufficient group united by consciousness of kind; it is 'essentially a center of feeling'" (Lowie 1948:3). Translating such notions of community to archaeological contexts has proven to be difficult or impossible due to problems of scale and boundary definition that plague archaeological considerations of both communities and regions (e.g., Canuto and Yaeger 2000). Often, archaeologists treat sites as communities even though community spaces as defined by residents often stretch beyond a site's boundaries. Differences in excavation sizes and the absence of studies that uncover anything approaching an entire community's space limit current understanding of the communal scale in the James River Valley, as in most regions.

Nonetheless, archaeological evidence reflecting the arrangement of structures and pit features in James River settlements, combined with colonial accounts of Chesapeake-region settlements, provides a basis for understanding key elements of Native communities. In this chapter I consider the spatial organization of residential settlements in order to evaluate changes in settlement nucleation, elite architecture, and pit feature use. The archaeology of communal space records the appearance of nucleated settlements containing elite residences and large food preparation features used in communal feasting during the centuries when villages first appeared. A long-term shift in feature usage within residential settlements, toward the increased prominence and formalization of mortuary contexts, reflects important changes in the activities conducted on the floodplain. Taken together, changes in the use and spatial organization of architecture and pit features signal new conceptions of community within the villages of the James River Valley.

Ethnohistory Of Powhatan Community Organization

Strachey (1953:77) wrote of Powhatan settlements: "Theire habitations or townes, are for the most parte by the rivers; or not far distant from fresh springs, commonly upon the rice [rise] of a hill, that they maie overlooke the river and take every smale thing into view which stirs upon the same, their howses are not manie in one towne, and those that are stand dissite and scattered, without form of a street, far and wyde asunder." Most Powhatan "towns" were composed of houses dispersed ("dissite") along floodplain levees or overlooking bluffs in what appeared to English eyes as haphazard arrangements. Villagers raised maize and other cultigens in small garden plots measuring 100 to 200 square feet (9–19 square meters) in the spaces surrounding their houses (Strachey 1953:79). Gabriel Archer's (1998b:123) contention that "they dwell as I guess by families of kindred and alliance some 40tie or 50tie in a Hatto or small village" provides a somewhat conservative estimate based on the archaeological record but most closely approximates the archaeological evidence of Contact period settlement demography. Chapter 4's analysis of pottery discard behavior suggests that two distinct settlement size categories appeared on James River floodplains after A.D. 1200, including those with 4 to 8 households in residence and those with at least 10 resident households.

Powhatan ethnohistory likewise offers indications that community organization took several forms. John Smith's (1986b) *Map of Virginia* differentiated "Kings' Howses" from "Ordinary Howses" in the Powhatan and Monacan regions. Smith tied these categories to the settlements' political status, though colonists' accounts also indicate that the distinction had implications related to population size, architectural components, and spatial organization. Keying on Smith's map and related ethnohistorical references, Binford (1964:85) hypothesized that Powhatan "villages" housed *weroances* and included mortuary temples and more than 12 houses, while "hamlets" lacked these distinguishing features and included fewer than 10 houses. Though Binford did not have access to the archaeological data with which to evaluate these ideas on the ground, the two settlement categories isolated in chapter 4 accord roughly with demographic aspects of his settlement typology.

Jamestown colonists emphasized the presence of *weroances* and their large residential structures as the distinguishing characteristic of populous and politically prominent village communities. The length of the Mamanatowick's residence impressed Smith (1986d:126), stretching as it did some 30 to 40 yards (27–37 meters) on the long axis. Henry Spelman (1998:487) reported that the houses of chiefs were all broader and longer than those of ordinary Powhatans. *Werowance's* villages were not necessarily palisaded, though Robert Beverley noted that high-status residences were encircled by a palisade in some villages: "They often encompass their whole Town: But for the most part only their Kings Houses" (1947:177). Nondomestic architecture appeared in the context of politically prominent villages as well. The seat of a district chief incorporated what the English labeled "treasuries" and "temples" tied to the political and sacred status of *weroances*. Toward the end of the seventeenth century, colonist John Clayton (1968:435) encountered a council session held in the "wiochisan house that is their temple."

Powhatan ethnohistory, then, describes a rather diverse seventeenth-century settlement landscape along the floodplains and adjacent bluffs of major rivers dominated by small, dispersed settlements lacking (to the English) a sense of planning or order. Residents of a select set of communities lived in nucleated arrangements of houses surrounded by palisades, though, and some villages included the unusually long residences of chiefs. The presence of council houses and temples within or near important communities suggests the construction of sacred spaces and structures designed to house communal events. References to settlement population indicate that *weroances'* villages contained larger numbers of residents than those lacking political elites.

In the following section I evaluate archaeological evidence of settlements in the James River Valley in order to trace these elements of community organization during the precontact era. As suggested by the model of James River social dynamics, a reorganization of communal space during the precontact era likely paralleled changes in social relations between domestic groups in the region.

Archaeology of James River Community Organization

Spacing of Domestic Architecture

Ethnohistorical references point to the political, religious, and economic significance of large, nucleated villages. Settlement nucleation may be evaluated in terms of the distribution of domestic architecture within a community. The spacing of houses provides an architecturally based measure of settlement concentration useful for evaluating trends in this attribute of settlement form. Figure 6-1 summarizes settlement nucleation as measured in terms of the shortest distances between each domestic structure in an occupation and the

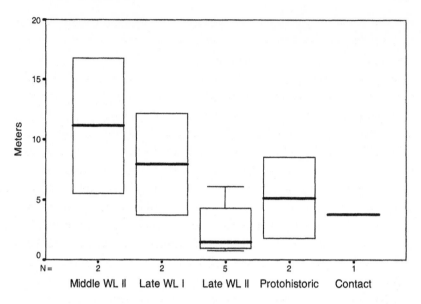

Figure 6-1. Mean distance between houses

nearest neighboring house. The figure reflects decreasing spacing between houses during prehistory, with particularly low values during the Late Woodland II when villages first appeared. For the James River data, house spacing correlates negatively with occupation date, indicating a significant decline in the distance between adjacent houses as viewed through time.[1]

This pattern demonstrates that Powhatan and Monacan communities in the James River Valley concentrated house construction within increasingly nucleated settlements, especially with the establishment of villages between A.D. 1200 and 1500. What drew these village residents together into nucleated communities during the Late Woodland II phase? What were the ramifications of community arrangements that tethered concentrated populations to a floodplain location? The patterning in settlement nucleation raises questions concerning the nature of social interaction in village settlements that may be addressed in part through the archaeology of elite residences, communal facilities, and feature use.

Elite Residences

Powhatan ethnohistory indicates that unusually large domestic structures served as *weroances'* residences during the early seventeenth century on the Coastal Plain. The emergence of village leadership is likely one factor behind

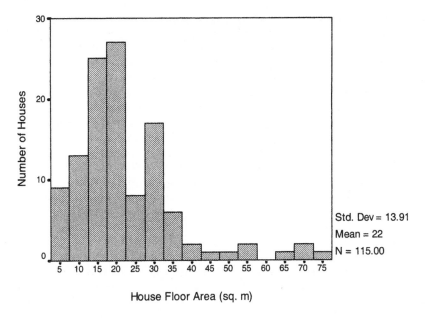

Figure 6-2. Floor area histogram

increasingly nucleated settlements on the James River floodplain. The following consideration of architectural patterns is intended to detect evidence of structures with dimensions and layouts similar to the elite architecture described ethnohistorically.

The histogram of house floor area in the James River Valley sample (figure 6-2) represents the number of cases in the James River data set that fall within each size range. The relatively long tail on the right side of the floor area histogram reflects a considerable range of variation at the high end of house floor areas, variation that may be associated with the homes of elites or other forms of special-use architecture. At the extreme end of this tail is a small concentration of cases centered at approximately 70 square meters. Each of these values is roughly three times the size of the average house in the James River Valley as measured by floor area. The attributes of these four houses are listed in table 6-1.

The possibility that these structures form a distinct category of architecture in the James River Valley may be evaluated on the basis of floor plan in addition to size. Figure 6-3 depicts the distribution of length-to-width ratios of James River Valley architecture in a histogram format. Two distinct peaks, or modes, are visible in the histogram at length-to-width ratios of 1.0 and

Table 6-1. Attributes of architectural patterns with large floor areas

Site	Feature	Date A.D.	Length (m)	Width (m)	Area (sq. m)	Length-to-width ratio
Huffman(44BA5)	House 2	1200	9.1	9.1	65.6	1.0
Bessemer (44BO26)	Structure 1	1325	15.3	6.3	71.8	2.5
Great Neck (44VB7)	Structure A	1450	15.5	6.3	76.7(est.)	2.5(est.)
Perkins Pt. (44BA3)	Feature 36	1600	15.2	6.1	72.9	2.5

1.4. Stated simply, Native American architecture in the James River Valley generally matches one of two typical floor plans that include circular and elliptical forms. Beyond the two distinctive styles reflected in figure 6-3 that correspond with circular and elliptical floor plans, a third concentration of cases appears at length-to-width ratios approximating 2.5. As listed in table 6-1, the three structures in this concentration all fall within the group of particularly large floor plans greater than 60 square meters in area. With the exception of the circular house 2 at Huffman, all of the "large" structures as defined by the figure 6-3 histogram of floor areas fall within the high length-to-width ratio category of approximately 2.5.

The three houses with both particularly large floor areas and unusual floor plans provide evidence of a distinct architectural category, perhaps best labeled "longhouses" to highlight the similarities with the Iroquoian house form (Warrick 1996) and dimensions that differ from those of most wigwam structures associated with eastern Algonquin groups (Rapoport 1982). The combination of unusually large structures and longhouse shapes results, in part, from the construction techniques employed by Native American groups in the Middle Atlantic. The potential width of post-in-ground architecture on the James River and in surrounding river valleys was constrained by the use of tree saplings for structural frames. House sizes could be enlarged by adding to the length, while increases in width beyond a certain range greatly weakened a house's structural integrity due to the length of trees suitable for use as framing material in house construction (Callahan 1985:125).

Hariot's (1972:24) statement about early-seventeenth-century Powhatan houses that "the length of them is commonly doubled to its breadth, in some places they are but 12 and 16 yeardes long" is generally not matched by late precontact and early colonial archaeological data from the James River Valley. Structures rarely matched a length-to-width ratio of 2.0, and the only recorded houses greater than 10 meters in length are the large structures described above. In fact, the three structures in the archaeological sample

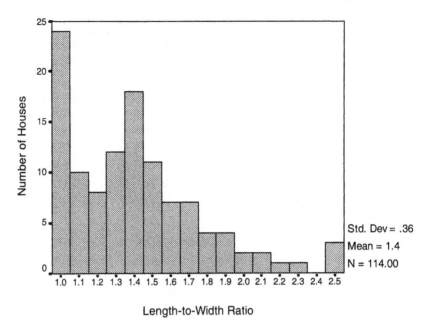

Length-to-Width Ratio

Figure 6-3. Length-to-width ratio histogram

that fit Hariot's description—structure 1 at Bessemer (44BO26), structure A at Great Neck (44VB7), and feature 36 at Perkins Point (44BA3)—are quite unusual features in the archaeological record, and the distinctiveness of these structures has already been noted (Hodges 1993; Thompson 1989:30–35; Whyte and Geier 1982:102–104). Thompson (1989) and Hodges (1993) suggest that the Bessemer and Great Neck examples resemble ethnohistorical descriptions of either elite residences or communal structures.

With a comprehensive regional context in which to situate these structures, several aspects of these structures become prominent. A palisade enclosed the Dan River settlement of Bessemer's structure 1. Similarly, palisades encompassed structure A at Great Neck and feature 36 at Perkins Point. Disagreement persists concerning the existence of a palisade at the Huffman site (L. Johnson 1982:40; Geier and Warren 1982a:4), although the excavation plan of the initial fieldwork provides evidence for such a feature. Including Huffman, 6 of the 38 distinct occupations considered in this study have evidence of a palisade. Only two of these six palisaded settlements did not include evidence of one unusually large structure. These were Wright (44GO30), a site whose interior remains unexcavated, and Beaver Pond (44BA39), whose postmold evidence was poorly preserved following the use of earthmoving equipment (Geier and Dutt 1978). Even without comprehensive architectural data from these two sites, a clear association between palisaded settlements and unusually long structures is apparent.

Inferring the purpose of this distinctive architecture requires consideration of ethnohistorical analogy and archaeological context. Early colonial accounts describe several types of architecture distinct from the typical domestic residence, all constructed "arbour wise" (Strachey 1953:88) with the same basic materials and techniques as ordinary houses. Chiefs' houses impressed colonists not only by their length, as noted above, but also in their segmentation. Spelman (1998:487) wrote that Powhatan "kings' houses" have "many dark windings and turnings before any cum where the king is." Beverley (1947:176) reiterated this when he wrote that "there's never more than one Room in a House except in some Houses of State, or Religion, where Partition is made only by Mats, and loose poles."

Structures such as those described by Beverley with multiple purposes tied to political or sacred authority appear often in Powhatan ethnohistory, notably in Clayton's (1968:435) description of a council house and in Smith's (1986b:169) descriptions of Powhatan's feasting house and the unusually long structure that housed his "treasure." The Powhatans located some temples apart from village settlements, though these structures paralleled other special-use architecture in their unusual lengths (up to 100 feet [30 meters] by Strachey's estimate) and by their segmented "wyndings and pillers" (Strachey 1953:88, 89). By the late seventeenth century when Beverley (1947:195) and several other Englishmen entered and desecrated a Powhatan temple, the structure included a partitioned room of "dismal dark" that housed sacred wooden images and human remains. Clearly, long structures and architecture with interior divisions played a special role in Powhatan social life.

Three of the four unusual structures isolated above have length-to-width ratios that correspond with the ethnohistorical accounts of elite or communal structures. The Powhatan accounts come from a somewhat different cultural context than that of the late precontact Ridge and Valley, though the floor plans of the Ridge and Valley longhouses include evidence of partitions that match those within Powhatan special-use architecture. Bessemer's structure 1 encompasses a line of interior postmolds running along the long axis of the structure and a second line perpendicular to the long axis near the southern end of the structure. Feature 36 at Perkins Point incorporates a similar line of postmolds that segregates 4 to 5 meters of the elliptical structure at the southern end. Structure A at the Coastal Plain's Great Neck site encompasses an array of interior postmolds suggesting large roof support poles, bench posts along the walls, and a central post line on the long axis that partitioned the structure into rooms (Hodges 1993:76–77). Other architectural patterns in the James River Valley with smaller dimensions also encompass interior posts, but none imply the presence of partitioning walls as clearly as the longhouses described above.

An additional line of evidence relating to the purpose of the longhouse architecture comes in the form of associated pit features. Little discussion of associated pit features appears in Powhatan ethnohistorical accounts beyond the occasional mention of interior hearths that appear within houses and nondomestic architecture alike (e.g., Beverley 1947:195). However, the association of domestic architecture and pit features established in chapter 5 provides a means of evaluating the function of James River Valley longhouses. If they served as larger versions of residential structures, longhouses should share the association with pit features seen in other domestic architecture. Presumably, communal architecture such as council houses or temples would not manifest the same suite of associated features, especially storage pits.

The archaeological evidence is ambiguous with regard to the purpose of structure 1 at Bessemer. Structure 1 did not incorporate any interior pit features. Unlike other Late Woodland II houses with interior storage pits, none were found in Bessemer structure 1, supporting the interpretation that the structure did not serve as a residence. However, a contemporary structure at Bessemer, structure 2, also lacked interior features. Structure 2 was smaller, was less structurally complex, and probably represents domestic architecture. Among the seven features immediately exterior to the structure 1 longhouse was a large storage pit. As noted by Thompson (1989:34), Bessemer structure 1's function cannot be stated with any certainty.

Despite the presence of multiple soil stains within structure A at Great Neck, no clear evidence of deep pits occurred within or immediately adjacent to the postmold pattern. Again, the lack of interior storage during the Late Woodland II points toward a nondomestic function for structure A. However, none of the Late Woodland II structures at Great Neck had interior storage. A general Coastal Plain shift to aboveground storage limits the usefulness of interior storage pits as a criterion for determining architectural function. Feature 36 at Perkins Point contained one interior storage pit feature and at least one interior hearth. Two storage pits occurred among the five interior features of Huffman's house 2.

Thus, the archaeological evidence regarding the purpose of the four unusual structures remains inconclusive. At least three of the four conform to ethnohistorical descriptions of Powhatan structures that may represent special-use architecture, elites' houses, or a combination of these. With the exception of the Protohistoric Perkins Point postmold pattern, the unusual structures date between A.D. 1200 and 1500. That three of the four structures occurred in the Ridge and Valley province does not necessarily indicate their concentration in that portion of the drainage. Rather, the structures appear to be associated with palisaded settlements. Archaeologists have investigated and reported evidence of palisaded settlements more intensively in the Ridge and Valley than in more easterly portions of Virginia. The only reported excavation of a palisaded settlement in the James River Coastal Plain included evidence of a longhouse. The one identified palisaded settlement in the Piedmont, the Wright site, may reveal similar evidence of unusual architecture once the site is excavated intensively.

The architectural evidence considered here suggests that, beginning during the Late Woodland II phase, palisaded communities saw the construction of remarkable buildings that housed some combination of elites, feasts, councils, wealth items, and the bodies of important ancestors. The longhouse structures may, in fact, record the emergence of village leaders. Alternatively, longhouses may correspond with the sort of new integrative communal institutions identified in other newly sedentary contexts (e.g., Byrd 1994; Lipe and Hegmon 1989) and signified in Powhatan society by council houses and temples. It is especially intriguing that the evidence for either elite residence or communal architecture appears in all of the intensively investigated (and well-preserved) palisaded settlements of the James River Valley rather than solely in the Coastal Plain, which has abundant ethnohistorical accounts of seventeenth-century social inequality and political complexity.

Roasting Pit Use

Archaeologists have recently begun to recognize evidence of communal feasting ceremonies of the past and to consider the implications of these events for understanding social organization and culture change (e.g., Dietler and Hayden 2001; Hayden 1993:225). Feasts may serve to reinforce social relations and cosmologies, or, in the hands of some sponsors, feasts may transform the social order.

Accounts of feasts in the colonial era Chesapeake generally involved massive quantities of food provided by *weroances* to English visitors of Powhatan villages. These feasts correspond with political strategies whereby *weroances* sought to develop social ties with the English as a means of enhancing networks of alliance, wealth, and power. Powhatan ethnohistory records the communal consumption of food and drink in a variety of other contexts as well. The Powhatans held celebratory feasts following the birth of a child, after a woman agreed to marry a man, and as part of the mortuary ritual for elites (Spelman 1998:490, 491; Strachey 1953:112). Large-scale feasts brought together the residents of several villages for the *huskanaw* ceremony, after military triumphs, and following the harvesting of first fruits (Smith 1986b:170). Food fit for feasting among the Powhatans included venison, walnut milk, and corn bread (Rountree 1989:108). Generally, feasting events served to cement social ties within and between Powhatan communities and to create new social relationships that brought outsiders within the orbit of a Powhatan community.

Archaeological evidence of feasting may be found in the form of roasting pits, hearths, and refuse deposits or in the presence of special decorative ceramics (Dietler and Hayden 2001). In the Chesapeake region's archaeological record, roasting pits appear to be facilities used to prepare considerable quantities of food, most likely more food than would be consumed by a single household. Indeed, early colonial accounts describe roasting pits as essential equipment for community-wide feasting rituals. Roasting pits constitute a feature class tied to events that incorporated a community and sometimes included the residents of multiple settlements.

In the James River Valley, roasting pits occur sporadically within Middle Woodland II through Protohistoric settlements. As depicted in figure 6-4, roasting pits generally increased in size from the Late Woodland I through protohistory. By the Protohistoric period, median roasting feature volume exceeded 0.5 cubic meter—a fairly impressive space that comprises a basin-shaped pit measuring more than 1 meter in surface diameter and 50 centimeters in depth. Across the James River Valley, roasting pit volume correlates positively with occupation date.[2]

Roasting pits in the James River Valley became larger through time while remaining a relatively unusual feature type. Viewed as the by-product of feasts, such a change likely signals a trend toward food preparation facilities designed to incorporate ever larger numbers of people. Native societies in the James River Valley may have prepared food for multiple households in roasting pits throughout prehistory and enlarged these pits as community size increased. Alternatively, roasting pits may have become ritually oriented feast

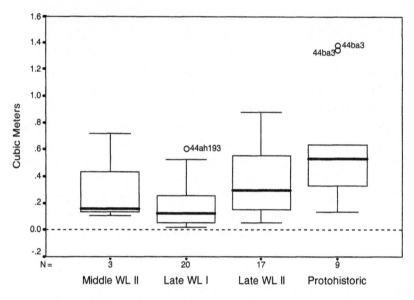

Figure 6-4. Boxplot of roasting pit volume by period

preparation features for the residents of multiple communities only during the final precontact centuries and during protohistory.

These explanations are not mutually exclusive. The evidence of expanding roasting pit size occurs during the centuries when most production activities were associated spatially with domestic architecture and when villagers moved storage pits to house interiors. The intermittent use of large pits to prepare feasts that incorporated an expanding number of participants suggests the possibility of events designed to establish crosscutting social ties counterpoised against the concentration of economic relations within the household. By the end of prehistory roasting pits may reflect communal, or even multicommunal, feasts during which village residents expressed a wide range of social obligations. The emergence of particularly large roasting pits by the end of prehistory provides evidence of new forms of communal events with the establishment of village communities.

Feature Usage

The evidence of James River communities considered thus far suggests that floodplain settlements hosted an altered set of daily practices and social arrangements with the establishment of village communities. Powhatan ethnohistory indicates that colonial era villages housed durable facilities designed

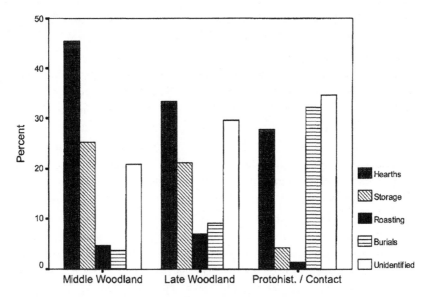

Figure 6-5. Mean percentage of feature types by period

for multiseason use—palisades, temples, and council houses—that required a commitment to floodplain locations lacking in earlier settlements that were occupied relatively briefly and infrequently. One method of evaluating the history of practices carried out in residential settlements is to consider archaeological evidence of the array of features used in floodplain settlements. Accordingly, figure 6-5 depicts the changing suite of feature types in the James River Valley.[3]

Figure 6-5 indicates that the relative importance of hearth use declined through time, with the percentage of hearths per occupation correlating negatively with occupation date.[4] By contrast, burials as a proportion of features increased from the smallest percentage of the four categories to become the dominant category. The percentage of burials per occupation correlates positively with occupation date.[5] The feature data confirm that burial increased within James River floodplain settlements from the Middle Woodland through Contact periods. Roasting pits occur in low frequencies during these centuries. Their use changes only modestly through time, with a slight peak during the Late Woodland period. Storage pits as a percentage of a settlement's features declined slightly between Middle and Late Woodland occupations before dropping substantially by the sixteenth and seventeenth centuries. Assuming that some form of storage continued to play a role in the increasingly sedentary horticultural settlements of the Late Woodland and subsequent centuries, a shift away from subsurface storage toward above-ground forms is indicated by these patterns.

These data indicate that daily practices conducted in floodplain settlements changed rather dramatically through time. Middle Woodland settlements dominated by hearths and storage pits gave way to settlements containing a more diverse range of feature types. Eventually burials assumed a prominent role in the array of facilities used in James River villages. The increasing concentration of burials and the Late Woodland formalization of communal burial ritual in the Piedmont (Gold 1998; Dunham 1994) and in the Coastal Plain (Curry 1999) likely corresponded with changes in the ways that village residents conceived of these settlements. The use of formal burial areas over multiple years may be associated with efforts to project a social connection to the landscape backward through time (Dunham 1994, 1999), expressions tied to notions of territoriality and claimed hereditary rights to important local resource (Charles and Buikstra 1983). The history of feature usage on the floodplain reflects practices intertwined with a communal "center of feeling" mentioned previously. Through changes in the practices conducted in riverine locations, village settlements came to embody a commitment to a location absent in preceding centuries.

Village Communities as Central Places

Comparative analysis of residential settlements excavated thus far suggests that a fundamentally new type of community appeared after A.D. 1200 along the James River. A built environment of more closely spaced houses accompanied this transition, as did the appearance of longhouse structures in palisaded communities. By the Protohistoric and Contact periods, floodplain villages were no longer dominated by hearth features, as burials assumed a more prominent role. Roasting pit use signals large-scale food preparation events that occurred in James River floodplain communities from the earliest stages of the sequence considered in this study. The appearance of particularly large roasting pits, however, did not occur until the final centuries of prehistory and the Protohistoric period.

Other elements of James River community organization discussed previously in chapter 3 reinforce the idea that a reorganization of community practices accompanied the final precontact centuries. Feature diversity increased markedly during the Late Woodland II phase, paralleling increased sedentariness but also indicating a settlement pattern whereby residents concentrated numerous activities in one location: the floodplain village. Together with evidence of increasing feature volume and burial density, these patterns indicate that villages became more central places on the social landscape, a centrality that incorporated economic production, communal feasting, and communal mortuary rituals. The increased prominence of long-term village settlement sanctified through dense concentrations of burials (or mass burial features such as mounds and ossuaries) supports the notion that floodplain communities became focal nodes on the late precontact landscape. Villagers may have identified more closely with these nodes than did residents of preceding floodplain communities that lacked these elements. Community organizational changes that culminated in the Late Woodland II establishment of villages generated funds of economic power, interhousehold inequality, and communal institutions that undoubtedly altered the region's social dynamics.

Chapter 7

Regional Interaction

Complementary changes in the domestic economy and in the organization of riverine communities introduced a new cultural landscape on the James River during the final Late Woodland centuries. Fundamental transformations at the regional scale accompanied the increased sedentariness and settlement population of the Late Woodland II phase as well. In this chapter I consider evidence of social interaction within the James River Valley in order to characterize changes in regional networks and the social connectedness of neighboring communities. As with the changes in household and community organization, the late precontact alteration of regional social interaction appears to be rooted in the increasing sedentariness and settlement population that marked the period between A.D. 1200 and 1500. In these centuries, new forms of interaction and expressions of style produced geographically bounded exchange networks and corresponding social identities that came to play prominent roles during the Contact period.

Previous archaeological studies of regional interaction in the late precontact Chesapeake suggest that increasing population densities and rising sedentariness during late prehistory led to the social circumscription of Native communities in the Chesapeake region (cf. Carneiro 1981). Greater regional populations and the proximity of potentially hostile neighbors limited the role that mobility could play as a solution to social and economic problems (Turner 1976; Potter 1993:167; Jirikowic 1990:367). Archaeologists have suggested that the formation of multiple-community, hierarchical polities (i.e., chiefdoms) in this context resulted from the need to build military alliances and to defend constituent communities from competing groups. Ethnohistorical evidence of chronic warfare in the Chesapeake region during the sixteenth and early seventeenth centuries offers support for this scenario, as do the palisaded settlements that appeared during the final precontact centuries, when populations reached their greatest magnitude.

Evidence collected for this study allows comparison of these interpretations against exchange relations and the use of style in the James River Valley. As detailed below, changes in ceramic style and house form suggest that spatially compact social networks developed in the region along with the Late Woodland II establishment of village communities. Lithic exchange patterns demonstrate that communities in the interior portions of the river basin also intensified their social interaction during these centuries. The emergence of these geographically constricted interaction networks in the James River Valley likely mirrors the advent of the Monacan cultural identity in the interior and the Powhatan identity on the coast.

Exchange, Style, and the Archaeology of Regional Interaction
Exchange relations of some sort occur in all societies, whether as gifts or commodities (Gregory 1982) or through media as varied as blankets (Benedict 1959) or wives (Levi-Strauss 1969). As Marcel Mauss (1990) wrote in *The Gift*, exchange generates social relationships whose significance hinges on cultural and historical context. At one level these social relationships involve notions of reciprocity, obligation, and indebtedness; at another level with particular relevance to archaeology, exchange results in the movement of things, innovations, and sometimes people.

One framework for integrating exchange, style, and the archaeological record draws on theories regarding the link between stylistic patterns and the exchange of material and information (e.g., Wobst 1977; Conkey 1978; Hodder 1977). The information-exchange approach to style provides a set of concepts useful for conceiving artifact style in terms of its dynamic (i.e., active and variable) role in the maintenance of social networks (e.g., Hantman and Plog 1982; Braun and Plog 1982; Plog 1995a, 1986; Hantman 1983; Hegmon 1986). According to this approach, style serves as a means of conveying information nonverbally, information that often concerns group membership. Such information may be communicated most effectively through visible and durable artifacts viewed periodically by socially distant people. This notion of the social use of style accords well with the indexical role that domestic architecture fulfills as an indicator of social identity (Blanton 1994:10). The particular meanings connoted by pottery decoration, architectural design, or other expressions of style cannot be determined in any simple manner from archaeological patterns, though the significance of stylistic variation may be interpreted within the broader context of social organization and culture change.

Ethnohistorical and Archaeological Evidence of Regional Interaction
Ethnohistorical evidence of regional interaction in the James River Valley, perhaps best considered in terms of the Monacan/Powhatan relationship, reflects a highly dynamic context. A buffer zone between the Coastal Plain

and the Piedmont in the area of the fall line separated the Powhatans from the Monacans during the seventeenth century. English colonists reported that both groups conducted fall and winter hunts in this zone that involved hundreds of men who used fire drives to take large numbers of deer (Strachey 1953:83). Despite this social boundary, protracted and varied interaction marked social relations between the Monacans and Powhatans. Exchanges of copper eastward across the fall line likely played a role in prestige-good relationships between elites (Hantman 1990). References to cross fall-line invasions by the Monacans and Powhatans found in Spanish and English accounts suggest a fluctuating balance of power between these groups (Hantman 1993:108–111). Eventually, in 1611, the Monacans and Powhatans struck an alliance in the face of English expansion westward from the Virginia Tidewater.

Archaeological evidence of a precontact fall-line boundary in the distribution of ceramic types appears circa A.D. 200 (Egloff 1985). After this time Coastal Plain groups tempered their Mockley pottery with crushed shells, while groups in the interior continued to use crushed rock or sand temper, a difference that may reflect the distinction between coastal Algonquins and interior Siouan-speakers. The boundary between these areas, though, exhibited a permeability in both the precontact and colonial eras (Hantman 1993). Archaeological evidence of shared ceramic style on either side of the fall line during the Middle Woodland (Gleach 1987) and Late Woodland (Mouer 1983) periods reflects the movement of Algonquin and Siouan groups across the falls or a porous boundary through which stylistic innovations flowed. The Blue Ridge served as a similarly permeable geographic boundary. During the first four Late Woodland centuries, groups on both sides of the Blue Ridge shared quartz-tempered Albemarle series ceramics, while differences in the use of ceramic temper characterized these areas subsequently. By the Late Woodland II phase, Piedmont and Ridge and Valley groups shared similar mound burial practices.

The proliferation and spatial segregation of Late Woodland pottery types in Tidewater Virginia provide evidence that spatially compact social networks developed during the Late Woodland period (Turner 1993:83). Four Late Woodland period pottery wares (Townsend, Potomac Creek, Gaston/Cashie, and Roanoke) took the place of one Middle Woodland ware (Mockley) in coastal Virginia, raising the possibility that social identity in the Coastal Plain was constricted to increasingly limited geographic zones by the end of prehistory. Even while the distributions of pottery wares became more spatially constricted during the Late Woodland period, ceramic attributes tied to stylistic aspects of pottery production—surface treatments and rim decorations—regularly crossed these boundaries.

Evidence of exchange relations in the form of nonlocal lithic artifacts indicates an overall attenuation of long-distance exchange relations during the Late Woodland period throughout the Middle Atlantic region. Stewart's (1984, 1989, 1991) analyses of Middle Atlantic exchange point to a Middle Woodland context involving the widespread movement of important lithic resources through long-distance exchange networks. The spatially extensive interregional networks through which rhyolite and other "exotic" lithic materials moved during the Middle Woodland period had evidently collapsed after A.D. 900. Some geographically smaller exchange networks within a river drainage appear to have intensified over the same period, however. One study (Parker 1989) identified an increased flow of chert projectile points from the Ridge and Valley province into the Piedmont during the Late Woodland period.

Thus, regional interaction in the late precontact Chesapeake was quite variable. Changing geographic distributions of pottery wares (defined largely by differences in temper) support the notion that material culture assumed a spatially bounded distribution circa A.D. 200. Meanwhile, ceramic stylistic attributes continued to cross these boundaries. Exchange relations that linked distant portions of the Middle Atlantic region during the Middle Woodland ended during the Late Woodland, possibly replaced by exchange relations between geographically adjacent areas that included the Ridge and Valley and the Piedmont. Jamestown colonists reported the existence of a social boundary during the colonial era between the Powhatans and Monacans, two groups with strongly developed social identities. Nonetheless, these groups continued to establish relationships across those boundaries throughout the colonial encounter.

Information Exchange in the James River Valley

In conjunction with this history of regional interaction in the Chesapeake, the information exchange approach to style raises several expectations with regard to the use of style in the James River Valley. Prior to the Late Woodland establishment of villages, the relatively low-density, mobile societies of the drainage likely participated in the sort of open, undifferentiated social networks shared by many foraging societies (e.g., Plog 1990a:191). Information exchange in such a context is expected to be unbounded, as social interaction linked far-flung groups in open networks that intermittently conveyed information, things, and people (Hantman and Plog 1982:250). Stylistic innovations, along with information and goods, likely flowed in a relatively unrestricted fashion within and between the major river basins of the Chesapeake region.

Stylistic variation in this phase of James River prehistory is expected to reflect what some researchers refer to as "isochrestic" variation, or stylistic patterns acquired by "rote learning" and employed automatically (Plog 1990b:62; Sackett 1986; Wiessner 1985:160–161). Ceramic and architectural styles in the James River Valley may reflect such open social interaction in the form of "clinal" variation (Hantman and Klein 1992:147). Clinal variation implies gradations of subtly differing style across a region and an absence of sharp boundaries. Clinal variation in ceramic attributes and domestic architectural forms entails a lack of boundedness across the geographic space of the river drainage.

Changes in the Late Woodland distribution of ceramic wares in the Chesapeake raise the possibility that geographically smaller social networks developed during the Late Woodland period. The greater sedentariness and larger storage volumes associated with Late Woodland II household clusters indicate that residents in the village communities of the James River Valley altered their primary means of buffering environmental variation from spatial-averaging mechanisms (e.g., mobility) to temporal-averaging mechanisms (e.g., storage) (Hantman and Plog 1982:252). With this shift in emphasis, the widespread social ties characteristic of relatively mobile societies likely declined in importance as information exchange networks became increasingly local.

These developments are expected to coincide with stylistic patterns that become more divergent over a large area. Ceramic style and house form, for example, should become more distinct with the end of clinal variation in the James River Valley. Interaction between groups residing in adjacent portions of the valley is not expected to have ceased, however. Archaeological evidence suggests that in some portions of the Middle Atlantic the exchange of nonlocal lithics continued into the Late Woodland, possibly through what Stewart (1991) refers to as "focused exchange." In contrast with the broad-based exchange networks of earlier periods, focused exchange involves the regular movement of certain items between individuals. In the James River Valley, a similar Late Woodland shift in regional interaction toward focused exchange may have occurred. The new forms and media of Late Woodland exchange such as those documented by Parker (1989) may signal the development of more frequent and regular social interaction within a geographically smaller social network.

Within individual communities, the establishment of relatively large and permanent villages created settings of more concentrated populations with important implications for the use of style on the communal scale. In such a setting "social symboling" and increased amounts of stylistic behavior may occur with the establishment of large communities characterized by a wider range of social groups and intracommunity tensions less resolvable through mobility (Braun 1991:367; Hegmon 1986). Archaeological evidence of style coinciding with the emergence of larger settlements and less mobile communities may include an increased amount of stylistic behavior as measured in terms of diversity. While the issue of stylistic diversity relates most immediately to the community scale discussed in the preceding chapter, it is addressed here due to the relevance of principles related to the information exchange approach to style.

With the emergence of the village as a settlement form, the use of style in the James River Valley may require explanations that entail "symbolic" variation rather than isochrestic variation. Wiessner (1985:160–161) defines symbolic variation as incorporating social identification through stylistic and social comparison. Individuals compare their ways of decorating artifacts with those of others and then imitate or differentiate these methods according to efforts to express social and personal identities. In this way, style becomes a more conscious effort to highlight or manipulate social relationships.

Ceramic Surface Treatment: Regional Variation
In order to evaluate stylistic variation in James River Valley pottery, I draw on an attribute-based approach to ceramic analysis. This classification method differs from the ware and type categorization that has become normative in the Chesapeake region (e.g., Evans 1955; Egloff and Potter 1982; Mouer et al. 1986). Ceramic types, defined by the presence of consistently covarying attribute states, need not be present in all cultural and historical contexts (Plog 1995b:373). Even with the emergence of well-defined ceramic wares in the Chesapeake, the same stylistic attributes continued to appear across the region. Temporal and geographic patterning in stylistic attributes offers an indication of information exchange and regional interaction.

The stylistic attributes most relevant to information exchange include those visible within a community setting. As a conspicuous attribute that varies considerably, rim decoration served as a stylistic domain for conveying

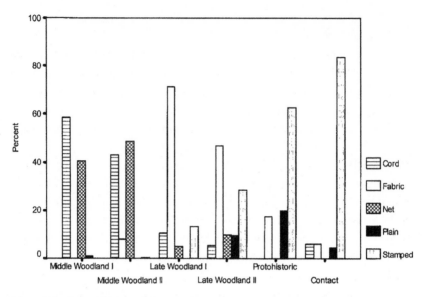

Figure 7-1. Coastal Plain surface treatment

information in the precontact Eastern Woodlands (e.g., Braun 1991). However, rim decoration does not occur consistently in precontact Chesapeake
region assemblages. A general increase in the amount of rim decoration
through late prehistory is apparent in some portions of the Chesapeake region. Even so, decoration of the rim or neck portion of a vessel appears to be
particularly scanty in the Piedmont and Coastal Plain portions of the James
River Valley relative to Late Woodland pottery from the Shenandoah River
Valley to the west, the Roanoke drainage to the south, and the Potomac River
basin to the north.

Surface treatment, on the other hand, provides a more easily accessible
stylistic attribute. Surface treatments include fabric impression, net impression, cord marking, and simple stamping. Potters applied these patterns to
ceramic vessels before firing by impressing textiles or paddles covered with
cordage or carved designs. Fabric impression refers to marks left by wicker
fabrics and other closely spaced textiles. Net impressions result from impressing knotted and looped textiles with visible spacing between the elements,
in contrast to the closely spaced fabric elements. The cord-marked category
includes ceramics with clear cord impressions. Simple stamping applies linear
or parallel grooves produced by a thong-wrapped paddle, a carved paddle,

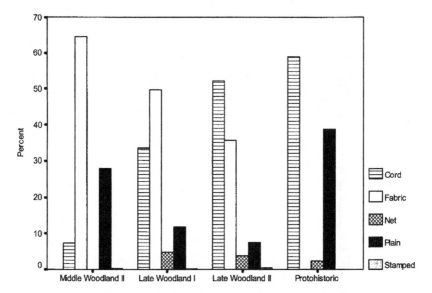

Figure 7-2. Piedmont surface treatment

or scraping with a tool that leaves a similar impression. Vessels may also be scraped or smoothed to produce a "plain" surface treatment.

Although not as visually prominent as rim decoration or laden with the same rich variability, surface treatment adds texture to the exterior of ceramic vessels that is visible within the confines of the household and community settings. As a practical matter, surface treatment may be identified on most sherds recovered archaeologically. Accurate identification of surface treatment does not require knowledge of the competing and often inconsistent ceramic typologies used in the Chesapeake. Ceramic analysts in the region sometimes consider surface treatment as a "technological" rather than a "stylistic" attribute due to its role in the ceramic production process. Surface treatment patterns may in fact provide a conservative indicator of the existence of symbolic variation and may overstate the importance of isochrestic style during the final stages of late prehistory and the early colonial era when stylistic variation in several parts of the Chesapeake region focused on rim decoration.

Figures 7-1, 7-2, and 7-3 depict the relative percentages of the surface treatments in the three physiographic provinces in the James River Valley.[1] In the Coastal Plain, Middle Woodland patterns differ markedly from those of

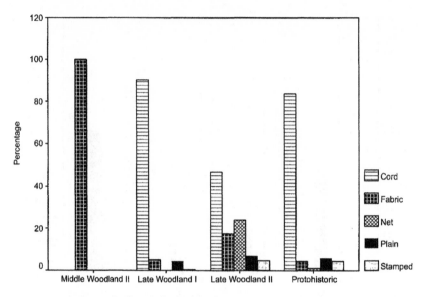

Figure 7-3. Ridge and Valley surface treatment

later periods in the predominance of cord-marked and net-impressed pottery.
Fabric impression dominates Late Woodland I assemblages but declines in importance thereafter, as simple stamping increases in popularity. This temporal
distinction between cord-marked and fabric-impressed pottery echoes the
break between Mockley and Townsend wares described by Egloff and Potter
(1982). Fabric impression dominates Middle Woodland II assemblages in the
Piedmont, then occurs in decreasing percentages as cord marking became
more frequent. A Protohistoric rise in plain surface treatments in the Piedmont corresponds with the occurrence of plain and cord-marked pottery
bearing rim decorations similar to those found on Potomac Creek vessels. In
the Ridge and Valley, a shift from fabric impression to cord marking occurs
early in the sequence, and cord marking dominates Late Woodland and early
colonial contexts.

Although these trends are important in the reconstruction of the region's
culture history, by themselves they reveal little concerning the social use
of style. Previous ceramic analyses have demonstrated that, beginning in
the Middle Woodland period, ceramic tempering agents differed across the
Chesapeake region's physiographic provinces, suggesting a spatial constriction
of social interaction and mobility. The Middle and Late Woodland use of
locally available tempering materials that differed across the drainage (i.e.,

shell in the Coastal Plain, quartz and sand in the Piedmont, and limestone and gastropod shell in the Ridge and Valley) does suggest declining mobility and increasingly localized social interaction. Yet the presence of the same surface treatments and rim decorations across the James River Valley, and indeed throughout much of the Middle Atlantic, indicates that some forms of social interaction continued to span physiographic boundaries during late prehistory. The ceramic stylistic data collected for this study may be used to evaluate the extent to which ceramic stylistic innovations flowed within and between physiographic provinces through relatively open social networks and clinally varying patterns.

As used with reference to biological phenomena, clines are gradual changes in the attributes of adjacent populations. Applied to ceramics, clinal variation refers to a gradient of differing style across space. Influenced by late precontact settlement focused on floodplains, such variation was channeled in part by the configuration of the river system. Structured in this way, clinally varying ceramic style should reflect distance decay patterns associated with down-the-line exchange and interaction (e.g., Hantman and Klein 1992:147).

One means of evaluating whether ceramic style varied clinally in the James River Valley involves comparing the prevalence of surface treatments to settlement location. The locations of pit features containing ceramics in the James River data set may be recorded in terms of distance to the James River's mouth at the Chesapeake Bay. Given the flow of the James, this measure accounts for a feature's westward distance from the Bay. This approach allows consideration of the distribution of different surface treatments in the context of the principal transportation network in the Chesapeake region—the river system. I do not mean to imply that the James River's mouth necessarily served as the geographic source of stylistic innovation. Rather, this location provides a convenient reference point from which to consider relative spatial patterns for the data set.

Table 7-1 lists statistical measures of the observed correlations between surface treatment (measured in terms of percentage per feature) and the distance to the James River's mouth. A high r^2 value and a low significance level indicate the likelihood that ceramic style, measured as the prevalence of a surface treatment, correlates strongly with the distance measure and varies clinally.

During the Middle Woodland II phase, the percentages of fabric impression, net impression, and plain surface treatments correlate in a statistically significant manner with distance to the James River's mouth. The value of

Table 7-1. Correlation between surface treatment percentages and distance to James's Mouth

Period	n(pits)	Cord			Fabric			Net			Plain			Simple Stamped			Mean
		r	r^2	Sig.	r	r^2	Sig.	r	r^2	Sig.	r	r^2	Sig.	r	r^2	Sig.	r^2
Middle Woodland II	17	-0.27	0.08	0.29	0.81★	0.65	<0.01	0.70★	0.48	<0.01	0.52★	0.27	0.04	-0.15	0.02	0.59	0.30
Late Woodland I	65	0.81★	0.66	<0.01	-0.73★	0.53	<0.01	-0.26★	0.07	0.04	-0.16	0.03	0.20	-0.27★	0.08	0.03	0.27
Late Woodland II	93	0.48★	0.23	<0.01	-0.20	0.04	0.05	-0.01	0.00	0.90	-0.02	0.00	0.82	-0.40★	0.16	<0.01	0.09

★Correlation is significant at the .05 level (two-tailed)

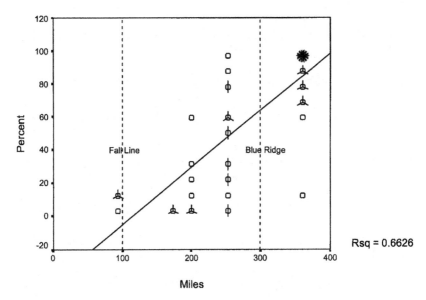

Figure 7-4. Cord marking against distance to James River's mouth, Late Woodland I

r^2, the coefficient of determination, measures the proportion of all variation in the Y axis (percentage of surface treatment) that is explained by X (the distance from the James River's mouth). Fabric impression increases in popularity west of the Chesapeake Bay such that distance to the James River's mouth accounts for over 65 percent of the variation in fabric impression for the Middle Woodland II features considered.[2] The high r^2 values and a low significance level suggest that fabric impression varied clinally during the Middle Woodland II phase. Similarly, net impression declines west of the Chesapeake Bay during the Middle Woodland II phase, producing a negative correlation with the distance measure. Almost half the variation in net impression may be accounted for by relative location within the James River Valley. These patterns indicate that the use of fabric impression and net impression in the James River Valley varied clinally during the Middle Woodland II centuries.

By the Late Woodland I phase, the percentage of all surface treatments per feature except one (plain) correlate in a statistically significant manner with distance. Cord marking and fabric impression produce high r^2 values, indicating that distance accounts for over 50 percent of the variation in the prevalence of these attribute states. Figures 7-4 and 7-5 depict the percentages of cord and fabric impression against distance from the mouth of the

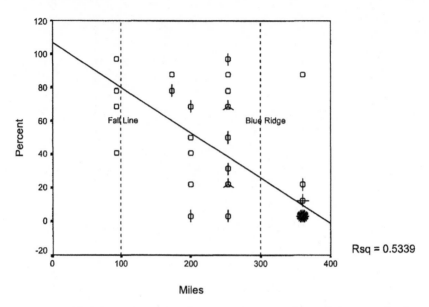

Figure 7-5. Fabric impression against distance to James River's mouth, Late Woodland I

James.[3] Fabric impression reverses the direction of its correlation over the Middle Woodland II phase, so that during the Late Woodland I phase fabric impression declines as a proportion of total surface treatment moving west of the Chesapeake Bay. Surface treatment usage in the Piedmont reflects a greater diversity than in areas to the east and west. This pattern suggests that substantial levels of social interaction spanned both the Blue Ridge and the fall line, while the Piedmont became a province that shared stylistic elements of surrounding areas.

Table 7-1 demonstrates that during the Late Woodland II phase, the prevalence of cord marking and simple stamping continues to correlate in a statistically significant manner with distance. This pattern does not meet the expectations raised above, which suggest that village formation led to an interruption of the open social networks and clinal variation that characterized preceding eras.

Closer examination of the patterns indicates that the clinal variation in surface treatment apparent in earlier periods did not continue into the Late Woodland II phase. This argument may be made on several grounds. As reported in table 7-1, Late Woodland II coefficient of determination values for cord marking and simple stamping were substantially lower than the co-

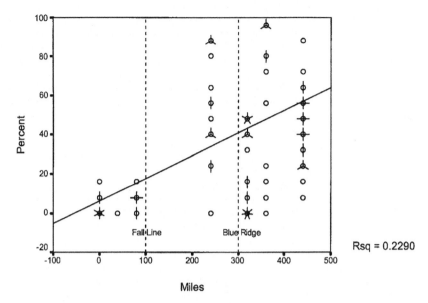

Figure 7-6. Cord marking against distance to James River's mouth, Late Woodland II

efficient of determination values for these surface treatments during previous periods. Most of the variation in cord marking and simple stamping is not accounted for by the distance measure. The overall mean r^2 value for Late Woodland II (0.087) is the lowest of all the periods considered. The mean Late Woodland II r^2 value is less than a third the Late Woodland I mean. Fabric-impressed pottery, which exhibited particularly high coefficients of variation during the Middle Woodland II and Late Woodland I phases, no longer correlates in a statistically significant manner with river distance during the Late Woodland II phase.

Second, scatterplots of the percentage of cord marking and simple stamping against distance record patterns that deviate sharply from the linearity of earlier centuries. Figure 7-6 indicates the possibility that the regression line has been "forced" between two distinct groups—Coastal Plain features with low percentages of cord-marked sherds and interior (i.e., Piedmont and Ridge and Valley) features with more variable but generally higher percentages of cord marking. Consideration of solely the interior portion of the James River drainage indicates that the correlation between cord marking and river distance suggested by table 7-1 is misleading. Little change in the

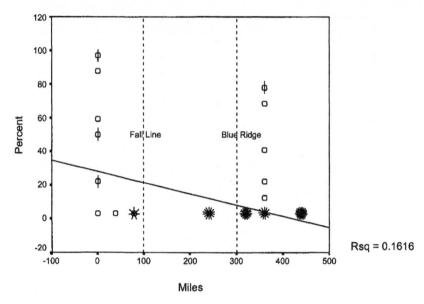

Figure 7-7. Simple stamping against distance to James River's mouth, Late Woodland II

percentage of cord marking occurs in the interior, and the correlation is not statistically significant.[4] At least in this portion of the drainage system, cord marking does not appear to vary clinally during Late Woodland II.

Figure 7-7 depicts rather low frequencies of Late Woodland II features containing simple-stamped pottery throughout the entire James River Valley. Features near the Chesapeake Bay and west of the Blue Ridge do have substantial percentages of simple-stamped sherds, though, while none of the Piedmont features with 10 or more sherds contain this surface treatment. Again, isolating the interior portion of the drainage results in the absence of a statistically significant correlation between the surface treatment percentage and river distance.[5] While this pattern differs in potentially meaningful ways from the distribution of features with cord-marked sherds, neither pattern supports an interpretation of continued clinal variation in ceramic style during Late Woodland II.

Nonclinal ceramic stylistic distributions might reflect such strategies as boundary maintenance, social alliances, or the reinforcement of social identity (Plog 1995b:372; Hantman 1984). The data set considered in this study does not allow these possibilities to be evaluated thoroughly but does provide grounds for additional studies aimed at addressing these issues. The distribution of cord-marked sherds during Late Woodland II provides evidence of continued Late Woodland II social interaction between the Piedmont and the Ridge and Valley. That such interaction relates to alliance formation is an intriguing possibility given the long tradition of shared ceramics (Gardner 1986) and mound burial practices (Hantman 1998) that spanned the Blue Ridge. I will examine this issue further in the discussion of chert exchange later in this chapter.

Surface treatment information from the Protohistoric and Contact periods provides a less detailed picture of ceramic stylistic variation than do data from previous periods due to the scarcity of excavated Piedmont features with more than 10 identified ceramics (n = 2). The general absence of data from the spatially intermediate Piedmont renders calculation of correlation coefficients for the Protohistoric and Contact period data inappropriate. Sherds from the few Piedmont features dating to this era are generally cord marked or have plain surfaces. Determining whether a return to more open networks and clinal variation characterized the Protohistoric and Contact periods or if the bounded networks continued after A.D. 1500 awaits additional excavation.

Pottery recovered during excavations at the Wright site (44GO30) on Elk Island raises a possible alternative to these options. As described in appendix 1, Wright site pottery is dominated by sand-tempered sherds that are either cord marked or plain. Rim sherds are generally decorated with incised motifs similar to those found on Potomac Creek pottery. In tracing the origins of Potomac Creek ceramics, Potter (1993:126–138) argues for the "Montgomery Complex hypothesis," in which Piedmont groups from the middle Potomac Valley migrated eastward to the inner Coastal Plain of the Potomac River during the Late Woodland centuries. Following Schmitt (1965:30), Potter sees evidence of this population movement in the form of a pottery tradition whereby the descendants of Shepard ware makers produced Potomac Creek ceramics. By the early colonial era Potomac Creek has been associated with the Piscataway chiefdom (Clark 1980:8) and related groups located in the James River Coastal Plain (Potter 1993:138).

During the late precontact and Protohistoric eras, however, Potomac Creek pottery may represent something more than a marker of a single political, ethnic, or linguistic unit, and understanding stylistic variation of ceramics such as the Potomac Creek series may require explanatory alternatives to migration. In a provocative argument, Moore (1993) rejects Clark's equation of Potomac Creek pottery with the Piscataway chiefdom, pointing out that similarities of material cultural may mask nonmaterial cultural diversity.

Moore (1993:131) argues that Potomac Creek pottery, especially in its latter stages, represents the archaeological correlates of a precolonial "contact situation" that incorporated a diversity of political, linguistic, and cultural entities.

In fact, Potomac Creek ceramics have a remarkably wide distribution by the late precontact and Protohistoric centuries. Potomac Creek pottery appears, sometimes as a minority ware, in the Coastal Plain of the Potomac and Rappahannock rivers (Egloff and Potter 1982:112), the Rappahannock Piedmont (Hantman 1993:105), the northern Shenandoah Valley (Gardner 1986:83), and at the Wright site in the James River Piedmont. At Rapidan Mound (44OR1) located in the Piedmont on a tributary to the Rappahannock, Potomac Creek ceramics occur in the context of a large mound burial site with ritual significance.

The groups embracing this use of ceramic style did not correspond geographically to a single river basin, as the distribution of Potomac Creek ceramics indicates. Based on the linguistic distribution that characterizes the Contact period, these groups likely did not all share the same language. By the end of prehistory and the beginning of the colonial era, the rim decorations on Potomac Creek pottery and similar wares may correspond to stylistic behavior expressed through decorative attributes other then surface treatment.

In sum, surface treatment patterns provide support for the notion that a late prehistoric shift from relatively unbounded social interaction to spatially discrete social networks occurred in the James River Valley. The ceramics suggest the prevalence of clinal variation through much of late prehistory, including the millennium between A.D. 200 and 1200, which corresponds to the Middle Woodland II and the Late Woodland I phases. Between A.D. 900 and 1200 most of the surface treatment categories vary in gradations of style viewed across the geographic space of the James River drainage. During the Late Woodland II phase, this clinal variation largely disappears, and explanations of stylistic behavior in terms of isochrestic variation no longer account for surface treatment variation. This disappearance coincides with a Late Woodland decline in the exchange of lithic artifacts such as rhyolite over long distances in the Middle Atlantic region (Stewart 1989). Finally, the distribution of surface treatments during the Protohistoric and Contact eras cannot be evaluated quantitatively given the available data. The widespread appearance of rim decoration in the Chesapeake region introduces the possibility that important aspects of ceramic stylistic variation shifted to this portion of the vessel.

Domestic Architectural Style

Architectural style provides an additional line of evidence for evaluating regional interaction among Native societies of the James River Valley. Ethnohistorical descriptions confirm that the Powhatans designed buildings, notably nondomestic structures and chiefs' houses, in ways that indexed such structures' special statuses. The Powhatans' storehouses bore beastlike images of "sentinels" (Smith 1986b:173–174), while chiefs' houses were particularly large and intricately partitioned. Presumably, the design and construction of domestic architecture conveyed meaning as well. Although much of this stylistic expression may be unrecoverable archaeologically due to the use of perishable building materials, the layouts of domestic floor plans offer an avenue for examining variation in the domestic built environment.

As discussed previously, two modal patterns appear in the James River Valley's architectural floor plans that correspond with circular or elliptical structures. Native communities in the James River Valley may have varied the floor plans of their houses as a result of stylistic choices or, alternatively, out of utilitarian decisions relating to such factors as household size and floor space needs that were largely distinct from stylistic considerations. As discussed in chapter 6 with regard to longhouses, structural limits on the width of James River houses led to the use of elliptical floor plans for particularly large houses. If house floor shape relates primarily to the intended size of the structure and not to stylistic considerations relating to the appearance of the architecture, then the length-to-width ratio should vary according to house floor area. In fact, the length-to-width ratios of domestic structures in the James River Valley do not increase along with floor area, suggesting that decisions regarding floor shapes did not respond to considerations related to structure size.[6] No apparent difference of function explains the circular and elliptical floor plans either, as each are associated with hearths and storage pits in roughly the same frequencies. Floor plan shape appears to have been at least partly stylistic.

If circular and elliptical floor plans do indeed reflect meaningful aspects of architectural style, their distribution provides evidence of stylistic behavior independent of the ceramic data. Distributions of house forms may be evaluated to determine the extent to which Native communities shared ar-

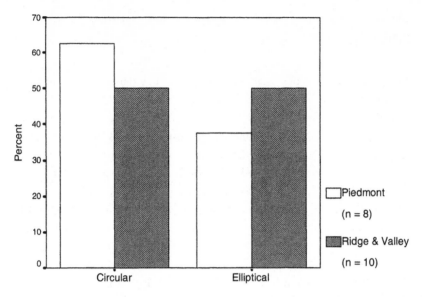

Figure 7-8. Late Woodland I floor plan shapes

chitectural styles across the physiographic boundaries of the fall line and the Blue Ridge. As identified in the analysis of ceramic surface treatments, such divergence is not expected until the Late Woodland II phase.

During the Middle Woodland II phase, the four house patterns with recognizable floor plans all occur in the Coastal Plain. Three of these fall in the elliptical range of length-to-width ratios, and one has a circular floor plan. Late Woodland I floor plan information has been collected from the Piedmont and Ridge and Valley provinces but not from the Coastal Plain. Figure 7-8 depicts the percentages of different floor plans by province for the Late Woodland I phase. No statistically significant relationship exists between house form and province during the Late Woodland I phase, indicating that the slight variation in house construction depicted in the graph does not parallel sharp differences across the physiographic provinces.[7] These results support the interpretation that domestic architectural style, at least as expressed through floor plan, was not impeded by the Blue Ridge Mountains between A.D. 900 and 1200.

Unfortunately, information concerning architectural style covers only the western portion of the James River Valley during Late Woodland I centuries. Potential distinctions between the architectural style of interior groups and those of the Coastal Plain cannot be detected without evidence from the

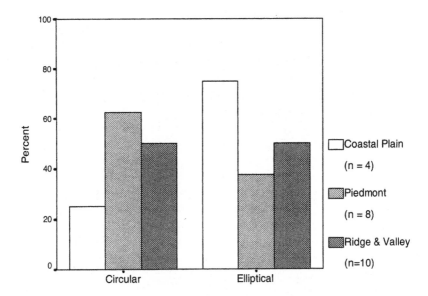

Figure 7-9. Combined Middle Woodland II and Late Woodland I floor plan shapes

coastal region. Figure 7-9 combines Middle Woodland II and Late Woodland I floor plan data in order to make this comparison. Compared with houses in the interior, a higher percentage of Coastal Plain houses during this era were elliptical. Given the wide chronological range associated with these data, the evidence of contrasting architectural styles in this graph may be the product of temporal variation rather than the expression of stylistic boundaries. Nonetheless, the frequencies of house forms from the three provinces indicate that no statistically significant relationship exists between province and house form during the Middle Woodland II to Late Woodland I centuries.[8] Similarly, there is no statistically significant relationship between province and house form when the Coastal Plain data are compared with houses from the Piedmont or the Ridge and Valley.[9] While limited in terms of sample size, the archaeology of architectural style prior to A.D. 1200 provides no evidence for sharp boundaries in the James River Valley.

The Late Woodland II data suggest a more distinct contrast between domestic architectural style in the Ridge and Valley compared with the eastern provinces. Coastal Plain and Piedmont floor plans include only elliptical forms, while circles dominate the Ridge and Valley (figure 7-10). Only one Piedmont floor plan in the James River Valley has been identified, an elliptical structure at the Little River site (44GO30b). This house offers a sample size

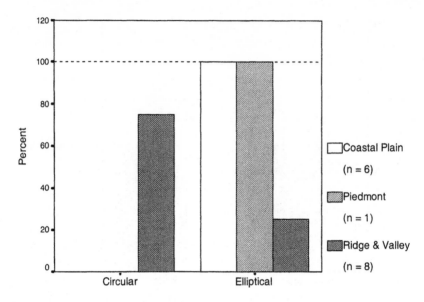

Figure 7-10 Late Woodland II floor plan shapes

too small to evaluate Piedmont patterns against those from other provinces using significance testing. Coastal Plain and Ridge and Valley values indicate that there is a statistically significant relationship between province and house shape during Late Woodland II centuries, a result that supports the notion that architectural style contrasted sharply across these portions of the James River Valley.[10] Recall that the comparison between Coastal Plain and Ridge and Valley house forms prior to Late Woodland II produced no evidence of a significant difference. These contrasting results suggest that architectural style became spatially bounded during Late Woodland II as it had not been previously.

House shapes of the Protohistoric sixteenth century indicate that the Late Woodland II contrast between architectural style in the eastern and western portions of the drainage persisted through time. As depicted in figure 7-11, circular forms predominated in the Ridge and Valley, while the Coastal Plain groups favored elliptical floor plans. No complete Protohistoric floor plans have been excavated in the Piedmont. Significance testing confirms that the relationship between province and floor plan remained statistically significant during protohistory, supporting the notion that domestic architectural styles continued to differ across the James River Valley during the early colonial era.[11]

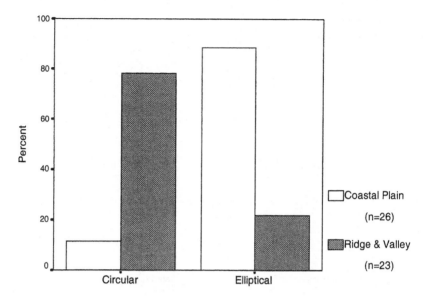

Figure 7-11. Protohistoric floor plan shapes

In sum, evidence of domestic architectural style in the James River Valley is limited largely to differences in the layout of floor plans, and small sample sizes place constraints on their interpretive potential. Nonetheless, evidence suggesting the existence of unbounded architectural style between A.D. 200 and 1200 provides independent support for the inference that open social networks characterized the James River Valley during this interval. After A.D. 1200 architectural style that differed between the physiographic provinces suggests that social boundaries were in place in the James River Valley and that social networks decreased in geographic scope.

The patterns identified above indicate that the geographic distribution of architectural style in the James River Valley changed measurably after A.D. 1200. Whether post–A.D. 1200 stylistic variation in house form represents deliberate efforts to achieve regionally distinctive styles or the variation re- sulted from less daily interaction between relatively sedentary groups with ge- ographically diminished social networks is difficult to determine. Among the seventeenth-century Powhatans, stylistic attributes marked chiefs' residences, storehouses, and temples as locations of power, implying the conscious ma- nipulation of architectural style. In a range of cultural and historical contexts, the domestic built environment results from considerable deliberation, much of it concerned with issues of status and identity. Similar issues likely played

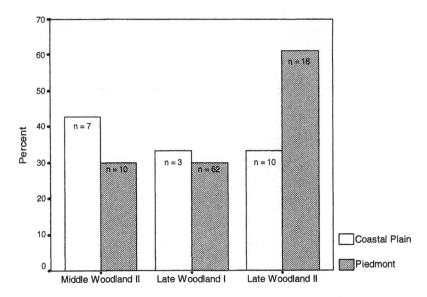

Figure 7-12. Percentage of features containing chert debitage, Coastal Plain and Piedmont

a role in the regionally distinctive architecture of the Late Woodland II phase and the early colonial era in the James River Valley.

Nonlocal Lithics East of the Blue Ridge

The Late Woodland II contraction of social networks mirrored by patterning in ceramic and architectural styles does not imply that regional interaction ceased. Evidence of an increase in exchange relations across the Blue Ridge Mountains appears in the James River interior during the Late Woodland, raising the possibility that exchange relations on a more limited spatial scale accompanied the attenuation of long-distance exchange. Drawing primarily on surface collection data, Parker (1989:119) determined that the overall diversity of raw materials in Late Woodland Piedmont settlements decreased while the frequency of chert projectile points increased over earlier periods. Chert, a fine-grained stone, is a far more suitable material for stone tool production than are quartz and quartzite. Though widely available through-out the Piedmont, quartz and quartzite tend to fracture in unpredictable ways. Other tool types were not produced from chert in similarly increasing frequencies during the Late Woodland period in the Piedmont, raising the possibility that an exchange sphere focused on small, triangular chert points developed during the Late Woodland (Hantman and Klein 1992:149).

The source chert for these projectile points most likely originated from outcrops located in the Ridge and Valley province and from float chert present in Piedmont and Coastal Plain river gravels. Small amounts of chert do occur east of the Blue Ridge, primarily in the form of cobbles transported by rivers such as the James from sources in the Ridge and Valley (Hantman 1987). The floodplain settlements included in this study all had direct access to at least some float chert, though the alluvial transportation of float chert does result in declining amounts of such chert to the east. Assuming that Native communities on the James River floodplain were aware of the chert cobbles present in river gravels throughout the centuries studied here, variation in the presence of chert artifacts in a given location likely reflects changes in exchange relations involving the material.

Figure 7-12 depicts the percentages of features in the Coastal Plain and Piedmont that contain chert debitage. Most dramatic is the Late Woodland II increase in the Piedmont, whereby over half of the features in the sample contained chert debitage. The percentage of features with chert debitage declines slightly in the Coastal Plain over the periods considered.

These results support the notion that the increased Late Woodland II presence of chert debitage in the Piedmont was associated with an increased movement of chert into the province and more intensive exchange relations between Piedmont and Ridge and Valley groups. [12] By contrast, no significant changes are apparent in the Coastal Plain.

Exchange relations between the Ridge and Valley and Piedmont apparently intensified during the Late Woodland II phase, even as long-distance interaction and exchange decreased throughout the Middle Atlantic. The slight decline in Coastal Plain features containing chert debitage raises the possibility that access to this material deteriorated in the eastern reaches of the drainage with the decreased settlement mobility of the Late Woodland period, though the small number of features with debitage information do not provide firm patterns with regard to this issue.

As proposed by Parker's (1989) study, chert projectile points may have served as a particularly important medium of exchange in the Late Woodland Piedmont. The data collected for this study allow Parker's findings to be evaluated with a data set of tightly dated feature contexts. Figure 7-13 depicts the percentage of features in the James River Piedmont and Coastal Plain containing chert projectile points, indicating that less than 10 percent of the features prior to Late Woodland II contained chert projectile points. During Late Woodland II the Piedmont percentage jumped to over 25 percent. Par-

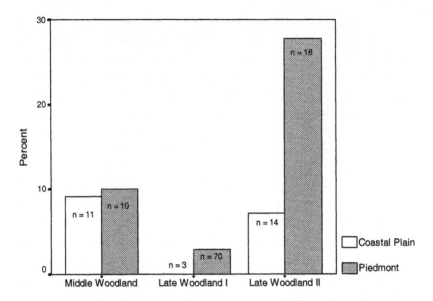

Figure 7-13. Percentage of features containing chert projectile points, Coastal Plain and Piedmont

alleling the chert debitage pattern, Piedmont features included a substantial increase in chert projectile points after A.D. 1200.[13]

The changing presence of chert debitage and projectile points in Piedmont features suggests that exchange relations across the Blue Ridge intensified during the Late Woodland II phase. A shared surface treatment, cord marking, also links these portions of the drainage circa A.D. 1200–1500. In conjunction with evidence of mound burial practices shared between Ridge and Valley and Piedmont societies, these social connections and cultural affinities highlight close links between central Virginia groups residing in the two provinces by the end of prehistory.

These patterns indicate that a social interaction network linking Piedmont communities to settlements in the Ridge and Valley emerged in conjunction with the establishment of village communities in both provinces. Information concerning domestic architectural style is largely absent from the Piedmont during Late Woodland II, preventing comparison of house form between these areas. The Late Woodland II intensification of Piedmont–Ridge and Valley interaction occurred amid a general attenuation of broad-based exchange relations in the Middle Atlantic. A spatially constricted social network apparently emerged in the interior portion of central Virginia. The results

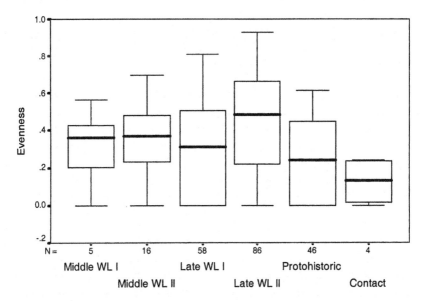

Figure 7-14. Boxplots of surface treatment evenness by period, James River Valley

obtained here provide independent support for Parker's (1989) findings, with the timing of the increased flow of chert into the Piedmont narrowed to the latter half of the Late Woodland period.

Ceramic Surface Treatment: Intracommunity Diversity

The stylistic patterns identified above raise the possibility that a shift in stylistic behavior toward symbolic variation occurred within village communities of the Late Woodland II phase. Symbolic variation involves social comparison and more conscious communication of identity through style. It may be reflected in a greater amount of stylistic behavior and more diverse ceramic style (e.g., Braun 1991; Hegmon 1986) such that higher levels of stylistic diversity correspond with greater social heterogeneity within floodplain communities.

Such stylistic behavior may be evaluated through diversity measures, particularly "evenness," which records the uniformity of stylistic attribute states within a given assemblage (Kintigh 1989). The most diverse assemblage, according to this measure, includes all potential attribute states in the same frequencies; the least diverse assemblage includes only one of the potential attribute states in any frequency. Potential surface treatments include cord marking, fabric impression, net impression, simple stamping, and plain surfaces.

Surface treatment diversity increased during the Late Woodland II (figure 7-14). A decline in these values during the Protohistoric and Contact periods is also evident.[14] Surface treatment diversity and, inferentially, the intensity of stylistic behavior within floodplain communities increased substantially during the Late Woodland II phase before declining during the sixteenth and seventeenth centuries. These results indicate that stylistic diversity peaked within Late Woodland II settlements, likely paralleling heightened social symboling in this context. Based on these patterns, Late Woodland II village communities appear to represent contexts with particularly frequent expressions of social differences.

Figure 7-15 breaks these data down using a finer level of spatial and chronological detail, with diversity measured by physiographic province and by century. Gaps in the chart indicate centuries for which no data are available. Within each province, surface treatment diversity peaked during the Late Woodland II phase. These data record increased symbolic variation of ceramic style with the establishment of village communities throughout the river basin.

Figure 7-15 also suggests that mean diversity values by century in the Coastal Plain and Piedmont changed in a generally similar sequence. By contrast, Ridge and Valley diversity remained lower than in the eastern provinces until the seventeenth century. The Middle Woodland trends in the Piedmont and Coastal Plain may parallel shifts in settlement patterns recorded by Potter (1993) in the Potomac Coastal Plain that are matched by survey data from the James River Piedmont (Gallivan 1994). In his Chicacoan survey, Potter identified large midden sites dating to A.D. 700–900, the final centuries of the Middle Woodland period. Potter (1993:81) suggests that these sites, especially Boathouse Pond (44NB111), reflect locations of large, seasonal population aggregations. A Late Woodland I dispersal of the Chicacoan population into intermediate-sized sites along the neck lands of the Coan River followed. As described in appendix 1, a similar increased frequency of small to intermediate-sized sites occurred circa A.D. 900–1200 along the Wingina floodplain in the James River Piedmont.

The Middle Woodland II seasonal aggregations on the floodplain likely incorporated groups with a wide range of social categories, as would subsequent Late Woodland II villages. In such contexts, stylistic diversity increased as ceramic style began to vary symbolically. By the early Late Woodland period the declining prominence of large base camps and the increased prevalence of

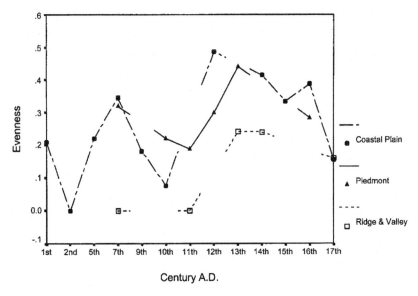

Figure 7-15. Mean evenness of surface treatments per century

smaller, dispersed hamlets apparently resulted in a decline in social symboling and, as a result, less stylistic diversity within floodplain settlements.

Transformation of Regional Interaction in the James River Valley

Regional interaction changed measurably in the James River Valley, as reflected in ceramic surface treatment, architectural style, and exchange relations. Native communities in the James River Valley embraced a transition circa A.D. 1200–1500 from relatively open, undifferentiated interaction networks to those that were localized and spatially discrete. Along with the establishment of relatively large and permanent villages, ceramic style ceased to vary clinally across the drainage, and house construction differed between physiographic provinces as never before. Within James River villages, increased stylistic diversity signaled a range of variable social identities within the same community.

These patterns force us to revise our understanding of regional social relations in the late prehistoric James River Valley. Surface treatment varied clinally even after A.D. 200, when Native Americans in the Chesapeake region began to produce ceramics tempered with locally available materials (i.e., shell, sand, quartz, and limestone). With the Late Woodland II establishment of relatively large and permanent village communities, though, the spatial distribution of surface treatments reflects the interruption of clinal variation, while house shapes began to differ between physiographic provinces. At the same time, exchange relations between Piedmont and Ridge and Valley groups became more intensive. To the east, coastal groups were excluded from these exchange relations.

The heightened sedentariness and settlement population size of the Late Woodland II link these changes at the regional scale to developments related to the household and communal scales documented in previous chapters. The creation of a cultural landscape of relatively permanent settlements resulted in a geographic scale of social interaction considerably more limited than that of mobile societies. The management of economic uncertainty during the Late Woodland II phase appears to have shifted in emphasis from a strategy of high mobility toward regular and intensive interaction over a more limited distance. With this understanding of regional social interaction in the James River Valley, the Late Woodland II phase emerges as the scene of a dramatically transformed social landscape in which new relationships developed at the domestic, community, and regional levels.

Chapter 8

Historical Anthropology of Native Societies in the Chesapeake

With its remarkably rich ethnohistorical and archaeological records, the Chesapeake region offers much to those interested in understanding the culture histories of Native societies. The written accounts produced by European sources during the early years of the colonial era highlight the actions of the Powhatans and Monacans, some of whom competed for wealth, power, and influence. However, evidence of the social changes that produced the figures shaping this political arena in the years leading up to Jamestown has been difficult to recognize. Archaeological patterns apparent in other North American contexts reflecting the centralization of authority in political and ceremonial centers are absent from the region. Long-distance exchange networks that conveyed items crafted with sacred connotations played a rather modest role in the Late Woodland Chesapeake, judging from the archaeological evidence. Mortuary practices generally lacked expressions of the social differentiation that might convey differences of wealth or power during this period. Clearly, the Native societies of the late precontact Chesapeake produced a unique culture history in the years leading up to Jamestown that deserves consideration on its own terms.

By identifying changes in the practices of Native communities, this study recovers important elements of Powhatan and Monacan culture history and provides a means of reuniting the region's ethnohistory with its archaeology. I have identified a set of social changes that coincided with the establishment of relatively large and permanent village communities in the James River Valley. During the three centuries between A.D. 1200 and 1500, Native societies transformed elements of their domestic economy, community organization, and regional interaction, resulting in social inequality and funds of power absent during preceding centuries. These changes altered the social organization and political economy of Native societies from the Appalachian Highlands to the Chesapeake Bay, though some important differences do distinguish the Powhatan and Monacan portions of the drainage. The creation of a landscape of village communities in the James River Valley triggered social dynamics that contributed to the political hierarchy of the late sixteenth and early seventeenth centuries in the Chesapeake region.

Nonetheless, the archaeological record of Native societies in the Chesapeake demonstrates that the early colonial era entailed a social context that differed in fundamental ways from the preceding era, complicating efforts to trace a regional culture history. A new set of developments within the domestic, communal, and regional spheres emerged rather abruptly during the sixteenth and early seventeenth centuries, changes coinciding with the colonial encounter. By linking this archaeological evidence to written accounts of the Powhatans and Monacans, a new historical anthropology of Native societies in the James River Valley begins to emerge. In this chapter I retrace precontact developments before turning to a narrative account of the colonial encounter in order to consider ways in which Native societies of the colonial Chesapeake drew upon funds of power originally generated by precontact social changes. In combining ethnohistorical and archaeological evidence from the sixteenth and early seventeenth centuries, it becomes apparent that the Contact period presented a unique and transformative historical setting that prompted a reorganization of village life in Native communities across the region.

Late Precontact Social Dynamics in the James River Valley

Household, Community, and Regional Dynamics

Throughout the sixteen centuries prior to the settlement of Jamestown, Native Americans in the James River Valley altered their behavioral practices in small and profound ways that created the archaeological record considered in this study. Middle Woodland hunter-gatherers left evidence of briefly occupied hamlets on the James River floodplain with relatively low reoccupation rates. The introduction of domesticates at the outset of the Late Woodland period originally produced a relatively modest alteration of social life on the floodplain. A focus on riverine environments and floodplain settlements with limited residential permanence had been in place for over three millennia prior to the sporadic A.D. 900–1000 appearance of maize. Horticulture initially represented a minor adjustment in terms of settlement and subsistence. Nonetheless, the decision to raise corn, beans, and squash tethered households to specific locations and resulted in new production relations critical to the gradual elongation of floodplain residence. The extension of riverine subsistence resources through floodplain gardening and increased storage also allowed households to produce previously unattainable surpluses.

The adoption of domesticates and the decision to remain committed to a single floodplain location for a longer portion of the year appear to have comprised triggers of social change in the late precontact James River Valley. The modest increases in Late Woodland I settlement permanence within some communities drew upon a long cultural history of seasonally aggregated, riverine-focused settlement. However, these extensions of floodplain-based food production and residential permanence became considerably more revolutionary with the creation of village communities during the Late Woodland II phase. Combining greater sedentariness with horticulture presented social opportunities and challenges to village residents. Native communities on the James faced these opportunities and challenges during an era that may be characterized as the "time lag" of the first three Late Woodland centuries (A.D. 900–1200).

During this interval modest changes in the domestic economy accompanied a trend toward greater settlement permanence at the core of the social transformations identified in this study. Domestic groups altered important elements of their daily practices and social reproduction amid decisions to add domesticates to the subsistence regime and to lengthen settlement on the floodplain. As household size increased during the Late Woodland I phase, interhousehold differentiation also increased. Households in some settlements stored surpluses in subsurface pits dug immediately outside of domestic structures, suggesting that domestic groups exerted a measure of control over surplus stores. Settlement population size did not increase appreciably during the Late Woodland I time-lag interval. The general absence of communal or public facilities in the archaeological record may reflect the absence of institutions of social integration that eventually attracted larger, nucleated, and more permanent communities.

Sedentariness and settlement population increased abruptly during the Late Woodland II phase. From A.D. 1200 to 1500 social organizational changes within the domestic, communal, and regional spheres permitted some Native communities in the James River Valley to cross a threshold represented by the establishment of village settlements. While not all floodplain settlements in the James River Valley during these centuries may be characterized as villages, enough communities chose to incorporate longer residence times, larger numbers of resident households, and altered community organization to create a social landscape radically different than that of preceding centuries.

The Late Woodland II reorganization of production around domestic groups appears to be tied closely to the institutionalization of social inequality. Increasing domestic group size and household differentiation indicate a continuation of trends in the domestic sphere that began during the preceding centuries. By contrast, Late Woodland II changes in community organization record developments that differed qualitatively from those of earlier centuries. The appearance of communal architecture and public facilities (i.e., palisades, large roasting pits, and longhouses) implies that villagers balanced communally integrative institutions against the potentially fragmentary nature of village communities. Paralleling the increases in household autonomy and village populations, social heterogeneity increased within Late Woodland II villages, as indicated by stylistic patterns present on domestically produced ceramics.

In this landscape of village communities perched between integration and segmentation, regional social organization reflected alterations as well. Stylistic patterning in the James River Valley records the development of social boundaries that appeared as more sedentary groups intensified and formalized interaction with neighboring communities. These linkages between large and socially diverse communities allowed James River villagers to buffer economic uncertainty through smaller, more intensive social networks than those of preceding centuries.

Political Strategies

Accompanying evidence of greater social differentiation during the Late Woodland II phase, a different set of symbols may be seen in the archaeological record that imply a generally corporate emphasis throughout the James River Valley. In fact, such corporate symbols appear to have been instrumental in the establishment of village communities in much of the James River Valley. Accretional burial mounds appeared in the Piedmont after A.D. 1200, indicating that the formalization of mound-related ritual accompanied the establishment of village communities. These collective burial features and contemporary ossuaries in the Coastal Plain suggest an emphasis on themes of social solidarity and corporate identity as opposed to those of individual differentiation within a population. Ridge and Valley mounds that have a somewhat longer history included some grave offerings and fewer interments than those in the Piedmont, patterns that reflect coexisting expressions of solidarity and individual status in the mortuary practices within this part of the drainage. In the Coastal Plain, the palisaded village at Great Neck (44vb7) incorporated elite mortuary treatment alongside ossuary burial during the Late Woodland II phase. Nonetheless, these expressions of social differentiation in mortuary ritual appear amid a general emphasis on corporate symbols in burial practices throughout the river basin, especially in the central Piedmont.

Beyond the mortuary evidence, the domestic and communal settings of the Late Woodland II reflect practices that conform with corporate political strategies (Blanton et al. 1996). Domestic production of subsistence increased during the Late Woodland II, while prestige-good exchange during this phase was limited largely to the sporadic movement of shell artifacts. Such patterns suggest a political economy in which Native communities emphasized staple production (i.e., intensified subsistence production) over more externally oriented wealth finance (i.e., exchange relations involving prestige goods). The increased size of roasting pits implies the use of facilities related to multi-household institutions and communal events that likely echoed the expression of corporate solidarity in mortuary ritual. While "home production" tactics of expanded household size and elevated subsistence production inevitably produced surpluses that differed between domestic groups, it appears that Native societies' emphasis on "group-oriented" themes during the Late Woodland II phase entailed cultural constraints on the ability to translate the social inequality of the domestic sphere into the exclusionary strategies of elite politics. In fact, during the precontact era such constraints appear as a critical cultural element within Chesapeake societies, an element that crossed cultural and linguistic boundaries in the James River Valley.

Regionally, intercommunity relations involving shared symbols (i.e., collective burial and longhouse architecture) and increased exchange in geographically limited areas (i.e., chert projectile point flows across the Blue Ridge) also appeared during the Late Woodland II phase. The presence of nucleated and palisaded villages with elite or communal architecture alongside smaller hamlets matched the two-part settlement hierarchy that continued into the colonial era, as documented by Smith's (1986b) *Map of Virginia*. While there is little in the archaeological record implying the emergence of a dominant regional center in any portion of the river drainage, the establishment of such large villages with unusual architectural components does suggest the creation of political centers absent during the preceding Late Woodland I phase. Based on these patterns of the Late Woodland II centuries, regional-scale social relations appear to have been shaped by intensive interaction, by symbolic emulation, and possibly by intergroup competition between relatively large, palisaded communities.

In the absence of a controlling political center, these social relations suggest Late Woodland II political dynamics driven by interaction between village-centered "peer polities" (cf. Renfrew and Cherry 1986). Throughout the James River Valley, these polities appear to have been group oriented, with an overriding corporate orientation, rather than individualizing chiefdoms structured by networks centered solely on powerful elites (cf. Renfrew 1974). Interaction between such peer polities in the absence of a dominant regional center often becomes instrumental in the long-term evolution of political systems. Political change in such a context of peer polity interaction results from social relationships between sociopolitical units situated in close proximity rather than from the diffusion of ideas from a cultural center or from a political core's dominance of its periphery.

The Early Colonial Conjuncture

How did political agents in the Chesapeake region capture individual-centered political authority within a cultural context that emphasized corporate symbols? What strategies allowed an individual such as Powhatan to manipulate the political economy to place himself at the center of a regional network of wealth and power? During the sixteenth through early seventeenth centuries in the Chesapeake region, historical events tied to intercultural contact introduced a historical conjuncture that altered cultural categories amid the events of contact, a historical process involving intercultural linkages not unlike those documented elsewhere as the modern world system began to take shape (e.g., Sahlins 1985; Mintz 1985). As reflected in both the archaeology and ethnohistory of this historical conjuncture in the Chesapeake, the corporate ethos of societies throughout the region gave way to network strategies shaped by Native culture brokers who placed themselves as intermediaries during the colonial encounter.

Protohistoric Encounters in the Chesapeake

During the Protohistoric sixteenth century Native societies in the Chesapeake region saw two parallel developments: intermittent contacts between European colonists, missionaries, slavers, and pirates and the emergence of a paramount chiefdom under Powhatan. By the 1520s Spanish maps of North America began to depict the Chesapeake Bay—*la Bahia de Santa Maria*—

indicating that vessels from that nation had explored the Bay during the early years of the sixteenth century (Lewis and Loomie 1953:7). French and Spanish ships sailed on the Bay and into the Virginia Tidewater in subsequent years, though accounts of these explorations and of contact with Native societies are few, and those that do exist are complicated by an imperfect knowledge of the regional geography. In 1549 a vessel—likely French—traveled on the Chesapeake and traded with several hundred Native Americans there (Lewis and Loomie 1953:13).

These sporadic and poorly documented contacts culminated in 1561 when a Spanish vessel entered the Chesapeake, captured a young Virginia Algonquin boy, and brought him to Spain to be educated in Spanish and converted to Christianity. Christened Don Luis, the boy was said to be from a ruling Algonquin family and the son of a chief. After traveling to Mexico and Havana, Don Luis joined a missionary expedition of Spanish Jesuits that returned to coastal Virginia in 1570. Eventually settling along the York River, the mission faced a land "chastened" with six years of famine and death (Lewis and Loomie 1953:39). Almost immediately, Don Luis abandoned the Jesuit priests to live with his kin, compounding the clergymen's difficulties. The Jesuits, soon facing starvation themselves, demanded that Don Luis return and aid the mission in February 1571. Don Luis responded by leading a group of Algonquins to the mission to kill the priests. In keeping with Algonquin practices, a Spanish boy named Alonso was allowed to live through the attack. Alonso's description of these events provides a rare account of Native actions during the sixteenth century. Researchers have suggested that Don Luis's assault stemmed from a desire to avoid public shame with his people (Rountree 1990:17), out of efforts to provide the martyrdom that the Jesuits truly desired (Gleach 1997:95), or in the context of his decision to abandon Christian mores for Algonquin practices (Lewis and Loomie 1953:47–48). After a relief expedition discovered what had happened, the Spanish sent a punitive force of soldiers to the area led by the governor of Cuba. In the process of winning Alonso's return and failing to seize Don Luis, the governor's men punished the local population by slaying more than 20 Algonquins through gunfire or hanging (Lewis and Loomie 1953:51–55).

Don Luis represents the first of several culture brokers to appear in early colonial accounts of the Chesapeake, culture brokers who had a hand in the social transformations of the early colonial era (cf. Fausz 1985:239). Several oblique references in the early Jamestown accounts hint that Don Luis may have been from the same matrilineage as Powhatan (Rountree 1990:18;

Gleach 1997:142), linking the European world of guns, conversion, and empire to powerful *weroances* of the Virginia Tidewater. Some ethnohistorians (e.g., Lewis and Loomie 1953:58–62) have suggested that Don Luis may in fact have been Powhatan's brother and successor Opechancanough, an intriguing possibility that is now impossible to verify. Regardless of his exact identity, Don Luis served as a mediator between the world of Native societies in the Chesapeake and the coming invasion of Europeans by providing accounts of European colonial activities, including the military, religious, and economic forces of empire and their devastating effects on Native societies under Spanish rule. Though the Powhatans immediately recognized distinctions between the English and the Spanish, they also likely saw similarities in the intermittent violence of men associated with the two colonial powers. Upon Don Luis's arrival in Virginia, his people reportedly assumed he had returned from the dead (Lewis and Loomie 1953:89). Subsequently, Indians throughout the Chesapeake region described the European colonists using metaphors that drew upon similar notions of an otherworldly origin. Following a 1608 skirmish between a group of Mannahoacs and Englishmen under Smith's command, a Mannahoac named Amoroleck told Smith that he heard that the colonists were a people who had come from under the world in order to take the world away from them (Smith 1986d:175–176).

English colonial efforts in the region began between 1584 and 1587 when Sir Walter Raleigh organized three expeditions to Roanoke Island, located approximately 75 miles (120 kilometers) south of the James River's mouth (Quinn 1985; Hariot 1972). During the first exploratory voyage in 1584 to the Carolina coast, the English encountered Algonquins led by Chief Wingina and recruited two Algonquins to serve as translators—Manteo and Wanchese. A subsequent expedition in 1585 brought 100 men to Roanoke Island under the command of Ralph Lane, a soldier by training with a deeply suspicious disposition. The Roanoke colonists explored the surrounding region, venturing as far north as the Chesapeake Bay where they encountered the Chesapeacks, with whom they established friendly relations. Later, through a series of overly aggressive responses to perceived challenges from coastal Algonquins, Lane managed first to alienate Wingina, then to have him killed and beheaded as a preemptive strike against a rumored attack. Weeks later, Lane abandoned the colony, bringing Manteo and Wanchese with him to England. The English mounted a second effort to establish a colony on Roanoke Island in 1587 under the governorship of John White. White returned to England to resupply the colony, only to be delayed by English efforts to counter the Spanish Armada. When White did finally return to Roanoke he found the settlement abandoned. These "Lost Colonists" may have moved to the mainland, possibly joining the Chesapeacks to the north, though their fate is unknown to this day.

Amid the intermittent violence of this Protohistoric context during the latter half of the sixteenth century, Wahunsunacock, the man known to the Jamestown colonists as Powhatan, began to expand the scope and magnitude of his power and to build a large-scale polity centered on himself. Powhatan reportedly inherited authority over six groups near the James River fall line and on the upper York River. From this core area lying between the Monacans and Tidewater Virginia, Wahunsunacock enlarged his influence over virtually the entire Virginia Coastal Plain through conquest and shrewd manipulation of marriage ties. Strachey (1953:68) offers an account of Wahunsunacock's Protohistoric tactics in the conquest of the Kecoughtans: upon the death of the Kecoughtans' *weroance*, Wahunsunacock "subtly stepped in" by killing the new chief and some of his people, relocating the remnant Kecoughtans, and placing loyalists in the principal village. During the subsequent conquest of the Piankatanks, Wahunsunacock had his men visit the Piankatank village on a friendly pretense before staging an ambush from within the settlement (Smith 1986b:175). The Piankatanks' *weroance*, women, and children were spared and brought to Wahunsunacock, echoing Don Luis's actions against the Spanish Jesuits.

Early Jamestown

On the evening of April 26, 1607, the date of their arrival at the mouth of the Chesapeake, the Jamestown colonists were attacked by an unknown group of Indians (Percy 1998:90; Smith 1986a:27). Though this brief assault and retreat into the woods near Cape Henry ushered in the early-seventeenth-century Contact period, earlier cross-cultural engagements had already deeply affected both sides of the colonial encounter. The intermittent confrontations between Indians and Europeans during the Protohistoric era shaped Algonquin perceptions of and tactics toward the people who came from under the world. On the other side of the equation, appealing descriptions of Virginia and its rich "commodities" encouraged the English to form the Virginia Company that brought settlers to Jamestown. Accounts from travelers and the failed Roanoke colony also offered an ambiguous picture of the "natural inhabitants" as simultaneously pliant and cunning, submissive yet "inconstant." In a letter from the Roanoke colony advertising its prospects,

Ralph Lane (1955) wrote in glowing terms of Virginia's greatness and of the courteous Natives while providing important details regarding the symbolic value that red copper objects held in the Native political economy. In fact, Hariot's (1972) *A Briefe and True Report of the New Found Land of Virginia*, an account of the Roanoke colonial effort and its encounters with the local Algonquin inhabitants, became required reading for the Jamestown colonists (Haile 1998:9).

Jamestown colonists' contacts with local inhabitants during the first years of the colony hint at early Native strategies in the face of the colonial encounter. These contacts occurred most often as the colonists explored the region by boat and sought to obtain corn from the Indians. The resulting confrontations throughout the coastal Chesapeake and, in a few instances, into the Piedmont involved warfare and trading, sometimes experienced in rapid succession and generally followed by a feast sponsored by a village *weroance*. During these events *weroances* of the coastal region played a prominent role, insisting on serving as intermediaries between the Virginia Algonquin communities and the newly arrived Tassantasses (Gallivan and Hantman 1996; Kupperman 2000:36–37). *Weroances* often received the colonists as "friends" and expressed their "love" of the English, all the while seeking to determine their intentions and to obtain their copper, glass beads, and iron implements. The Jamestown colonists struggled badly during the first years of the colony, enduring appallingly high attrition in the face of a "starving time," poor water quality, and local pathogens to which they had no immunity. Though the Indians who faced the English were well aware of these weaknesses, the Tassantasses's red copper and blue beads represented potential media of sacred power from an exotic, outside world. These objects proved meaningful in Powhatan society due largely to the connotations attached to red and shades of blue and black in the Powhatans' symbolic system. Among Algonquin groups, red metal objects conveyed associations to the spirit world, while black's significance for the Powhatans appears to have involved mediation with the sacred (Gleach 1997:56–58). As Hantman (1990) has suggested, it is their access to such media of power that may have kept the colonists alive during the earliest years of the colony.

Colonists George Percy (1998:90–99) and John Smith (1986d: 136–153) offer the most detailed account of the initial contacts between the Powhatans and the English, events that are worth considering in some detail. Following the brief raid and retreat near Cape Henry that greeted the colonists, the English encountered a group of Kecoughtans who brought them to their principal village on the north shore at the mouth of the James River. The Kecoughtans greeted the English with a "doleful" cry, laying on the ground and scratching at the earth. The "chiefest" of the Kecoughtans sat together, feasting the English then offering tobacco in a large pipe decorated with a piece of copper. After the Kecoughtans entertained the English with dancing, Captain Christopher Newport gave them glass beads and other small objects. The colonists then departed, traveling upstream to the Paspaheghs' village, where the *weroance* welcomed them and made a point of delivering a fervent speech, which the English failed to understand. At this point the *weroance* of the Rappahannocks arrived at Paspahegh by canoe, insisting angrily that the English quit the Paspaheghs and travel to his own village. When the colonists acquiesced the following day and met the Rappahannock *weroance*, he appeared before the English wearing a red crown, a large copper plate, pearls, and birds' claws festooned with copper. His body was painted crimson and his face blue. After departing from the Rappahannocks' village, the colonists encountered a hostile force of Appomattucks. Upon attacking the colonists, an Appomattuck, again one of whom the English perceived as the "chiefest," stood with a bow in one hand and a tobacco pipe in the other. The colonists conveyed signs of peace, choosing the pipe for the time being.

Having explored the James as far as the mouth of the Appomattox River, the colonists then sailed back down to an island in the Paspahegh territory that seemed ideal for settlement. On May 14, 1607, they started constructing James Fort and what would become the English toehold in North America at Jamestown. Captain Newport then led a group of colonists to explore beyond the Appomattox River, traveling as far as the fall line. After meeting Powhatah, the son of the Mamanatowick and *weroance* of Powhatan village located near the falls, the colonists traveled back down river and returned to their fort under construction. While absent, a large force of Indians had attacked the fort but were repulsed by the colonists.

During the first six weeks of the Jamestown colony, we see Native political tactics and symbolic systems operating in the face of European intervention in the Chesapeake. *Weroances* greeted the English at each village and competed for the colonists' attention, conveying their status with copper objects and body adornment. Copper represented a symbolic embodiment of sacred and political authority in the Chesapeake and was the material that Indians sought most (e.g., Potter 1989; Hantman 1990). Copper's symbolic importance was widespread among North American Indians (Miller and Hamell 1986), a symbolism with deep roots in the precontact world (Trigger 1991). For the Powhatans, much of the power conveyed by copper and those who wore it derived from its origins outside or beyond the Powhatan world. As Gleach (1997:56–57) has noted, the Powhatans identified the world outside their villages as a place of dangerous and powerful forces. Priests' temples, Powhatan's treasure house, and the *huskanaw* rituals were all contexts of sacred and political potency too dangerous to be located within the village proper. Initially, at least, the Powhatans appear to have comprehended the Tassantasses in similar terms—as dangerous forces from outside, or perhaps under, the known world (Gallivan and Hantman 1996).

The periodic raiding and sniping on the colonists at James Fort came to a halt on June 15, 1607, apparently at Powhatan's command. The following months entailed a period of starvation at Jamestown during which half of the colonists died. Once the fall harvest arrived in the Powhatans' villages, the colonists sent John Smith to trade with the Indians for corn. On one of his expeditions Smith encountered a hunting party of Powhatans from several villages, at which time he was taken captive by Powhatan's younger brother, Opechancanough. Opechancanough brought Smith to a camp in the woods beyond any village, where priests were summoned to divine the intentions of Smith and his compatriots. Smith was placed before a great fire when seven priests painted black, red, and white entered the structure (Smith 1986d:149). A ceremony ensued as the priests sang a series of songs while placing a ring of cornmeal around the fire. The priests then surrounded the meal with grains of corn and divided the corn with sticks. Smith reported that the circle of meal "signified their country," the circle of corn connoted the bounds of the sea, while the sticks represented Smith's country (Smith 1986d:150).

Though Smith likely failed to comprehend much of the meaning conveyed through the ritual, his account does demonstrate the influence of priests in Powhatan society and their association with red and black symbolism. As *quioccosuks*, the priests had been initiated into a divine status through the *huskanaw* ceremony that produced "black boys" (Smith 1986d:124). Upon completing the rite of passage the *quioccosuks* played a prominent role shaping Powhatan affairs. The *huskanaw* endowed *quioccosuks* with "a state of equality and perfect freedom, to order their actions, and dispose of their persons, as they think fit" (Beverley 1947:209). If indeed we accept Smith's explanation of the ceremony as divining his intentions and those of the Tassantasses, the priests appear to have used the ritual to determine whether a potentially dangerous group of outsiders could be incorporated into the Powhatan world.

In the following days Opechancanough took the captive Smith on a tour of the central part of the Powhatan paramountcy, ending at Werowocomoco, where Smith confronted the Mamanatowick Powhatan for the first time. Powhatan received Smith lavishly as an important *weroance* and urged that he and the colonists abandon their fort near Paspahegh and settle in a village closer to Werowocomoco under Powhatan's protection. Powhatan promised corn and venison if the English would reciprocate with copper and iron tools. Smith feigned acceptance of the arrangement, never really intending to abide by it. Two days later Smith was taken to a temple in the woods outside Werowocomoco whereupon Powhatan, appearing "more like a devil then a man," and a large group of others similarly painted black made the "dolefullest noyse" within the temple's inner room (Smith 1986d:151). After this ceremony Powhatan instructed Smith that he should go to Jamestown and procure two great guns and a grindstone in return for Powhatan's protection and some territory nearby. Subsequently Powhatan sent his daughter Pocahontas with provisions to feed the colony.

Powhatan's actions during these events indicate how he successfully incorporated the English into his expanding paramountcy. The steps through which the Indians sought to integrate Smith, and by extension the Tassantasses, within the Powhatan world expose elements of the political and sacred realm within which the Powhatans made decisions and wielded authority. Originally, priests defined the proper course of action with regard to Smith and his compatriots through a divination ritual. Later, a second group of men—likely also *quioccosuks*—gathered for further ceremony with Smith in attendance. With the corporate will of the *quioccosuks* expressed, Powhatan offered to protect the colonists as his subjects. In demanding guns and a grinding stone, he sought objects with both practical and symbolic significance that originated from outside the Powhatan world. The corresponding accoutrements within the Powhatan world—wooden or stone mortars for processing corn and the bows, arrows, and clubs used in warfare—served as important tools of power as Powhatan expanded his domain through military exploits and gift exchange, including the food supplied by his daughter to the struggling English colonists.

During these events Powhatan effectively built an individual-centered authority upon the foundation of corporate will expressed by the priests and other *quioccosuks*. Powhatan pursued strategies designed to enhance his own centrality within networks that encompassed the English by building alliances and demanding symbolically resonant objects. In effect, the English briefly became Powhatan's subjects during the winter of 1608 as the Mamanatowick played the *werowance*'s role of a culture broker capable of assimilating the unrefined strangers into the Powhatan world (Gallivan and Hantman 1996; Gleach 1997:114). Powhatan had pursued similar strategies to build networks of power during the Protohistoric era prior to the settlement of the Jamestown colony, precluding the notion that the Tassantasses's arrival somehow produced the Mamanatowick and his paramountcy. Nonetheless, through his role in the Protohistoric and Contact period events that comprise his reign, Powhatan revealed himself as a canny manipulator of both the corporate symbols that were central to Powhatan culture and the exclusionary power that came to dominate the early colonial encounter. The intermittent violence and profound otherness that attended European visits during the Protohistoric and Contact periods likely contributed to the consolidation of chiefly authority in the Chesapeake, perhaps by encouraging some Virginia Algonquins to invest in the Mamanatowick and their *weroances* an unprecedented measure of authority.

During the summer of 1608 Smith led two expeditions northward to the upper reaches of the Chesapeake, events referenced previously. The resulting encounters involving various groups of coastal Algonquins and Piedmont Indians included an intriguing mix of hostilities, feasting, and exchange. In most of these encounters, *weroances* stepped in as intermediaries, first placing themselves between the Tassantasses and the villagers during perfunctory hostilities and then seeking to build ties through exchanges with the colonists.

In the fall of 1608 Christopher Newport sought to mollify Powhatan by crowning him as a vassal of King James and giving him gifts befitting English notions of royalty. Powhatan clearly saw through these motives and successfully framed the coronation in his own terms by forcing Newport to travel to Werowocomoco and to stage the event according to his schedule. Following the coronation, Newport led an expedition of 120 men up the James, across the falls, and into the Monacans' Piedmont country. Though Smith's accounts of this expedition (1986c:238, 1986d:184) are brief, they offer some of the few descriptions of the Monacans' reactions to the colonists' presence in the Chesapeake. The Monacans living in two villages, Massinacak and Mowhemcho, received their English visitors neither "well nor ill," though Newport did not hesitate to risk angering the villagers by seizing one of their "petty kings" to guide him while exploring the Piedmont.

Engagements between the English and Native communities each took their own turn, though many entailed a similar structure of events involving a brief skirmish followed by feasting and talk of "friendship" and concluding with the exchange of gifts. During these events the Powhatans probed the Tassantasses, while *weroances* forged social ties with a people from under the world, much as the Mamanatowick had done during the previous months. Smith (1986b:174) informs us that the Algonquin term *"weroance"* refers to "inferior kings," and *"weroansquas"* represented queens. Strachey's (1999:57) Powhatan word list similarly defines a *weroance* as a king or great lord. In parsing the Powhatan use of the term, though, Smith recognized that the title had a somewhat more complex connotation: "But this word *weroance* which we call and [construe] for a king is a common word whereby they call all commanders: for they have but few words in their language, and but few occasions to use but any officers more than one commander" (1986b:174). Other sources indicate that *weroance* is an Anglicization of *wirowantesu*, a term meaning "he is wealthy" (Gerard 1907), which highlights the importance of *weroances'* wealth accumulation. *Weroances* were "tyed to rule by customes" (Smith 1986b:174), raising the likelihood that their authority ultimately derived from collective will and a place among the *quioccosuks*. Powhatan *weroances'* structural importance rested in their mediation between the village and the world beyond—a world that included priests tending temples in the forested areas beyond villages (Williamson 1979) and Tassantasses traveling the Chesapeake and seeking corn. As with the *quioccosuks* who faced Smith in a ritual context, the *weroances'* copper and red or black body adornment may have signified a powerful "liminal," or structurally intermediate, status tied to their connections to this outside world (Gallivan and Hantman 1996; cf. Turner 1969).

While on one level Newport's efforts to force Powhatan to kneel and to receive his crown during the "coronation" entail a rather absurd incident in the colonial encounter (e.g., Smith 1986d:184), the event also signaled the transformation of Powhatan's role as a powerful *weroance* among the Virginia Algonquins into something far more comprehensive. After forcing Newport's compliance regarding the timing and location of this event and upon receiving exotic symbols of authority, purportedly from King James, Powhatan had in many ways reached the pinnacle of his status as Mamanatowick. He had established networks of authority and accoutrements of power that extended far beyond the known Powhatan world and into the world of the Tassantasses.

The picture of Powhatan that emerges from ethnohistory is of a transitional figure who recognized new social possibilities presented by the events of the colonial encounter. During the colonial conjuncture into which he and the English colonists stepped, the Mamanatowick constructed networks of authority even while relying on the collective will of the *quioccosuks*. In the process, Powhatan proposed a sweeping form of corporate solidarity through which the Tassantasses "and his people shall be all one, brothers, and friends" (Strachey 1953:58). In this way Powhatan sought to absorb the English through the metaphor of kinship and to make the starving colonists indebted to him through the feasting of their *weroance* Smith and through gifts of food to those still alive at Jamestown. Throughout these events Powhatan filled the traditional role of a *weroance* as a mediator capable of socializing dangerous outside forces. At the same time, he transformed the political field through strategies that became particularly effective amid the early colonial encounter. During the colonial encounter Virginia Algonquins revalued important elements of their political system amid the events of contact. This revaluation affected the actions of *weroances* and the Mamanatowick, even as these individuals complied with practices and meanings inherited from the precontact world.

Equally powerful figures likely appeared during the precontact centuries of the Late Woodland period. Potentially hostile outsiders, including the Massawomecks and Susquehannocks, intruded into coastal Virginia during this period, presenting intergroup contacts not unlike those of the colonial encounter. It is probably no accident that Powhatan began to play an important role in Chesapeake political dynamics from Powhatan village at the falls of the James, a location that served as the gateway to and from the Monacans' Piedmont country. Yet as the archaeological patterns considered below demonstrate, historical circumstances that allowed figures such as Powhatan to intrude upon practices at the household, community, and regional scales do not appear to have been in place until the Protohistoric sixteenth century.

In contrast with Powhatan and the *weroances* of the Algonquin world, the Monacans of the James River interior elected not to engage the colonists in trade, alliance, or strategies of manipulation during the early years of contact and throughout much of the colonial encounter, a historical pattern first identified by Hantman (1990). Despite the Monacans' long-term interaction with the coastal Algonquins and cultural similarities reflected in the archaeological records of the Piedmont and Coastal Plain, the colonial encounter elicited a profoundly different response from interior groups. Judging from their ambiguous reaction to the arrival of the colonists, the Monacans' disengagement from colonial contact appears to have been rooted in cultural strategies and a historical tradition that differed from the coastal region. The Monacans' cultural emphasis on corporate symbols continued into the early colonial era, in contrast with the transformations that marked other portions of the Chesapeake region.

Leveraging Funds of Power in the Colonial Encounter

While the early colonial context represents a unique moment in Chesapeake culture history, the strategies of *weroances* and the Mamanatowick witnessed by the English during the historical encounter drew in large part from social practices of the preceding Late Woodland period that are identified in this study. In comparing ethnohistorical and archaeological evidence from the Protohistoric and Contact periods, it becomes apparent that the developments of the Late Woodland II phase produced funds of power that were leveraged in novel ways in the colonial era Chesapeake. These efforts may be evaluated by turning from a narrative perspective to a multiscalar frame of reference and by linking archaeological patterns from the early colonial era to ethnohistorical references.

Intervention in the Domestic Economy

Archaeological patterns indicate that practices adopted during the Late Woodland II phase by villagers in the James River Valley changed with the Protohistoric sixteenth century. Two such developments prominent at the domestic scale involve the end of both storage pit use and household expansion. These patterns may in fact have responded to chiefly intervention in the domestic economy after A.D. 1500. Late Woodland II storage patterns indicate that households produced increasing surpluses and sheltered at least part of these in storage pits located inside domestic structures. In a parallel development, domestic groups continued to increase in size during these centuries, as reflected in expanding house floor dimensions. During the Protohistoric and Contact periods, though, most villages in the James River Valley lacked storage features altogether, implying the adoption of aboveground storage. Average house size began to decline after A.D. 1500, even as the range of house sizes within a village showed a growing gap between the largest houses and the rest of the domestic structures. Judging from the dimensions of domestic architecture, most household groups ceased to increase in size during the colonial era, even while a few of the largest domestic groups continued to expand.

Ethnohistorical references from the coastal region complement this evidence by demonstrating how *weroances* and the Mamanatowick leveraged funds of power originating in the domestic sphere. In describing Powhatan households, Strachey tells us that "the reason why each chief patron of a familie especially *weroances*, are desirous and (indeed) strive for manie wives is because they would have manie children who maie, if chaunce be fight for them, when they are old, as also then feed and mayntein them" (1953:114). Similar motives for augmenting the domestic workforce likely played a role in the expansion of household size recorded in the region's Late Woodland archaeology, a period when horticultural production grew in importance. The archaeological record of house sizes during the subsequent colonial era suggests that *weroances* may have accomplished this objective at the expense of "commoner" households, such that the average size of domestic structures actually declined.

The colonial histories also record tribute payments that Powhatan extracted from *weroances* and that *weroances* drew from domestic groups, tribute that included domestic staples—corn, meat, and deer skins—along with prestige items such as copper and pearls (Strachey 1953:63). Central storage of these items occurred in aboveground storehouses constructed by the Mamanatowick and, on a smaller scale, by *weroances*. In fact, *weroances'* considerable tribute demands may have induced some domestic groups to conceal corn and other valuables in storage pits in order to avoid tribute payment. Strachey noted of the Powhatans that "their corn and (indeed) their copper, hatchetts, howes, beades, perle and most things with them of value according to their own estymation, they hide one from the knowledge of another in the grownd within the woods, and so keepe them all yeare, or untill they have fit use for them . . . and when they take them forth they scarse make their women privie to the storehowse" (1953:115). Where storage pits located within domestic architecture offered adequate protection for surpluses of the Late Woodland II phase, Powhatans elected to hide corn and other valuables away from the village during the early colonial era. Similar tactics aimed at avoiding the loss of surpluses appeared amid the colonists' efforts to extract corn from Powhatan village at the James River falls, "[t]rade they would not, and finde their corn we could not; for they had hid it in the woods" (Smith 1986d:185).

Viewed in tandem, the archaeological and ethnohistorical evidence indicates that colonial era *weroances* successfully intervened in the domestic economy in order to extract surpluses. Through gift giving, feast sponsorship, and other forms of patronage, surpluses that remained within the domestic realm during the Late Woodland II phase became funds of power wielded in the political arena after A.D. 1500. Ethnohistorical references hinting that some Powhatan households and communities took steps to counter this process through concealment indicate that, even in the Coastal Plain, *weroances* had not established hegemony over the domestic economy. Nonetheless, the Powhatans altered their use of storage pits rather dramatically during the colonial era, concealing them in the woods rather than placing them within their houses in response to elites' intervention in the domestic sphere.

The Village as Social Stage

Changes in the use of community space also reflect important developments of the Protohistoric and Contact periods founded on the practices of the preceding Late Woodland II phase. These may be considered through the archaeology of palisade construction, mortuary practices, and settlement permanence, along with ethnohistorical references to these issues. Palisaded settlements first appeared in the Chesapeake region after A.D. 1200, and their numbers grew substantially in the James River Valley during the sixteenth century. Most of the Late Woodland II sites evaluated in this study were not palisaded, though palisades did surround settlements at Bessemer (44BO26) and Great Neck (44VB7) from this phase. By contrast, residents erected palisades at three of the four James River Valley settlements dating to the fifteenth century that archaeologists have studied intensively (Wright [44GO30]), Perkins Point [44BA3], and Beaver Pond [44BA39]). Palisaded settlements appear to have proliferated during the Protohistoric period.

Mortuary patterns from the Coastal Plain reflect expressions of social heterogeneity that similarly began in some settlements during the Late Woodland II and intensified thereafter. The Great Neck site's Late Woodland II component provides rare evidence for the emergence of marked social differentiation in the late prehistoric James River Valley (Hodges 1993:264). Individual and ossuary burials occurred at the site, with copper items found in association with two primary interments. The appearance of varying burial forms during the Late Woodland II phase provides unusual evidence for the expression of social distinctions during the precontact era in the region. The most thoroughly excavated Contact period site from the Coastal Plain, Paspahegh (44JC308), offers indications that Powhatan mortuary practices expanded upon social distinctions rarely expressed in precontact mortuary practices (Lucketti et al. 1994). Differentiation occurred in the contrast between primary interments and secondary ossuary burials, between cemetery burials and isolated interments, and in the inclusion of copper grave goods with 3 of the 21 excavated burial features. Analysis of the copper artifacts has indicated a European source for the material—an expected pattern given the proximity of the settlement to Jamestown and ethnohistorical indications of extensive exchange relations between the two communities. The excavators see evidence of three levels of social status in the relationship between rank-denoting artifacts, grave orientation, age of deceased, and the spatial organization of burial features. Whatever the symbolic connotations of mortuary patterning at Paspahegh, the variable burial forms support the notion that such practices expressed social distinctions that assumed a greater prominence during the colonial era.

Archaeological evidence of the village as a social context also records rather unexpected patterns indicating that Coastal Plain settlements after A.D. 1500 saw declining levels of sedentariness. In fact, the culture history of Native societies in the James River Valley does not match a simple evolutionary trajectory toward increasing sedentariness. Rather, coastal sites document briefer occupation spans than those of preceding centuries, while contemporary settlements in the interior continued to manifest relatively permanent settlements. Coastal communities that faced the most intensive European contact and encompassment by the Powhatan paramountcy appear to be the least stable in the river valley. This pattern raises the possibility that the appearance of European interlopers and aggrandizing *weroances* led some Powhatans to break their commitments to village communities more readily than they had during preceding centuries. Judging from these settlement patterns, fundamental elements of the Powhatan cultural context presented by the ethnohistory of the early colonial era diverged from social practices of the precontact era.

Documentary references to the ways that riverine villages became the primary stages for enacting political strategies aimed at drawing on funds of power include allusions to feasting and elite mortuary ritual. As noted above, the arrival of English visitors in a Powhatan village often resulted in a communal feast orchestrated by the local *weroance*. Almost from the moment the Tassantasses first sat down with the Kecoughtans in the opening days of the colony, the "chiefest" offered "friendship," tobacco, and enormous quantities of food. Particularly large roasting pit features representing the by-product of such events occur in the archaeological record beginning with the Late Woodland II phase, suggesting that such feasts rose in prominence with the establishment of village communities. During the colonial era English colonists reported that *weroances* and the "better sort" from Powhatan society sponsored these feasts, though it is clear that Kecoughtans lacking an elite status ultimately supplied the food for these meals. Colonist George Percy (1998:91) wrote that Kecoughtan elites feted the English after "the meanest sort brought us such dainties as they had, and of their bread which they make of their maize."

Smith (1986b:169) described how the Powhatans buried their *weroances* in a lengthy process that involved several stages and a familiar set of grave goods. Upon death, *weroances*' bodies were first dried in aboveground sepulchers. Priests then adorned the desiccated bodies with copper and pearls and wrapped them in skins and mats. Finally, the bodies were placed in temples maintained by priests. Such practices appear to be aimed at distinguishing *weroances*' status in death and perhaps also at reproducing a social structure among the living that sustained *weroances*' elite social position. The Powhatans buried their *weroances* collectively and did so in aboveground temples located outside of villages and designed for that purpose. Though evidence of these practices is not accessible archaeologically, they do appear to parallel elements of the multistage, communal burial rituals embraced by Late Woodland II villagers throughout the river basin. In burying their elites collectively in remote temples, the Powhatans modified the communal burial practices begun during the preceding era and invested these practices with new symbols of social hierarchy. Residents of a Late Woodland II village at the Great Neck site introduced similar expressions of social distinction among the dead at the end of the precontact era. Within the Contact period Paspahegh village, a diversity of practices continued to transform Native burials, including the interment of copper obtained from the English colonists in ossuaries.

Taken as a whole, evidence from the communal sphere reflects the advent of palisade construction, communal feasting, and elite mortuary ritual in the Late Woodland II archaeological record, though each took on a greater prominence during the colonial era. Palisades distinguished a space dominated by chiefly elites and possibly served as defensive features amid peer polity interaction that included hostilities. Mortuary practices that conveyed heightened social differentiation indicate that symbolically potent prestige goods with a sparse distribution in the precontact era assumed a substantial role with the early colonial era. The communal feasts that drew upon the surpluses of a horticultural economy became a critical part in the events of contact involving *weroances* and the Tassantasses. In short, through their association with palisade construction, elite mortuary ritual, and communal feasting, select villages of the early colonial era became physical landscapes that embodied expressions of sacred and political authority.

Building Social Identities on a Regional Scale

Jamestown colonists conceived of regional interaction in the Chesapeake world in terms of large-scale social identities. English colonists, "savages," Powhatans, Monacans, Massawomecks, and Susquehannocks—each appears in early seventeenth-century documents as a social category that encompassed multiple communities spread across a large geographic area. Ethnohistorical accounts demonstrate that these categories proved to be meaningful within Native societies as well. The Powhatans frequently spoke in geopolitical terms of these groups in the course of negotiating the changing political dynamics of the early colonial era. As noted in chapter 2, a Mannahoac named Amoroleck referred to the Powhatans, the Monacans, and the Massawomecks as the "worlds" that he knew.

A close reading of the colonial ethnohistory reveals that the perceptions and actions of individual Powhatans and Monacans actually involved an intricate blend of factionalism and solidarity, while social identity depended largely upon context. Whether Amoroleck chose to consider himself a part of a Monacan polity, a member of the Mannahoac branch of this "confederation," a resident of the village Hassinanga, a member of his matrilineage, or the head of a household depended, of course, upon the particular frame of reference. Based on his account of the Chesapeake social landscape (Smith 1986d:175–176), Amoroleck was well aware of the situational nature of his own identity. Compounding the fluidity of the colonial context, Algonquin *weroances* from the coastal region competed with one another to obtain English prestige goods from the opening days of the Jamestown colony. Algonquin communities at the geographic margins of Powhatan's influence often acted independently of the Mamanatowick's will, while the nearby Chickahominies remained autonomous in the early days of the Jamestown colony. During this period Indians residing within Powhatan's "empire" failed to follow the Mamanatowick's promises of "love," prompting Jamestown colonists to complain when his "subjects" continued to snipe at James Fort (Strachey 1953:58).

Amid this factional social context, the Mamanatowick strove to cultivate a Powhatan identity that absorbed diverse groups residing in coastal Virginia, efforts that eventually included the Tassantasses, whom he hoped would become "friends and forever Powhatans" (Smith 1986d:195). Taking into account such rhetoric, along with his efforts to influence or control Algonquin communities throughout the coastal region, it appears that the Mamanatowick sought to construct a cultural and political identity under the Powhatan label. Whether or not such efforts should be considered as part of the creation of an "ethnic" identity (Rountree 1993:7), they did reflect an important dynamic underlying events of the colonial encounter.

Precontact archaeological patterns considered in this study suggest that such efforts drew upon cultural transformations rooted in the Late Woodland II phase when regional social relations allowed a Powhatan identity to be placed in opposition to a Monacan one. After A.D. 1200 stylistic and exchange patterns imply the emergence of social networks in the James River Valley that were more sharply bounded and tightly integrated than those of preceding eras. In the James River interior, Late Woodland II phase settlements in the Piedmont and the Ridge and Valley established social ties through shared mortuary practices (i.e., the construction of accretional mounds), similar ceramic style (i.e., the use of cord marking), and social relations enacted through the exchange of chert artifacts. Together these developments may record the original archaeological footprint of an "ancestral Monacan society" (Hantman 1998) and the emergence of a cohesive social identity in the interior. Ceramic stylistic patterns in the coastal region similarly reflected the Late Woodland appearance of spatial boundaries tied to the Native social identities of the colonial encounter. The archaeological evidence compiled for this study suggests that, within the James River interior, an ancestral Monacan society became culturally cohesive with the post–A.D. 1200 establishment of village communities. Even as the social identities that marked the Native social landscape in the Chesapeake proved to be fluid and situational, the Monacan threat to the Algonquins of Virginia's Coastal Plain remarked upon so frequently in the colonial ethnohistory has its origins in social networks and shared cultural symbols of the Late Woodland II phase.

During the subsequent Protohistoric era, Powhatan's efforts to expand his authority included positioning himself at the center of an emerging Powhatan social identity. Wahunsunacock altered his principal residence several times over his lifetime, including relocation during the Protohistoric era from Powhatan village on the James to Werowocomoco, situated to the east on the York River. Finally he moved to Orapaks near the head of the Chickahominy, once he recognized the need to distance himself from the

English presence at Jamestown. Powhatan's residential history undoubtedly played a role in the emergence, coalescence, and decline of the chiefdom centered around him and therefore has important implications for regional-scale social dynamics in the early colonial Chesapeake.

Quantitative analysis of John Smith's *Map of Virginia* (Gallivan 1997b) offers a means of characterizing the spatial dimensions of Powhatan's strategies while moving his principal residence, strategies tied to regional-scale social relations. Ethnohistorical accounts imply that Powhatan began his efforts to consolidate a polity around himself from Powhatan village where he was born. Powhatan's move from Powhatan village to Werowocomoco may have been motivated by a shift in his strategic priorities from manipulation of exchange relations and other interaction with the Monacans (Turner 1993; Potter 1993) to military dominance, tribute collection, and ultimately the creation of a regional Powhatan identity from a central location among the coastal Algonquins of the Chesapeake.

One way of evaluating this possibility involves determining the coastal Chesapeake's geographic "center of gravity" (Steponaitis 1978) using data regarding the location of "Kings' Howses," the politically prominent villages depicted on Smith's *Map of Virginia*. Measured as such, the political center of gravity in the Coastal Plain inhabited by Algonquin speakers was located just north of the confluence of the Mattaponi and Pamunkey rivers in the Pamunkey district. In fact, the Pamunkey district represented an area of high population density at the core of the Powhatan chiefdom during the early seventeenth century. Smith's map depicts four "Kings' Howses" near the confluence of the Pamunkey and the Mattaponi, confirming the political importance of the area. Located down river of this political center of gravity, Powhatan's Werowocomoco residence established his presence immediately downstream of this central area. Powhatan's move there suggests that he sought to place himself in a highly central location in relation to the politically prominent villages of the coastal Chesapeake. From Werowocomoco, Powhatan was well placed to expand his influence over coastal Algonquins through intimidation, warfare, and tribute collection. Later, Powhatan moved to Orapaks in order to distance himself from the English at Jamestown, a motivation that accords with its peripheral location vis-à-vis the region's political center of gravity. As the colonial encounter drew to a close, Powhatan relinquished his central place in Chesapeake political dynamics for a more guarded role on the margins of the expanding English presence.

Native Culture History in the Chesapeake: Summary and Implications

As an effort to construct a historical anthropology of Native societies in the Chesapeake, this study focused on cultural changes marking the sixteen centuries leading up to colonial encounter. I have framed the social dynamics of James River groups through a multiscalar perspective and relied on quantitative methods and ethnohistorical accounts to interpret these cultural patterns. Though researchers have considered the ethnohistory of the colonial encounter in the Chesapeake numerous times and according to various perspectives (e.g., Feest 1978; Fausz 1985; Binford 1964; Turner 1976; Rountree 1989, 1990; Hantman 1990, 1993; Potter 1993; Gleach 1997), none has been able to evaluate the early accounts against a body of archaeological data as comprehensive as the one available for this study. This archaeological evidence may be understood best through a regional, comparative perspective that makes use of archaeology's greatest strength: access to long-term patterns of social change otherwise invisible to any single observer.

With this perspective, the culture history of the Chesapeake region unfolds as more intricate and intriguing than once imagined. By embracing social transformations associated with the Late Woodland emergence of village communities, Native societies in the James River Valley introduced a new cultural landscape between A.D. 1200 and 1500. As exemplified by the Powhatan paramountcy, these Late Woodland changes contributed to the development of multicommunity polities centered on powerful figures who dominated political decision making, sacred affairs, and economic wealth. In short, the social transformations of the Late Woodland II phase fostered the emergence of a complex chiefdom in the coastal region and a complex Monacan polity in the interior. However, the culture history also reveals two elements that complicate this narrative. First, the process of complex polity formation in the James River Valley combined internal social dynamics with historically contingent events tied to the colonial encounter. Second, the colonial context often viewed as a point of departure for understanding Chesapeake prehistory, and North American chiefdoms more generally, represents a social context that differed in rather significant ways from the pre-contact world. Both of these factors have important implications for Chesapeake culture history and perhaps for anthropological archaeology as well.

The sequence through which precontact social changes in the domestic, communal, and regional spheres fused with transformative historical events to shape the Chesapeake's complex political dynamics offers a model of chiefdom formation that may prove useful in other contexts. Whether or not such transformative events involved the arrival of strangers from Europe, complex polity formation may entail similar cultural changes tied to domestic production, communal integration, and ideologies of regional identity. Developments evident in the James River's precontact archaeology made funds of power available that Powhatan and other charismatic figures leveraged during the early colonial era, subverting a cultural emphasis on corporate symbols in the process. Events that introduced symbolically potent material culture and hostile outsiders comparable to those of the colonial era Chesapeake likely affected similar cultural transformations in other regions. Prior to the arrival of Jamestown colonists in Virginia, Powhatan represented a transitional figure through his efforts to place himself in the center of social networks in the Coastal Plain. As Powhatan commenced these strategies at a time when Europeans only began to encroach upon the Chesapeake, his original rise to power is largely independent of the colonial encounter. The early colonial era sustained his efforts, though, by providing a context allowing him to fulfill his role as an Algonquin *weroance* in the face of the Tassantasses' intrusion. Identifying comparable agents of change represents an important challenge for archaeological analysis of political dynamics.

Despite the corporate orientation and culturally sanctioned limits to the political centralization implied by the James River's late precontact archaeology, the colonial context that began in the sixteenth century produced the conditions in which political leaders, including coastal *weroances* and the Mamanatowick, adopted strategies designed to build networks of power. In the Coastal Plain, the Powhatan paramountcy and competing polities emerged from *weroances'* exclusionary strategies of prestige-good monopolization combined with military exploits and the mobilization of surplus staple production. Ideological and economic attributes of these political dynamics highlight the significance of events that unfolded during the Late Woodland II phase and during the early colonial era. The chiefdoms of the coastal region were responsive to expanding European intervention in the region and an increasingly cohesive Monacan presence in the interior. Though the nature of the Monacans' political system remains unclear, its far-reaching influence on events of the colonial encounter is no longer in doubt.

Native cultural practices of the colonial encounter differed from the precontact era, as reflected in the archaeology of the domestic, communal, and regional spheres. Efforts to link a region's archaeology to its ethnohistory represent a serious challenge in any cultural context, due partly to archaeology's ambiguities but also due to cultural practices that are responsive to historical events. Chesapeake ethnohistory and archaeology reveal both persistence and transformation across the precontact/colonial divide. These continuities and differences lie at the heart of Native societies' impact on the events of colonial encounter.

Postscript

Over half their number dead, the colonists decided to abandon Jamestown on June 7, 1610. During the time leading up to this decision, relations with the Indians soured badly. Smith, an English culture broker who met with some success in his efforts to obtain provisions, had departed for England the previous year after sustaining serious burns in a powder explosion. The colonists gradually exhausted their supply of metal tools and other goods critical for establishing exchange relations with the Indians. In the end, the colonists resorted to eating rats and cannibalizing the bodies of the dead for food. Floating down the James at the peak of their desperation, the departing colonists encountered an advance ship from a relief expedition led by Lord Delaware. The colonists reversed course for Jamestown, where Lord Delaware took command.

The tide had turned for the colony and for the Powhatans (Rountree 1990:54). With the subsequent introduction of Orinoco tobacco to Virginia, the English found a product that grew readily in Virginia and could be exported for a considerable profit. To accommodate tobacco production, the colonists expanded settlement outward from Jamestown up the James, claiming the same riverine settings that represented the geographic center of the Powhatan world. After Powhatan died in 1618, his charismatic younger brother, Opechancanough, assumed a leadership role among the Powhatans. Under Opechancanough's command, the Powhatans responded to English expansion with two violent strikes—large-scale, coordinated attacks mounted in 1622 and in 1644 (Fausz 1977). Though the attacks succeeded in slaying several hundred colonists, they failed to dislodged the Tassantasses or to alter their efforts to expand settlement and to constrain the Indians' movements across the riverine landscape.

The descendants of the Powhatans and Monacans remain a vital force in Virginia after weathering four centuries of encompassment within an English colony and the American republic. As told eloquently elsewhere (e.g., Rountree 1990), this history involves economic struggles, resistance to paternalistic attitudes, and defiance of racist policies. During the twentieth century Virginia's Indians turned to the tasks of reconstructing an Indian identity denied under the 1924 Racial Integrity Act and to reestablishing their political influence in Virginia (Moretti-Langholtz 1998). In the coastal region, the Pamunkeys and the Mattaponis continue to reside on reservation lands, and five additional tribes are recognized by the state—the Chickahominies, Nansemonds, Rappahannocks, Eastern Chickahominies, and Upper Mattaponis. The Monacans remain in the Virginia Piedmont, concentrated near Bear Mountain in Amherst County where social, economic, and political changes in recent years have allowed them to break away from the bonds of colonialism and dependency (Cook 2000). Recently, Virginia's Indians have formed a new coalition of Native societies seeking tribal recognition from the federal government. Though the outcome of this effort at this time is unknown, it is clear that Native societies will continue to insist on a meaningful role in shaping Virginia's political landscape.

A Descriptive Account
of Sites in the Sample

The following description of archaeological sites in the Chesapeake region provides a foundation for a culture-historical analysis of residential settlements in the James River Valley. The description begins with sites located in the Piedmont before turning to the Coastal Plain and Ridge and Valley provinces. The Piedmont context, including information from a stratified site and a floodplain survey, is presented in greater detail since excavation and analysis in this region comprise basic contributions of this study. I briefly describe the Coastal Plain and Ridge and Valley sites to account for my interpretive assumptions, most importantly in the construction of the settlement chronology. For these sites I drew from previous publications and from studying material archived at the Virginia Department of Historic Resources. Tables A-1 through A-3 list the results of radiocarbon assays and calendrical calibration for features included in this study. Gallivan (1999) contains tables that detail the pit feature and house pattern data used in the study.

Stratified Deposits at the Spessard Site (44fv134)

Few radiocarbon-dated contexts excavated in the James River Piedmont date prior to the seventh century A.D. near the end of the Middle Woodland period. Changes in Piedmont material culture throughout the Woodland period may, however, be evaluated in the context of stratified deposits at the Spessard site (44fv134). Situated near the center of the James River drainage, Spessard contained a combination of stratified deposits and pit features with preserved paleobotanical and faunal remains (figure A-1). Flooding of Piedmont portions of the James in 1985 scoured the Spessard site in several areas, exposing artifacts across a 6,000-square-meter area of the floodplain. Excavation revealed that Spessard included cultural levels representing Late Archaic through Late Woodland occupations along with features dating to the Middle and Late Woodland periods. The south wall profile in figure A-2 is representative of Spessard's stratigraphy. Cultural deposits occurred in levels 1 through 7 of this unit.

A-1. Selected radiocarbon dates, Piedmont

| Phase/Sites | Context | Uncalibrated Age (years B.P.) | Calibrated Dates (years A.D.) | | | | |
| | | | Lower Limits | | Calibration | Upper Limits | |
			2σ	1σ	Curve Intercept(s)	1σ	2σ
Middle Woodland II (A.D. 200–900)							
Spessard (44Fv134)							
	Fea 87-3	1380±50	603	640	660	677	768
	Fea 86-1	1350±80	561	640	668	561	881
Wood (44NE143)							
	Fea 1B	1120±60	782	883	898, 906, 961	998	1023
Late Woodland (A.D. 900–1200)							
Wingina (44NE4)							
	Fea 9	1030±80	880	967	1014	1042	1150
Point of Fork (44Fv19)		920±75	989	1024	1064, 1075, 1127, 1133, 1159	1220	1279
Wood (44NE143)							
	Fea 27	990±100	880	978	1025	1168	1269
	Post 94	910±80	989	1025	1162	1226	1283
	Fea 1A	850±80	1019	1052	1218	1278	1295
Partridge Cr. (44AH193)							
	Fea 10	980±50	983	1013	1028	1156	1180
	Midden	950±70	978	1016	1041, 1150	1177	1250
	Fea 24	930±75	983	1021	1052, 1085, 1121, 1139, 1156	1216	1277
	Fea 12	890±80	1004	1032	1168	1247	1287
	Fea 22	870±50	1126	1063	1195	1134	1279

Continued

| Phase/Sites | Context | Uncalibrated Age (years B.P.) | Calibrated Dates (years A.D.) | | | | |
			Lower Limits 2σ	Lower Limits 1σ	Calibration Curve Intercept(s)	Upper Limits 1σ	Upper Limits 2σ
Spessard	Fea 87-4	955±55	992	1019	1039	1165	1221
(44FV134)	Fea 87-1	930±80	978	1019	1052, 1085, 1121, 1139, 1156	1218	1279
	Fea 86-3(#1)	900±80	996	1028	1165	1229	1285
	Fea 86-3(#2)	790±80	1041	1192	1263	1290	1386
	Fea 86-3(avg.)	845±57	1036	1164	1220	1272	1287
Late Woodland II (A.D. 1200–1500)							
Partridge Cr.	Fea 40	830±70	1031	1165	1225	1280	1296
(44AH193)	Fea 37	790±70	1051	1213	1263	1288	1373
	Fea 39	680±50	1268	1285	1298	1386	1401
Little River (44Go30B)	Fea 1	750±60	1189	1239	1282	1295	1310
Leatherwood	House 1 floor	780±40	1212	1229	1275	1285	1293
Creek (44HR1)	House 4 pit	500±70	1307	1402	1431	1449	1616
Protohistoric (A.D. 1500–1607)							
Wright (44Go30)	Fea 2	370±40	1443	1459	1488, 1609, 1611	1631	1644
Contact (A.D. 1607—1646)							
Lickinghole Cr.	Fea 1a	370±60	1432	1448	1488, 1609, 1611	1638	1657
(44AB416)	Fea 1b	250±60	1486	1638	1657	1954	1954

Note: Radiocarbon date calibration: Stuiver and Reimer 1993.

A-2. Selected radiocarbon dates, Coastal Plain

| | | Uncalibrated | Calibrated Dates (years A.D.) | | | | |
| | | | Lower Limits | | Calibration | Upper Limits | |
Phase/Sites	Context	Age (years B.P.)	2σ	1σ	Curve Intercept(s)	1σ	2σ
Middle Woodland I (500 B.C.–A.D. 200)							
Hampton U #1 (44HT36)	Fea 42	1930±70	50 B.C.	A.D.12	80	141	245
Hampton U #2 (44HT37)	Fea 1003	1910±80	50 B.C.	A.D.19	88, 98, 115	223	261
Middle Woodland II (A.D.200–900)							
Hampton U #2 (44HT37)	Fea 1024	1650±80	234	267	415	535	601
Reynolds-Alvis	Fea 11	1675±85	318	256	401	446	594
(44HE470)	Fea 8	1615±85	246	381	429	548	633
	Fea 16	1445±70	447	557	632	661	689
	Fea 14	1180±70	679	779	883	967	1011
Great Neck (44VB7)	Fea 106c	1690±60	233	260	389	424	535
	Fea 106ae	1540±60	410	438	544	606	648
	Fea 106ab	1490±90	404	455	600	654	686
Late Woodland I (A.D. 900–1200)							
Irwin (44PG4)	Fea III	1110±40	880	890	967	990	1015
	Fea 3	910±120	890	1014	1162	1265	1300

Continued

| Phase/Sites | Context | Uncalibrated Age (years B.P.) | Calibrated Dates (years A.D.) | | | | |
| | | | Lower Limits | | Calibration | Upper Limits | |
			2σ	1σ	Curve Intercept(s)	1σ	2σ
Reynolds-Alvis (44HE470)	Fea 9	1030±75	883	970	1014	1039	1178
Carter's Grove (44JC118)	Fea 6069 (#1)	670±70	1237	1283	1300	1396	1416
	Fea 6069 (avg.)	618±55	1285	1299	1317, 1345, 1391	1405	1428
	Fea 6069 (#2)	540±90	1288	1310	1410	1444	1511
Late Woodland II (A.D. 1200–1500)							
Great Neck (44VB7)	Fea 29	620±80	1270	1293	1315, 1347, 1390	1410	1441
	Fea 163	440±50	1409	1433	1446	1478	1627
Reynolds-Alvis (44HE470)	Fea 2	630±100	1225	1286	1310, 1353, 1385	1416	1449
Contact (A.D. 1607–1646)							
Paspahegh (44JC308)	Bur 2	250±70	1476	1529	1657	1954	1954

Note: Radiocarbon date calibration: Stuiver and Reimer 1993.

A-3. Selected radiocarbon dates, Ridge and Valley

Phase/Sites	Context	Uncalibrated Age (years B.P.)	Calibrated Dates (years A.D.)					
			Lower Limits		Calibration	Upper Limits		
			2σ	1σ	Curve Intercept(s)	1σ	2σ	
Middle Woodland II (A.D. 200–900)								
Cement Plant (44AU51)	Fea 10	1340±60	615	654	671	767	790	
Late Woodland I (A.D. 900–1300)								
Cement Plant (44AU51)	Fea 1	1030±60	892	897	1014	1154	1160	
Huffman (44BA5)	Fea 15a	1065±65	826	894	993	1024	1158	
	Fea 29d	935±75	980	1019	1049, 1090, 1118, 1142, 1154	1214	1276	
	Fea E1	765±65	1166	1225	1279	1293	1383	
	Fea 28a	730±65	1213	1328	1286	1301	1396	
Late Woodland II (A.D.1200–1500)								
44WR300	Fea B-141	1030±100	786	895	1014	1156	1226	
	Fea C-14	1020±80	883	972	1017	1153	1215	
	Fea B-8	820±80	1028	1165	1229	1284	1303	
	Fea C-1	740±120	1028	1214	1284	1391	1431	
	Fea B-139	730±80	1168	1240	1286	1373	1403	
	Fea C-18	700±60	1229	1279	1293	1379	1401	
	Fea 101A	630±50	1285	1297	1310, 1353, 1385	1401	1417	
Noah's Ark	Fea 8	700±85	1190	1267	1293	1392	1416	
(44BA15)	Fea 45	695±70	1223	1278	1294	1389	1407	
	Fea 31	675±65	1242	1283	1299	1393	1409	
	Fea 12	645±80	1243	1287	1306, 1364, 1376	1404	1435	

Continued

| Phase/Sites | Context | Uncalibrated Age (years B.P.) | Calibrated Dates (years A.D.) | | Calibration Curve Intercept(s) | | |
| | | | Lower Limits | | | Upper Limits | |
			2σ	1σ		1σ	2σ
Bessemer (44BO26)	Fea 104N1	770±50	1188	1229	1278	1288	1300
	Fea 5	730±90	1162	1229	1286	1379	1408
	Fea 6	730±70	1190	1251	1286	1303	1398
	Fea 160N3	730±50	1225	1271	1286	1298	1386
	Fea 140S1	720±70	1213	1261	1288	1373	1401
	Fea 80S2	700±50	1245	1281	1293	1373	1396
	Fea 80S1	630±50	1297	1285	1310, 1353, 1385	1401	1417
	Fea 10S4	590±50	1295	1307	1398	1411	1434
	Fea 70S1	580±50	1297	1310	1400	1416	1436
	Palisade posts	540±70	1297	1321	1410	1439	1474
	Fea 60S4	530±50	1309	1400	1415	1436	1449
	Fea 140N1	510±50	1320	1405	1426	1441	1467
	Fea 90N2	380±70	1419	1443	1483	1638	1660
	Fea 1S4	230±60	1515	1644	1663	1954	1954
Protohistoric (A.D. 1500–1607)							
Perkins Point	Fea 62	440±130	1292	1403	1446	1638	1954
(44BA3)	Fea 69	435±50	1411	1434	1447	1481	1630
	Fea 1	315±60	1447	1484	1636	1655	1673

Note: Radiocarbon date calibration: Stuiver and Reimer 1993.

The Spessard site produced the only stratified deposits reflecting changes in James River Piedmont ceramics from the Early Woodland period through the beginning centuries of the Late Woodland period. Steatite-tempered ceramics from deeply buried deposits at Spessard indicate that these vessels were rectanguloid with flat bases, characteristic attributes of Marcey Creek ware dated to the Early Woodland period throughout the Chesapeake region (Egloff and Potter 1982:95). Pottery tempered with 10 to 25 percent quartz inclusions that are large (greater than 2.0 millimeters) and crushed (with angular or blocky edges) fell under the Albemarle series (Evans 1955) found throughout the central Virginia Piedmont and the Ridge and Valley province. A third category of sherds recovered from Spessard were tempered with sand (defined as particles smaller than 0.5 millimeters) and a variety of small (0.5–1.0 millimeter) to medium-sized (1.0–2.0 millimeters) lithic materials. These ceramics cannot be classified easily with the region's existing pottery classification schemes.

In an effort to classify Spessard ceramics that did not fit the Marcey Creek or Albemarle wares, each sherd was categorized according to temper and surface treatment. Three temper categories were used to classify these ceramics on an ordinal scale: fine sand tempered, coarse sand tempered, and mixed sand and grit tempered. In order to distinguish between this third category and Albemarle pottery, the mixed sand and grit–tempered ceramics were defined as having more than 25 percent aplastic inclusions (i.e., temper) and small to medium-sized (< 2.0 millimeters) lithic particles. With the exception of extremely small and eroded sherds, all Spessard site ceramics could be classified using the five categories of Marcey Creek, Albemarle, fine sand tempered, coarse sand tempered, and mixed sand and grit tempered.

Based on the distribution of pottery and projectile points at Spessard, strata at the site record cultural activity dating to the Early through Late Woodland periods. Level 1, which represents alluvium deposited recently in limited portions of the site, was combined with the level 2 plow zone deposits. Levels 6 and 7 were also consolidated due to the preponderance of Marcey Creek pottery in these deposits and the low numbers of artifacts recovered from these levels. Figure A-3 reflects a clear trend from Marcey Creek ceramics in the earliest deposits (levels 6 and 7) to Albemarle series pottery in the latest deposits (levels 1 through 3). In the intermediate levels 4 and 5, the various sand-tempered wares predominate. This pattern confirms the trend from steatite-tempered pottery dating to the Early Woodland period to sand-tempered wares from Middle Woodland contexts and finally to quartz-

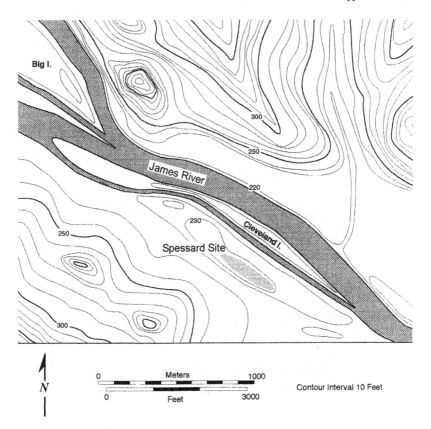

Figure A-1. Spessard site and vicinity

tempered pottery of the Late Woodland period. The sequence also provides new information regarding pottery design during the middle portion of the sequence. Radiocarbon-dated features at Spessard indicate that Albemarle fabric-impressed pottery dominates deposits from the latter portion of the Middle Woodland and the early Late Woodland centuries.

The sequence of projectile points recovered from the Spessard site provides independent support for the notion that the site's stratigraphic integrity remains intact. While minor mixing of deposits has probably occurred, the available projectile point and ceramic data indicate the following chronological sequence at Spessard: Late Woodland, levels 1 and 2; Middle Woodland, levels 3 and 4; Early Woodland, levels 5 and 6. Given the radiocarbon dates derived from Spessard's features described below, the Late Woodland deposits were limited to the first three centuries of this period. Evidence of a rather

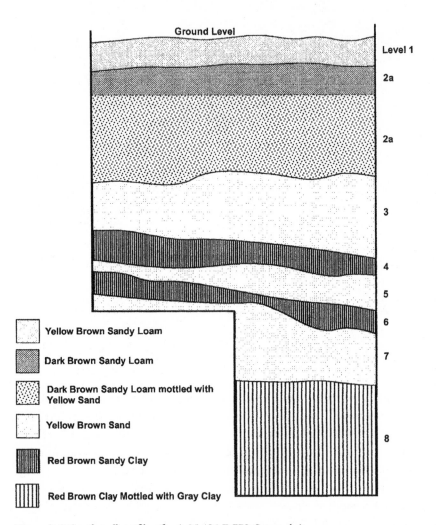

Figure A-2. South wall profile of unit N 484 E 772, Spessard site

ephemeral Archaic period presence at the site in the form of two projectile points also occurred in levels 6 and 7.

Assuming that this interpretation of Spessard's stratigraphy is correct, the distribution of pottery at the site reflects the sequence of ceramic attributes in the James River Piedmont from the Early Woodland through the opening centuries of the Late Woodland. Surface treatments applied to Spessard pottery suggest that the three varieties tempered with sand or sand and grit delineated in this study may have some validity as types, considered as pottery with consistently co-occurring temper and surface treatment. Excluding sherds lacking surface treatment, Spessard's sand and grit–tempered pottery was cord impressed, while coarse sand–tempered sherds were generally fabric impressed, and fine sand–tempered pottery was net impressed.

In general, then, Spessard's stratified deposits offer a sequence of chronologically diagnostic artifacts in the James River Piedmont. The site's stratigraphic deposits record continued use of the floodplain during the Early through Late Woodland periods. Marcey Creek ceramics identical to the pottery from the deepest deposits at Spessard occur over a broad portion of the Chesapeake. The Middle Woodland deposits at Spessard contain ceramics with a diverse mix of attributes, some of which likely entail localized forms of ceramic production. Albemarle ceramics of the terminal Middle Woodland and opening Late Woodland centuries returned pottery manufacture to a suite of attributes recognized across a broad region, though this region was smaller than the one that adopted Marcey Creek ceramics almost 2,000 years earlier.

Piedmont Floodplain Survey

The Spessard site's stratigraphic deposits provided a basis for recognizing temporally diagnostic artifacts in the James River Piedmont. An archaeological survey drawing on these patterns recovered evidence of floodplain settlement history in that region (Gallivan 1994). The survey, conducted in 1993 by University of Virginia archaeologists under my direction, combined shovel testing at 10-meter intervals with surface reconnaissance of plowed fields in the vicinity of the Wood (44NE143) and Wingina (44NE4) sites. Our survey universe consisted of a 200-meter-wide stretch of floodplain running for 3,000 meters along the James. We identified an increasing number of floodplain sites during the Woodland period that peaked circa A.D. 900. Table A-4 standardizes site frequencies by calculating the number of sites identified per 1,000 years. The highest settlement frequency occurs during the Middle

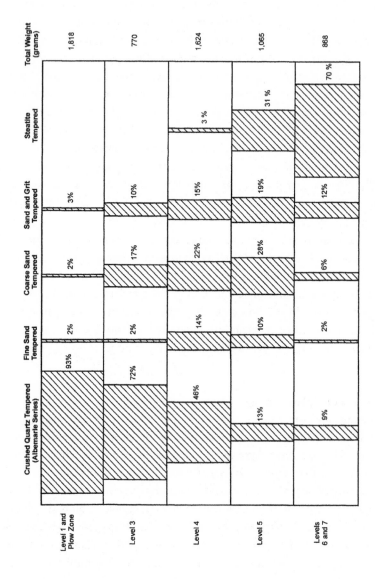

Figure A-3. Stratigraphic distribution of Spessard site ceramics

Table A-4. Results of the Wood and Wingina floodplain survey

Phase/Period	Diagnostic Artifacts	Number of sites	Sites per 1,000 years
LATE ARCHAIC (3000–1000 B.C.)	Savannah River point	3	1.0
EARLY WOODLAND (1000–500 B.C.)	Small stemmed point Marcey Creek pottery	1	2.0
MIDDLE WOODLAND I (500 B.C.–A.D. 200)	Large–medium triangles Thick-walled, sand-tempered pottery	2	2.9
MIDDLE WOODLAND II– LATE WOODLAND I (A.D. 200–1200)	Medium triangles Albemarle fabric-impressed pottery	6	6.0
LATE WOODLAND II–CONTACT (A.D. 1200–1650)	Small triangles James River cord-marked pottery	2	4.4

Woodland II through Late Woodland I phases, which are combined here due to the difficulty of distinguishing between their diagnostic artifacts.

Estimating site dimensions also proved to be a challenge due to the multiple occupations of elevated floodplain terrace locations which, in at least one instance, incorporated Late Archaic through Late Woodland II materials. However, four of the six Middle Woodland II/Late Woodland I settlements that were isolated from terraces containing multiple occupations measured less than 300 square meters in area, making them the smallest sites recorded in the survey.

In general, the survey indicates that the number of floodplain sites increased during late prehistory, though not necessarily in a continuous fashion or according to a linear sequence. The circa A.D. 900 peak in the number of floodplain sites parallels patterning in Potter's (1993) survey in the Potomac River Valley's outer Coastal Plain. As in that region, the proliferation of relatively small sites may reflect the dispersal of settlements comprised of a few households during the same era when Piedmont Indians adopted agriculture. A modest decrease in the number of floodplain sites during the last period isolated in the survey raises questions concerning settlement patterns on the eve of and during the colonial era. Piedmont groups may have consolidated their settlement in larger villages, as suggested by Mouer's (1983) survey data, and some Monacans may have withdrawn from floodplain settlement, a development suggested by excavations at the Lickinghole Creek site (44AB416) located on the eastern edge of the Blue Ridge Mountains (Hantman et al. 1993).

Middle Woodland II (A.D. 200–900)

The Middle Woodland II phase is the earliest for which features from all three provinces have been radiocarbon dated. Two excavated sites in the Piedmont, Spessard and Wood, include Middle Woodland II features. In the Chesapeake region as a whole, the Middle Woodland II phase is distinguished from the Middle Woodland I phase largely on the basis of a change in the Coastal Plain from sand-tempered net-impressed pottery (Pope's Creek ware) to shell-tempered vessels with cord, net, and plain surfaces (Mockley ware) (Egloff and Potter 1982). While a similarly sharp break in ceramic attributes is not apparent in the Piedmont, the Spessard site ceramics described above do suggest a shift in the terminal Middle Woodland period from a diverse range of surface treatments and tempering methods to the increased use of quartz-tempered fabric-impressed ceramics. Projectile points recovered from radiocarbon-dated Spessard site features are predominantly medium-sized quartz triangles. Archaeological survey in the central Virginia Piedmont (Holland 1978; Klein 1986) and the Maryland Piedmont (Kavanaugh 1983) suggest a continued shift in settlement focus to riverine settings during the Middle Woodland II phase, with an increase in the number of sites on the floodplain.

Spessard Site (44FV134)

The six pit features identified at the Spessard site contained artifacts, eth-nobotanical materials, and faunal remains (figure A-4). Five of these features yielded radiocarbon dates (table A-1). Other disturbances included 14 post-holes, none of which appeared to form any discernible patterns, and three amorphous charcoal stains that lacked clear boundaries. The Spessard features dating to the Middle Woodland II phase included two storage pits and a roasting pit. The lack of well-defined architectural patterning at Spessard places limits on any interpretation of community or household arrangements, yet the presence of storage pits and stratified deposits implies that Spessard residents remained committed to the site for a considerable occupation span. Two storage pits with virtually identical radiocarbon dates suggest the possibility that several households at Spessard returned to the same floodplain location over multiple settlement cycles.

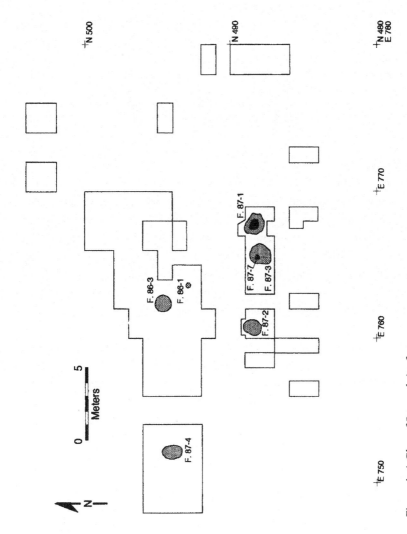

Figure A-4. Plan of Spessard site features

Table A-5. Dating Wood site stratigraphic contexts

Stratum/Arbitrary (10 cm) level	No. of Sherds	Mean Sherd Thickness (mm)	Mean Sherd Temper Size (mm)	% Dect'd. and Stamped	Years B.P.	Date A.D. (+/- 188)
I (plow zone)	30	6.98	0.77	0	925	1025
II/a	27	7.10	0.45	0	888	1062
Level II/b	10	7.20	0.70	0	933	1017
Level II/c	11	7.10	1.25	0	979	971
Level II/d	13	8.15	1.90	0	1088	862
Level III/e	17	8.35	1.75	0	1092	858

Note: Uses Klein's (1994:321) absolute seriation (uncalibrated).

The Wood Site (44ne143)

Excavations at the Wood site, located approximately 30 miles (48 kilometers) upstream of Spessard, uncovered evidence of pit features, postmold patterns, and buried deposits dating to the Middle Woodland II through Late Woodland I phases. Sorting the temporal history of the Wood site required the utilization of two distinct chronological methods—radiocarbon assays and an application of the absolute ceramic seriation developed by Klein (1994). These methods suggest a rather ephemeral presence at the site circa A.D. 900 marked by the use of a roasting pit. Subsequent, more intensive occupations occurred circa A.D. 1000–1200.

Excavation at the northern edge of the site identified a series of buried cultural horizons containing dark, organic soils beneath the plow zone. Pottery recovered from these buried A horizons was significantly larger than pottery recovered from the plow zone, suggesting that historic plowing has left a vertically shallow but horizontally extensive midden undisturbed. Klein's (1994) absolute seriation method allowed me to date pottery from each of the five buried levels and the plow zone (table A-5).

As table A-5 indicates, ceramics from the stratigraphic deposits at Wood returned dates ranging from the ninth through the eleventh centuries, providing results consistent with the site's radiocarbon dates. These dates suggest that Wood site occupations spanned a relatively limited period at the end of the Middle Woodland and the opening of the Late Woodland. Plow zone and stratum II ceramics were predominantly quartz tempered. Coarsely crushed feldspar–tempered sherds with cord-marked surfaces dominate the level III deposits and decline in percentage closer toward the surface.

Radiocarbon assays from feature contexts allowed refinement of this oc-
cupational sequence. The Wood site's feature 1 reflects two chronologically
distinct depositional episodes. The center portion of the feature (level a) had
relatively straight-sided walls that appeared to be lined with pieces of schist
(figure A-5). This portion of the feature returned a radiocarbon date of 850
± 80 B.P.. The encompassing basin-shaped soil zone (level b) generated a
radiocarbon date of 1120 ± 60 B.P. These radiocarbon dates are the earliest
and latest of the four dates obtained from Wood's features, bracketing occupation at the site. The dates differed significantly at the .05 level using
Thomas's (1986:206) and Long and Rippeteau's (1974:249) tests of feature
contemporaneity (F = 7.91, t = 2.70), indicating that feature 1b predates
feature 1a by a statistically significant margin. The inner portion of the pit
apparently represents a small Late Woodland storage pit excavated into an
earlier Middle Woodland feature. At the base of feature 1b a concentration of
fire-cracked rock and wood charcoal suggested that the feature likely served
as a large roasting pit.

The distribution of diagnostic ceramics within Wood site features provided the basis for an interpretation of feature chronology. Crushed feldspar–
tempered cord-marked sherds appeared in level b but not in level a of feature
1. These ceramics are present in the deepest buried midden deposits represented by levels II/b, II/c, II/d, and III/e but are absent from the plow
zone and the immediately underlying level II/a. As these ceramics occur in
the context of a pit feature radiocarbon dated to the Middle Woodland II
phase and within the deepest and presumably oldest Wood site strata, crushed
feldspar–tempered cord-marked ceramics appear to mark Middle Woodland
II settlement at Wood. The six other features containing crushed feldspar–
tempered cord-marked ceramics similar to those recovered from feature 1b
and diagnostic of the Middle Woodland II phase proved to be quite small
and shallow and contained few artifacts. None could be classified using the
feature typology used in this study.

In contrast with the Spessard site, which contained evidence of two Middle Woodland II storage pits, excavations of Middle Woodland II features
at Wood recovered no evidence of storage facilities. A single, large, basin-
shaped pit that may have served as a roasting facility occurs at both Wood
and Spessard. Viewed in tandem, these Middle Woodland II patterns suggest
that James River Piedmont groups periodically returned to floodplain locations for large-scale food preparation events. It is difficult to characterize
the internal organization of floodplain settlement from preceding periods in

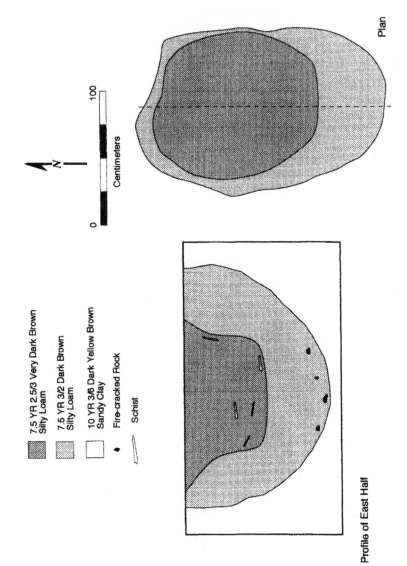

7.5 YR 2.5/3 Very Dark Brown
Silty Loam

7.5 YR 3/2 Dark Brown
Silty Loam

10 YR 3/6 Dark Yellow Brown
Sandy Clay

Fire-cracked Rock

Schist

N

0   Centimeters   100

Plan

Profile of East Half

Figure A-5. Wood site feature 1

the Piedmont since excavation data come from narrowly exposed deposits encountering few features (e.g., MacCord 1974) or from formerly buried sites badly disturbed by flooding (e.g., Mouer 1990). The stratigraphic deposits at Spessard and Wood along with Spessard's storage features point to a focusing of seasonal residence in favored locations during the Middle Woodland II phase. The lack of clearly discernible architectural evidence and the limited suite of features present at Spessard and Wood contrast with the Late Woodland occupations, though, when feature use implies a substantially greater intensity of settlement than that evidenced during the Middle Woodland II phase. Middle Woodland II settlements in the James River Piedmont most likely represent the periodic use of riverine locations in a settlement pattern that began centuries earlier during the Late Archaic period.

Late Woodland I (A.D. 900–1200)

Late Woodland I excavation data come from five sites that make this phase the best-understood portion of the James River Piedmont's prehistoric record. Broad horizontal excavations at the Wood and Wingina sites identified architectural patterns and associated pit features offering evidence of household organization and community patterning in the era when Piedmont groups supplemented their riverine-focused settlement and subsistence patterns with horticulture. Comparable data reflecting trends in subsistence and the regional distribution of style and exchange may be drawn from Late Woodland I contexts at Spessard, Partridge Creek (44AH193), and Point of Fork (44FV19). The archaeology of the tenth through thirteenth centuries in the James River Piedmont thus provides a baseline from which to gauge the social transformations of the Late Woodland period.

Diagnostic artifacts from the Late Woodland I Piedmont differ little from those found in the Spessard site features dated to the Middle Woodland II phase, raising the importance of radiocarbon assays and Klein's (1994) absolute seriation method. Macrobotanical evidence of domesticates occurs sporadically within Late Woodland I Piedmont and Coastal Plain sites, including within the Coastal Plain Reynolds-Alvis site (44HE470) and Piedmont sites such as Partridge Creek, Point of Fork, and Spessard (table A-6). Excavation of Late Woodland I contexts suggests that Native Americans in the Piedmont lived in small horticultural settlements on the floodplain, perhaps best termed "hamlets."

Late Woodland I components at the Wingina, Wood, and Spessard sites are described below. Analysis of the Partridge Creek site, which will be addressed

A-6. Early radiocarbon-dated contexts in the James River Valley contexts containing domesticates

| Site | Context | Cultigen(s) | Uncalibrated Age (years B.P.) | Calibrated Dates (years A.D.) | | | | |
| | | | | Lower Limits | | Calibration | Upper Limits | |
				2σ	1σ	Curve Intercept(s)	1σ	2σ
Reynolds–Alvis	F. 9	Bean, cucurbit	1030±75	883	970	1014	1039	1178
Partridge Creek	F. 10	Maize, bean, cucurbit	980±50	1041	1192	1025	1290	1386
Point of Fork	Pit feature	Maize	920±75	989	1024	1064, 1075, 1127, 1133, 1159	1220	1279
Spessard	F. 86–3(#1)	Maize cupules	900±80	996	1028	1165	1229	1285
	F. 86–3(#2)		790±80	1041	1192	1263	1290	1386
	F. 86–3(avg.)		845±57	1036	1164	1220	1272	1287

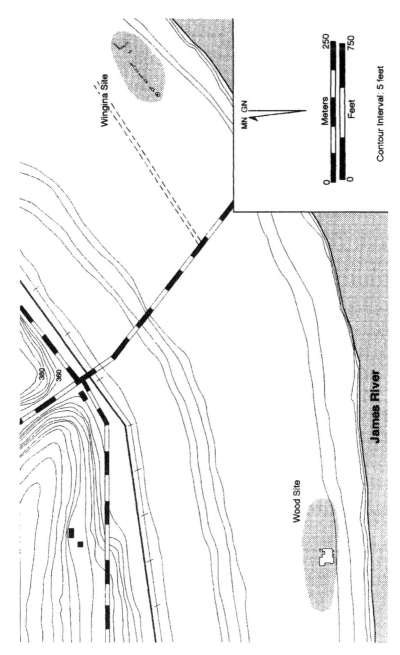

Figure A-6. Floodplain in the vicinity of the Wood and Wingina sites.

under the Late Woodland II section, required distinguishing features from multiple late precontact occupations. Excavations at the Point of Fork site, which yielded early evidence of maize, entailed limited salvage work not included in this study.

The Wingina Site (44NE4)

Evidence concerning organization of Late Woodland I Piedmont households and communities may be drawn from the Wingina and Wood sites (figure A-6). The Archaeological Society of Virginia's 1971 excavations at Wingina in the western Piedmont under the direction of MacCord (1974) produced postmold patterns, pit features, and artifacts diagnostic of periods ranging from the Middle Archaic to Late Woodland. Twelve features were identified, including three shallow pits containing pottery, four concentrations of fire-cracked rock, and four postmold patterns. An elliptical postmold pattern at the site measured approximately 5 by 6 meters. Charcoal from one of the postmolds associated with this pattern returned a Late Woodland I radiocarbon date. Two additional partial postmold patterns whose dimensions could be estimated from field drawings occurred at Wingina. A Late Archaic component at Wingina is marked by the presence of 31 steatite bowl fragments. The Wingina site reflects intermittent occupation of the floodplain during the Late Archaic and more intensive occupations during the Middle and Late Woodland. Application of Klein's (1994:321) absolute seriation equation to Wingina features produced dates of approximately A.D. 900–1000.

The Wood Site (44NE143)

Located 750 meters upstream (west) of the Wingina site, the Wood site is situated within a broad and slightly undulating east-west trending terrace that rises about 10 meters above the river. Systematic surface collection has indicated that the Wood site measures 200 meters east to west and 50 meters north to south, approximately the same dimensions as the Wingina site. Wood site excavations produced evidence of architecture and pit features dated to the Late Woodland I phase. Patterning in these features suggests that Piedmont groups resided in compact, unpalisaded communities composed of several household clusters that included small domestic structures with external storage pits.

Thirty-three pit features at the Wood site were assigned to the Late Woodland period through radiocarbon assays, absolute dating of ceramics, and diagnostic artifacts (Gallivan 1995). As reported in table A-1, the uncalibrated results of radiocarbon dates from feature 27 (990 ± 100 B.P.), feature 1a (850

Table A-7. Absolute seriation of Wood site feature ceramics

Feature	Number of Sherds	Mean Sherd Thickness (mm)	Mean Sherd Temper Size (mm)	% Dect'd. and Stamped	Years B.P.	Date A.D. (+/- 188)
18	10	7.5	0.45	0	913	1037
43	19	7.75	0.55	0	948	1002

Note: Uses Klein's (1994:321) absolute seriation (uncalibrated).

± 80 B.P.), and post 94 (910 ± 80 B.P.) overlap at the one-sigma level. Tests of radiocarbon assay contemporaneity indicate that the difference between these assays is not statistically significant at the .05 level (F = 1.53, t = 1.24), implying the features' approximate contemporaneity. Averaging the radiocarbon dates with Long and Rippeteau's (1974:206–210) method produced a result of 908 ± 54 B.P. (A.D. 1042 ± 54) from the feature 27, feature 1a, and post 94 assays, a result that calibrates to A.D. 1017–1257 at the two-sigma range. Absolute seriation of ceramics from two additional features (table A-7) also produced eleventh-century A.D. dates (uncalibrated).

Thus two independent chronological methods produced uncalibrated dates of circa A.D. 1000–1050 for Wood site features, indicating that much of the feature construction at Wood occurred during a relatively brief interval within the Late Woodland I phase. The five contexts dated with absolute chronological methods, in addition to the Wood site plow zone, contained almost exclusively Albemarle series ceramics with fabric-impressed or plain surfaces. Based on this pattern, Albemarle fabric-impressed and plain ceramics served as diagnostic indicators of the Late Woodland I occupation at Wood. The 33 Wood site features assigned to the Late Woodland I occupation through either radiocarbon assays, absolute ceramic dates, or diagnostic artifacts included five storage pits, four hearths, two postholes, and one structure floor.

Excavations uncovered a dense scatter of 350 postmolds at the Wood site. Five elliptical to circular postmold patterns were noted in the field (structures A–E in figure A-7). These hypothesized patterns roughly matched ethnohistorical descriptions of circular to elliptical domestic architectural floor plans. Each included at least one post stain containing Albemarle fabric-impressed pottery, suggesting chronological placement in the Late Woodland I phase. In an effort to introduce a level of objectivity and replicability to the recognition of Wood's postmold patterns and to evaluate the validity of the proposed

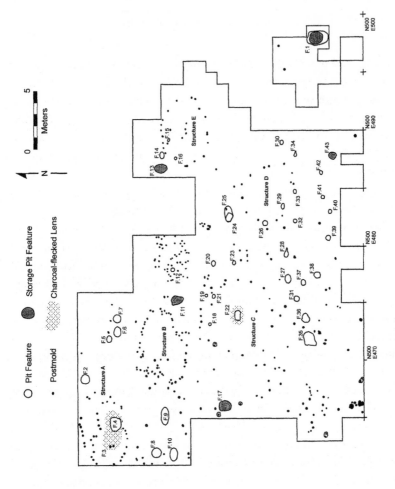

Figure A–7. Plan of Wood site features

structural patterns, I applied two methods of quantitative spatial analysis to the postmolds identified at the site. Prezzano's (1988) two-part evaluation of an Owasco site using *k*-means cluster analysis and a linear linkage method served as a model for this analysis. The Owasco tradition, centered in the Mohawk drainage and Finger Lakes region, represents the Late Woodland archaeological horizon in upstate New York of Native communities ancestral to the tribes of the Iroquois League. *K*-means procedures cluster data based on nonhierarchical divisive criteria, maximizing intercluster distance while minimizing intracluster variance (Prezzano 1988:30; Kintigh and Ammerman 1982). Additionally, Prezzano's (1988:36–42) linkage of postmolds located a set distance apart within an Iroquois site provided a second means of identifying postmold patterns.

The *k*-means cluster analysis generally supports the field interpretation of the postmold patterns at Wood. Figure A-8 depicts the seven-cluster solution of postmold patterns, with the numbers placed in the postmold locations referring to cluster numbers. In this figure, the postmolds thought to be part of structure C were not clustered together in any of the solutions arrived at by the *k*-means procedures. The initial interpretation of structure C as architectural evidence was based in part on the presence of a hearth feature (feature 22) near the center of a circular pattern of postmolds, corresponding with accounts of Native American houses in the region. John Lawson, a colonist who traveled extensively among the Indians of the North Carolina Piedmont in the first decade of the eighteenth century, wrote an account of Indians' domestic architecture that refers to internal hearths and overall construction techniques. Lawson's description is useful for interpreting the postmolds at Wood:

> They make the fire in the middle of the house, and have a have a hole at the top of the roof right above the fire to let out the smoke. . . . [T]hey set very long poles of pine, cedar, hickory, or any other wood that will bend; these are the thickness of a small man's leg, at the thickest end, which they generally strip of the bark, and warm them well in the fire, which makes them tough and fit to bend. Afterwards they stick the thickest ends of them in the ground, about two yards asunder, in a circular form, the distance they design the cabin to be (which is not always round but sometimes oval) then they bend the tops and bring them together, and bind their ends with bark of tree. (1967:187)

Assuming that Lawson's estimates are correct, postmolds up to approxi-

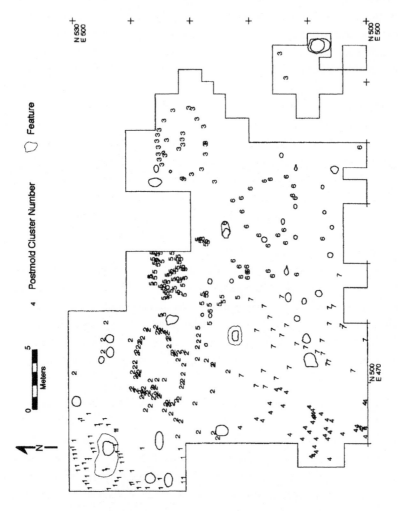

Figure A–8. Seven-cluster solution to cluster analysis of Wood site postmolds

mately 180 centimeters (2 yards) apart might be part of the same structure, a useful measure for the second analytical approach developed by Prezzano.

Prezzano's (1988:36–43) linear linkage method of associating postmolds at an Owasco village site is based on the principle that posts were spaced at regular intervals. Lawson's (1967) account provides the typical post-to-post distance drawn from a village close to the James River Piedmont. Figure A-9 depicts the linear linkage of each postmold to the two closest postmolds up to 180 centimeters (2 yards) distant. Since rebuilding episodes likely resulted in distances between related posts that were less than the original interval, each post is linked to its nearest neighbor. The map suggests that five circular to elliptical postmold patterns are identifiable, including those grouped together as part of structure C. Two other clusters of postmolds, one in the southwest corner of the excavated area and one near the center of the site, may represent additional post-in-ground facilities. Based on these two methods, it appears that the postmold distributions reflect five house patterns and two additional features constructed for aboveground storage, drying racks, or some other purpose. Table A-8 summarizes the attributes of the five postmold patterns interpreted as domestic structures due to their sizes, shapes, and associated pit features.

All Late Woodland I feature and midden ceramics were examined for potential cross mends to evaluate the potential contemporaneity of feature construction at Wood. Pottery from more than one feature context that cross mends does not necessarily reflect simultaneous feature construction; however, refits do suggest the presence of pits that were open and filled at roughly the same time (e.g., Nass and Yerkes 1995:89). Beyond the numerous intrafeature mends, four sherds cross mended with pottery from other feature contexts, resulting in two interfeature refits. All four of the cross-mended sherds were Albemarle fabric impressed. Pottery from features 2 and 3 and sherds from features 13 and 16 cross mended.

When compared to the location of postmold patterns at Wood, the spatial context of these temporally related features suggests the contemporaneity of at least some of the intramural and extramural features. Feature 3, the shallow, charcoal-rich deposits surrounding hearth feature 4 located on the interior of structure A, included a sherd that cross mended with another from feature 2 located less than 3 meters northeast of structure A. Feature 16, probably a large postmold associated with structure E's wall, included a sherd that was refitted to another from storage feature 13 located immediately northwest of the structure E wall. While it is unclear exactly what combination of

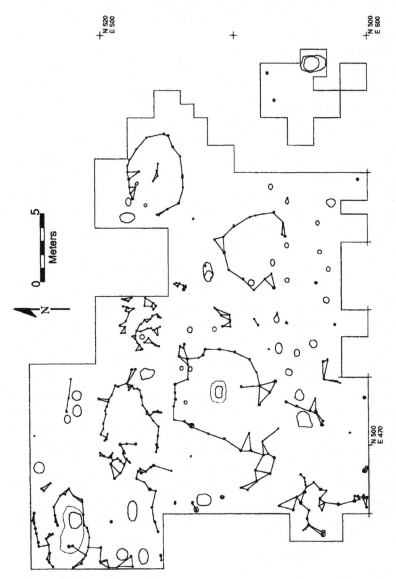

Figure A-9. Linear linkage of Wood site postmolds

Table A-8. Architectural attributes at the Wood site

Structure	Length (m)	Width (m)	Mean Post Diameter (m)	Mean Post Depth (m)	Floor Area (sq. m)
A	5.5	3.1	0.14	0.14	13.38
B	6.4	3.1	0.12	0.13	15.57
C	5.8	—	0.14	0.11	26.41
D	3.3	—	0.13	0.10	11.94
E	5.6	4.0	0.15	0.17	17.98

disposal practices and site formation processes resulted in the deposition of portions of the same vessel in these contexts, the resultant pattern supports the notion that domestic structures were contemporaneous with spatially proximate, external pit features containing Albemarle ceramics.

The Wood site reflects aspects of settlement structure at the community and household scales during the opening centuries of the Late Woodland period. Both the Wood and Wingina sites appear to represent multihousehold hamlets arrayed in a generally linear fashion parallel to the James. Relatively dense concentrations of artifacts that make up the Wood and Wingina sites are interspersed with smaller, outlying sites in close proximity. Given the diversity of artifacts (i.e., lithic debitage, stone tools, pottery, fire-cracked rock, and projectile points) recovered from the outlying locations, these may represent residential settlements rather than limited activity areas. Although not all settlements in the vicinity of Wingina were contemporaneous, the survey evidence records substantial floodplain use in this area during the opening Late Woodland centuries. The overall pattern does not clearly fit models of dispersed or nucleated settlement (Turner 1992; Potter 1993) or a model contrasting "compact clusters" and "linear arrangements" (Mouer 1983:27) but suggests aspects of all of these patterns.

Spatial patterning relative to the household arena appears in the Wood site's architectural patterns, pit features, and cross-mended ceramics. Five storage pits and five postmold patterns representing domestic structures occur in the excavation area. Cross-mended ceramics link internal and external pits at the Wood site. Given this association between houses and contemporaneous features located immediately outside the structure, four of the five houses at Wood appear to be associated with a storage pit. The spatial organization of households at the opening of the Late Woodland period in the James River

Piedmont likely involves domestic groups who stored surpluses in small pits immediately external to their residences.

The Spessard Site (44fv134)

Three pit features at the Spessard site returned Late Woodland radiocarbon dates (table A-1). Tests of radiocarbon date contemporaneity suggest no significant difference between the dates at the .05 significance level (F = 1.93, t = 1.39). The features produce an uncalibrated average of 906 ± 35 B.P., with a two-sigma calibrated date range of A.D. 1029–1224. Two of the features fell into the roasting pit category, and one pit could not be classified. Artifacts included predominantly Albemarle ceramics and small to medium-sized triangular points. Paleobotanical analysis of feature 86–3 resulted in the identification of corn cupules, *chenopodium*, and hickory and walnut shell.

Radiocarbon dates from Spessard indicate that Piedmont groups introduced horticultural production in the early centuries of the Late Woodland period, a conclusion supported by paleobotanical evidence from the Partridge Creek site in the western Piedmont and the Point of Fork site situated near the confluence of the James and Rivanna rivers downstream of Spessard. At the Partridge Creek site, described below, a Late Woodland I radiocarbon date was obtained from a feature that contained a bean seed and hickory nut shell (Tourtellotte 1990:19). At Point of Fork, a radiocarbon assay from a feature containing a maize cob fragment and *chenopodium* seeds also returned a Late Woodland I date. By contrast, paleobotanical analysis at the Wood site showed no evidence of domesticates but suggested the intensive gathering of wild seed plants, including *chenopodium* during a warm-weather occupation. Considered together, these ethnobotanical data suggest a mixed Piedmont economy in the early centuries of the Late Woodland in which cultigens were added to subsistence practices involving wild foods.

In general, the Late Woodland I Piedmont sites support the interpretation that the residents of small, seasonal floodplain settlements constructed a range of pit features and incorporated cultigens that included maize, beans, and squash. Domestic structures with adjacent storage pit features within one site raise the possibility that household groups exercised at least some control over surplus production.

Late Woodland II (A.D. 1200–1500)

Late Woodland II phase patterns in the James River Piedmont are less well understood than those of the preceding era due to the paucity of excavated sites. Survey in the James (Mouer 1983) and excavation data (Hantman and Klein 1992) from river basins surrounding the James imply the establishment of relatively large and nucleated floodplain settlements during Late Woodland II centuries. Excavation at the Leatherwood Creek (44HR1) site in the Roanoke River Piedmont immediately south of the James River Valley provides the most thoroughly excavated Piedmont context reflecting these trends (Gallivan 1997a). For this reason I have included the Leatherwood Creek site in the study. Ceramics from the James River Piedmont during the Late Woodland II phase are typically tempered with finely crushed quartz and are cord marked, falling under Mouer et al.'s (1986) description of "James River" ceramic ware. However, continuous variation in vessel wall thickness and temper size, in addition to the presence of fabric-impressed surfaces throughout the Late Woodland sequence, make any distinction between Albemarle and James River ceramics a relative one. Continuous variation also appears in the size of triangular projectile points, although a trend toward smaller, serrated projectile points that fall under the Clarksville or Fort Ancient types is apparent regionally.

The Partridge Creek Site (44AH193)

The Partridge Creek site is the only Piedmont site in the study with features dating to the Late Woodland I and Late Woodland II phases. The site is the westernmost Piedmont location included in the sample. In 1985 high-magnitude overbank flooding of the James scoured an L-shaped area of roughly 3,500 square meters immediately downstream of Partridge Creek's mouth (figure A-10). As described in Tourtellotte's (1990) initial report and a subsequent, more detailed analysis of the recovered material (Gallivan 2003), salvage excavations identified the remains of 48 pit features and midden deposits. The flooding not only stripped plow zone soils from this area to uncover a previously unrecorded site but also removed some of the subsoil surrounding features. This process created a bizarre landscape of cylindrical, tree stump–like features that protruded 20–40 centimeters above the scoured surface. The flooding disturbed feature deposits as well, removing the tops of many features. Nonetheless, careful excavation and recording of the features by Sweet Briar College students and Archaeological Society of Virginia members under Tourtellotte's direction produced a critical data set for understanding the late precontact Piedmont floodplain.

Fieldwork at the site included excavation of flood-exposed features adjacent to the James River and Partridge Creek, stripping of midden deposits

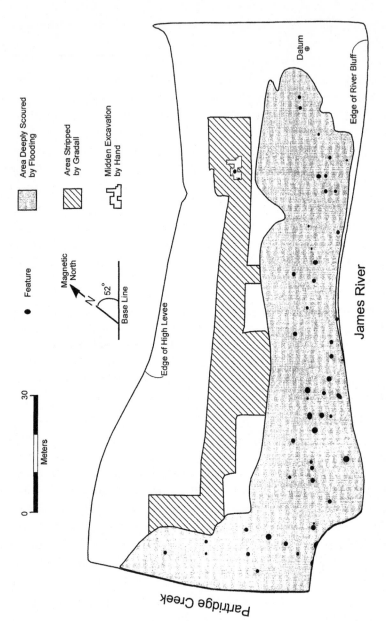

Figure A-10. Plan of Partridge Creek site features (redrawn from Tourtellotte 1990)

west of the scoured area, and hand excavation of a small portion of the midden. The majority of identified features occurred in the flood-affected area. Any postmold evidence of architectural structures that had existed in this area was destroyed by the flooding.

Evidence of subsistence practices from Partridge Creek site features included paleobotanical remains recovered during water screening and flotation of selected features. Maize kernels or cupules were recovered from 44.4 percent of the features subjected to flotation analysis (n = 18), implying that corn-based horticulture was more than a sporadic occurrence at Partridge Creek. Feature 10, radiocarbon dated to 980 ± 50 B.P. and interpreted as a roasting pit, contained carbonized evidence of corn, beans, and squash. Not only is the combination of cultigens recovered from feature 10 remarkable, but the feature provides the earliest date for evidence of domesticates in the Virginia Piedmont.

Features at the Partridge Creek site badly disturbed by flooding were excluded from my analysis. Classification of the remaining features using the typology presented in chapter 3 placed pits in all of the principal types. These results suggests that, despite the flooding, Partridge Creek site features had retained enough of their original shapes and contents to allow their inclusion in the James River Valley data set.

Constructing a chronology of occupation at the Partridge Creek site required drawing on a combination of radiocarbon dates and absolute seriation of feature ceramics. As listed in table A-1, the seven radiocarbon dates obtained from Partridge Creek site features span a substantial portion of the Late Woodland. Tests of contemporaneity indicate that the earliest radiocarbon date obtained from a Partridge Creek site feature (feature 10) differs statistically at the .05 significance level from the feature 37 date (F = 5.45, t = 2.21) and the feature 39 date (F = 18.00, t = 4.21), the two latest dates at the site. These results indicate that feature use occurred over multiple occupations at the site.

Thirty-four additional features that contained at least 10 ceramic sherds were also dated using the absolute seriation method. The figure A-11 histogram depicts the results of this analysis, pointing to a bimodal distribution of feature dates at the site with peaks centered near A.D. 1025 and 1200 (uncalibrated). Tests of radiocarbon assay contemporaneity indicate that the earliest and latest radiocarbon dates in the first hypothesized mode do not differ significantly at the .05 level (F = 3.4, t = 1.74), nor do the dates from the second (i.e., later) mode (F = 0.33, t = 0.58). The results of these tests and

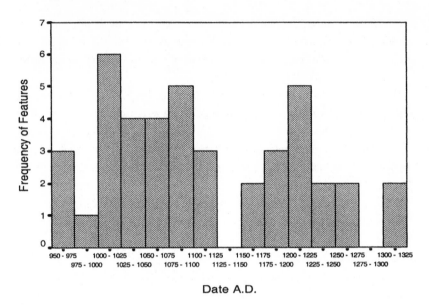

Date A.D.

Figure A-11. Uncalibrated dates for Spessard site features obtained through absolute dating methods

the figure A-11 histogram imply occupations at the Partridge Creek site that were concentrated within two distinct temporal intervals. It is unlikely that all of the materials recovered and features identified at the Partridge Creek site were deposited during two discrete settlement events. Yet the absolute dating of feature contexts provides a sound empirical basis for separating earlier and later occupations at the site rather than implying a continuous series of Late Woodland settlements. Averaging the radiocarbon assays that fall under the early mode results in an uncalibrated mean date of A.D. 925 ± 27, which calibrates to the one-sigma range of A.D. 1040–1166. The uncalibrated mean date for the latter mode of 717 ± 41 B.P. calibrates to the one-sigma range of A.D. 1276–1297 during the opening century of the Late Woodland II phase.

This chronological interpretation of Partridge Creek site chronology provides the basis for a comparison of Late Woodland I and Late Woodland II occupations of a single Piedmont location, as detailed elsewhere (Gallivan 2003). The ability to keep floodplain location constant while comparing feature contexts from different eras is unusual in the region and makes the Partridge Creek site particularly important for evaluating Late Woodland floodplain settlement and exchange patterns. Differences between the features and materials associated with the two occupations point to changes

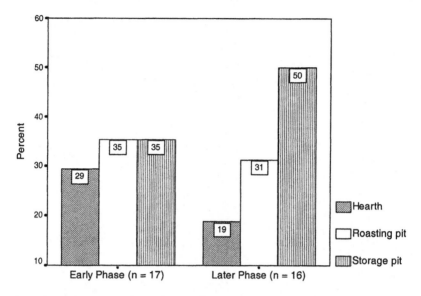

Figure A-12. Feature type by settlement phase

in the use of pit features and stone tool technology. Figure A-12 depicts the distribution of feature types by period at the site. A shift toward the construction of storage features is apparent at the Partridge Creek site, with storage pits making up half of identifiable Late Woodland II features.

Ceramics recovered from both occupations at Partridge Creek site features generally fall under the Albemarle series with crushed quartz temper and fabric-impressed or cord-marked surfaces. Seven limestone-tempered cord-marked sherds recovered from feature 3 fall under the Page series classification (Evans 1955). Figure A-13 summarizes the surface treatment data by settlement phase, indicating that fabric impression decreased slightly from the early to the late phase at the site while cord marking increased.

Despite the unusual circumstances surrounding the Partridge Creek site's discovery, the excavation provides clear evidence of Late Woodland patterns in the James River Piedmont related to subsistence patterns and material culture. The site provides the largest example of excavated pit features in the James River Piedmont and thus contributes substantially to this study.

The Wright Site (44Go30) and the Little River Site (44Go30b)
Elk Island, a 1-by-5-mile (1.6-by-8.0 kilometer) stretch of floodplain located 35 miles (56 kilometers) west of the fall line (figure A-14), contains a

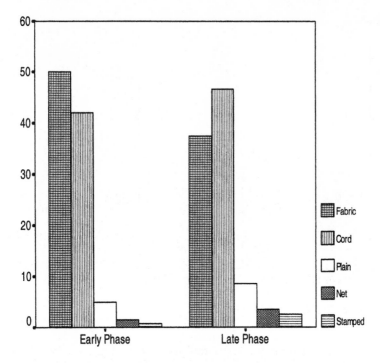

Figure A-13. Surface treatment percentages by settlement phase

large number of sites dating from the Late Archaic through Contact periods, including the Wright (44Go30) and Little River (44Go30b) sites. One of these, the Wright site, appeared as a dense concentration of ceramics with small triangular points in the context of circular midden deposits. Mouer (1983) characterized the core of the Wright site as 200 by 200 meters in size, highly nucleated, and defined by a black circular midden, part of which was exposed by flooding. Seventeenth-century bottle glass, gunflints, and Delftware pottery were collected along with Native American ceramics. The presence of decorated Potomac Creek pottery and a chert Fort Ancient triangular projectile point suggests a terminal Late Woodland occupation.

My resurvey of the Wright site vicinity identified two distinct concentrations of materials diagnostic of the final Late Woodland centuries, both of which were tested by small block excavations. Excavation in the southernmost concentration, designated as the Little River site, identified two pit features and postmolds (figure A-15). Deep, cylindrical feature 1 included James River cord-marked ceramics and returned an uncalibrated radiocar-

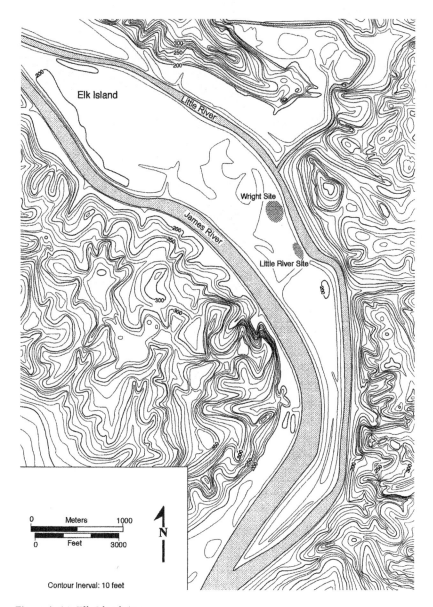

Figure A-14. Elk Island sites

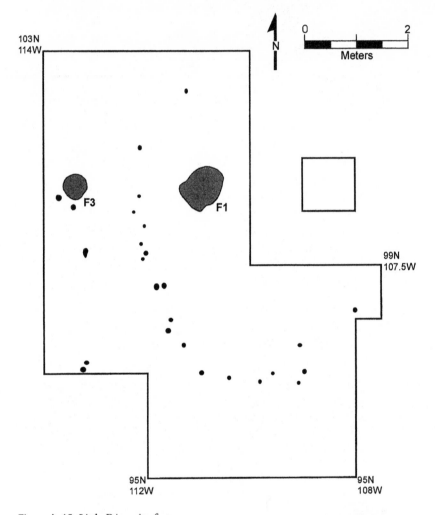

Figure A-15. Little River site features

bon date of 750 ± 60 B.P. This date has a calibrated two-sigma range of A.D. 1189–1310. A postmold pattern that appears to encompass the feature disappeared along the eastern portion of the excavation block along a modern farm road. Feature 3, an area of fire-reddened soil, contained no diagnostic artifacts. Little River site features may represent two domestic structures, at least one of which surrounds a storage pit feature. The limited excavation data from the Little River site suggest the possibility that a shift in storage pit location to house interiors may have occurred in the Late Woodland II Piedmont.

The Leatherwood Creek Site (44HR1)

Although located in a river basin adjacent to the James River Valley, the Leatherwood Creek site was included in the database as the sole Late Woodland II example of a Piedmont Virginia site containing multiple pit features, domestic architecture, and radiocarbon assays (Gallivan 1997a). Excavated in the late 1960s by avocational archaeologist Richard Gravely (1971, 1983), the site is distinguished by the presence of two distinct styles of domestic architecture: rectangular postmold patterns surrounding hearths and circular houses with deep, internal pit features. All of the structures were constructed on prepared floors consisting of shallow depressions. The artifact assemblage includes Dan River series pottery; small, triangular projectile points; bone tools; and clay pipes.

Evidence of chronological patterning at the Leatherwood Creek site suggests multiple Late Woodland II occupations of the location. A radiocarbon assay of a pit feature centered within a circular structure returned an uncalibrated date of 500 ± 70 B.P., which calibrates to the two-sigma range of A.D. 1307–1616. An uncalibrated date of 780 ± 40 B.P. was obtained from the floor associated with a rectangular structure, which calibrates to the two-sigma range of A.D. 1212–1293. Tests of contemporaneity indicate a significant difference ($F = 7.48, t = 4.95$) between these dates. These results imply at least two site occupations, the first of which was marked by rectangular structures and the second of which includes the construction of circular structures. Application of the absolute seriation approach to Leatherwood Creek site feature ceramics allowed pits from these two hypothesized occupations to be distinguished.

As detailed elsewhere (Gallivan 1997a), the Leatherwood Creek site provides an unparalleled data source concerning Late Woodland II architectural and pit feature construction in the Virginia Piedmont. A shift in the location of storage pits to house interiors occurred at the Leatherwood Creek site, a pattern paralleled at the Little River site to the north. The presence of sealed house floor deposits at the Leatherwood Creek site that contained large vessel sections provides evidence of domestic ceramic assemblages in late precontact Virginia, critical information used in the construction of a demographic model of floodplain settlement developed in chapter 4.

Protohistoric Period (A.D. 1500–1607)

Excavation data from the James River Piedmont dating to the sixteenth century is limited to the Wright site. Testing at Wright identified evidence of pits, burials, a palisade, and a radiocarbon-dated feature that suggests a Protohistoric date. Ceramics recovered from this site and diagnostic of the Protohistoric Piedmont include finely crushed James River cord-marked pottery and ceramics categorized as Potomac Creek ware (Egloff and Potter 1982:112; Potter 1993:135). Like James River ceramics (Mouer et al. 1986), Potomac Creek pottery is thin walled, tempered with sand and finely crushed quartz, and primarily cord marked. Unlike James River ceramics, Potomac Creek pottery is defined largely by the presence of decorative motifs on the rim portion of the vessel. Potomac Creek ceramics occur primarily in the Potomac River's inner Coastal Plain and outer Piedmont, although the ware has a wide distribution that crosses physiographic boundaries and extends to the Shenandoah, Rappahannock, York, James, and Shenandoah rivers. Small, triangular projectile points, especially isosceles triangles with serrated edges, appear frequently in Protohistoric contexts in the Piedmont.

The Wright Site (44GP30)

The Wright site is located on Elk Island near the confluence of the James and Rivanna rivers (figure A-14). The results of excavations by University of Virginia archaeologists in 1997 support Mouer's (1983) hypothesis that the site represents a substantial Protohistoric village. Feature 2 returned an uncalibrated date of 370 ± 40 B.P. Oscillation of the calibration curve near A.D. 1500 results in the large, two-sigma calibrated range of A.D. 1443–1644, preventing precise placement of the site vis-à-vis Jamestown's settlement. Calibration curve intercepts occur at A.D. 1488, 1609, and 1611 for the radiocarbon assay. No European artifacts were recovered from sealed feature contexts at Wright. Recovered ceramics include James River and Potomac Creek wares with incised or cord-impressed rim decorations and paddle-edge lip impressions.

Excavations at the Wright site identified what appeared to be narrow slot trenches that differ markedly from plow scars at the site in soil color and texture, artifact contents, and orientation (figure A-16). Within and adjacent to these features, labeled features 11 and 12, were postmold stains containing ceramic and lithic artifacts. Together, the trenches and the postmolds suggest the presence of palisade lines similar to those identified at the Potomac Creek site (44ST2) and the Accokeek Creek site (18PR8) in the Potomac River valley

(Potter 1993:121). A slight curve to these features implies that a palisade may have surrounded a settlement located primarily northeast of the excavation area. Burial features 2 and 3 included primary interments located either immediately within or outside of the palisade features. James River cord-marked ceramics and lithic artifacts appeared in all features at the site.

The Wright site excavations laid the groundwork for future study of the Protohistoric and Contact eras in the James River Piedmont. The site appears to represent the remains of a large, palisaded settlement from the period when European colonization began in the Middle Atlantic. The interpretation that Wright represents a Protohistoric settlement is preliminary, as the presence or absence of European artifacts is not a definitive indicator of a Contact period occupation. Given the proximity of Elk Island to the confluence of the Rivanna and James rivers, the Wright site may represent the location of Rassawek, depicted on John Smith's 1612 *Map of Virginia* and described as the Monacans' chief habitation (Smith 1986b). While our excavations recovered no European artifacts from feature contexts, such materials did occur in the plow zone.

Contact Period (A.D. 1607–1650)

Despite several intensive surveys, no large Contact period village settlements have been identified in the James River Piedmont. Additional study of the Wright site may clarify its chronological placement relative to the beginnings of an English presence at Jamestown. The one site that has been dated to the Contact period in the James River Piedmont—the Lickinghole Creek site—represents a small settlement near the base of the Blue Ridge Mountains far removed from any major stream. The few artifacts recovered from the site provided little information regarding changing material culture in the Piedmont. The lack of European artifacts at the site, though, challenges the assumption that European trade goods provide a diagnostic indicator of postcontact settlement.

The Lickinghole Creek Site (44AB416)

The Lickinghole Creek site is located on a low-order tributary of the Rivanna River and occupies a relatively broad section of the floodplain where several ancillary tributaries join Lickinghole Creek (figure A-17). University of Virginia archaeologists identified the site through shovel testing. At the time of investigation, the area was a pasture, and there were no surface indications of the presence of an archaeological site.

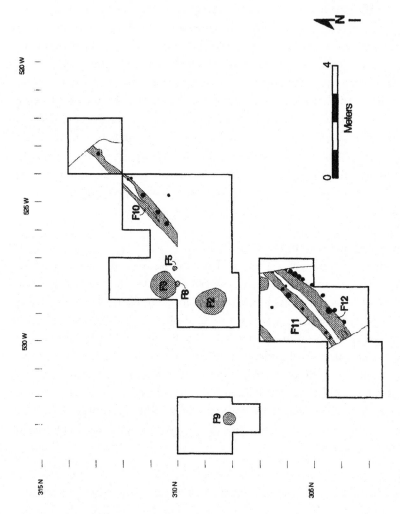

Figure A-16. Wright site features

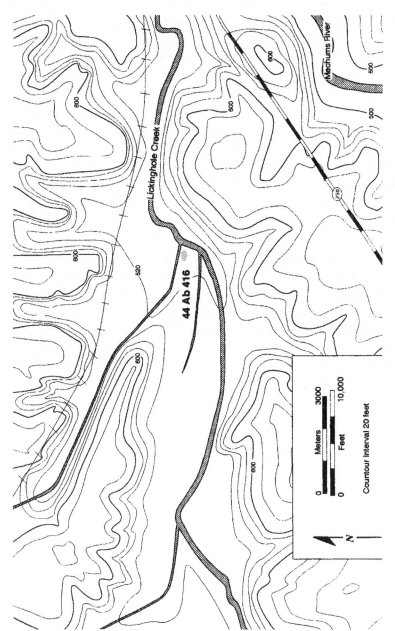

Figure A-17. Lickinghole Creek site vicinity

Excavations identified an irregularly shaped, buried, charcoal-rich lens (figures A-18 and A-19) in the context of the densest concentration of artifacts at the site. The sedimentary characteristics of the overlying strata indicate that high-intensity flooding from the nearby permanent creek during the historic era had buried cultural deposits within this level. The burned materials in this level were primarily grasses and bark, with some charred wood on the perimeter of the staining. The relatively high amounts of lithic debitage at this depth, as well as ceramics, flat-lying stones, and fire-cracked rock, suggest that this level probably represents a former habitation surface. No postmolds, hearths, or pits were identified. Excavations uncovered the sharply defined boundary of the lens, suggesting an irregular, roughly circular shape in plan. Concentrations of wood charcoal located 45 to 50 centimeters below surface and immediately south of the charcoal lens may represent charred posts of domestic architecture. The lens measured 14 meters east-west by 7 to 10 meters north-south—roughly the dimensions of late precontact houses identified in other Piedmont settlements.

The feature appears to reflect the burned remains of a structure. One radiocarbon date derived from a charred post dated to 250 ± 60 B.P. (uncalibrated). An accelerator mass spectrometry assay of the charred material that made up the bulk of the lens yielded a date of 370 ± 60 B.P. (uncalibrated). Test of contemporaneity indicates no significant difference at the .05 level between these dates (F = 1.37, t = 1.41). The two dates produce an uncalibrated average of 310 ± 42 B.P., which calibrates to the two-sigma range of A.D. 1474–1674 and has a calibration curve intercept at A.D. 1638. Precise chronological placement of the feature is thus difficult due to the complexities of the calibration curve, although a seventeenth-century occupation at the site is supported by the single calibration curve intercept. This buried, low-artifact-density site is the first site in the central Virginia Piedmont dated (tentatively) to the Contact period.

In addition to a high density of quartz lithics, the charcoal lens deposits yielded a Clarksville projectile point and quartz-tempered ceramics. Pottery recovered from the lens is tempered with finely crushed quartz. The small assemblage was so badly eroded that surface treatment and decoration could not be determined. The Lickinghole Creek deposits did not contain European trade goods. Only the radiocarbon assays of the oddly buried and preserved charcoal lens allow placement of this site in the seventeenth century.

As discussed elsewhere (Hantman et al. 1993), the elusiveness of Contact period sites in the James River Piedmont may be due to several factors,

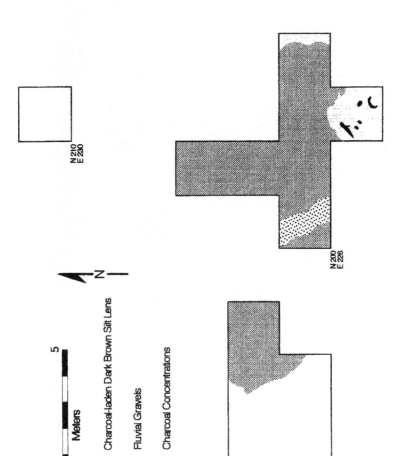

Figure A-18. Lickinghole Creek site charcoal lens feature

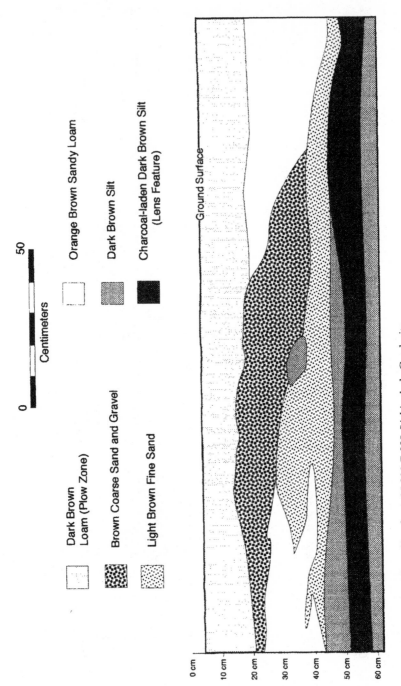

Figure A-19. South wall profile of unit N 200 E 228, Lickinghole Creek site

including those related to chronologically diagnostic artifacts, cultural strategies, and geomorphological dynamics. With regard to the first of these issues, there may in fact be no artifacts clearly diagnostic of the Contact period in the James River Piedmont. Neither the ceramics nor projectile points appear to be qualitatively different in the pre- and post-1607 eras. As a result, Contact period sites identified by surveys may be mislabeled as dating to the Late Woodland. Settlements of the Contact period Piedmont may typically be small hamlets, even small, single-household homesteads located away from major rivers that are difficult to identify with current survey methods.

Second, a lack of European trade goods on seventeenth-century sites in central Virginia may be the product of cultural factors particular to the Monacans, as Hantman (1990, 1993:110) has proposed. Ethnohistorical references suggest that the Monacans chose not to interact with the English as part of a deliberate cultural strategy. European trade goods, when recovered from other Middle Atlantic archaeological contexts, frequently appear in burial contexts. Unlike those of neighboring groups, the Monacans' mortuary practices did not entail the inclusion of wealth items, or any artifacts, with interments. Thus the most common locus of trade goods is not pertinent to the Monacans.

Finally, late precontact and Contact period sites frequently occupy dynamic alluvial landforms, such as those associated with floodplains. The size, duration of occupation, and relative permanence of such sites were affected by landform stability. As demonstrated by the Lickinghole Creek site, a rapidly aggrading floodplain contributed to the preservation of a small archaeological site. Evidence of similar sites elsewhere may no longer exist or may be difficult to identify without intensive survey methods and subsurface testing.

Late Precontact Piedmont Culture History
The archaeology of the late precontact James River Piedmont allows reconstruction of a culture historic sequence involving changes in material culture, subsistence, and settlement organization. A substantial floodplain presence is indicated by stratified deposits dating as early as the Late Archaic period in the Piedmont, although evidence of architecture and diverse pit features suggestive of a demographically large, relatively permanent floodplain presence awaited the Late Woodland. As determined by previous archaeological survey, settlement patterns involved an increase in floodplain sites through the Late Woodland I phase, with a possible settlement dispersal concurrent with the

appearance of domesticates. James River surveys and excavation data from adjacent regions hint at a Late Woodland II appearance of large, nucleated settlements. By the Protohistoric period a large, palisaded village site was present at the Wright site on Elk Island. Contact period settlements have proven to be elusive in the Piedmont, possibly due in part to a seventeenth-century withdrawal of Monacans to small sites located away from the floodplains of major rivers. Household organization within at least one site at the outset of Late Woodland horticultural production in the Piedmont involved the storage of surplus in public areas located immediately adjacent to domestic structures. A developing household control of surplus production is suggested by the subsequent Late Woodland II appearance of houses with internal storage pit features.

Floodplain Archaeology of the Woodland Period in the James River Coastal Plain

Woodland period archaeology within Virginia's Coastal Plain reflects a complex history of social change summarized in a number of publications (e.g., Rountree and Turner 2002; Dent 1995; Blanton 1992; Turner 1992; McLearan 1991; Waselkov 1982). Evidence of increasing sedentariness and population may be drawn from survey data that are punctuated by a Late Woodland intensification of production, population growth, sedentariness, and investment in floodplain settlement infrastructure. Excavation and survey data suggest a shift from an estuarine-focused subsistence regime centered on shellfish beginning during the Late Archaic to a Late Woodland horticultural economy among groups "preadapted" to such a regime. The following section briefly describes the sites included in the sample and the interpretive framework applied to these data.

Middle Woodland I (500 B.C.–A.D. 200)

With the advent of the Middle Woodland period in the Tidewater region, floodplain settlements containing hearths, storage pits, and burials reflective of a lengthy and repeated commitment to riverine locations first appear in the James River drainage. Diagnostic ceramics of the Middle Woodland I phase include primarily sand-tempered and net-impressed Pope's Creek ware.

The Powhatan Creek Site (44JC26)

Located 3 miles (5 kilometers) southwest of Williamsburg and along a small tributary to the James, the Powhatan Creek site (44JC26) represents a rare stratified site in the Virginia Coastal Plain with evidence of stacked Middle Archaic through Middle Woodland deposits (Reinhart 1976; Malpass 1976). While archaeologists from the College of William and Mary identified no pit features at the site, evidence of two rock hearths and the remains of a possible structure were located within the stratified deposits. The evidence of a possible structure consists of a circular concentration of fire-cracked rocks, lithic artifacts, and ceramic sherds. Measuring approximately 2.5 meters in diameter, the feature encompassed a tight cluster of fire-cracked rock interpreted as the remains of a hearth (Reinhart 1976:44). This evidence occurred in the context of pebble-tempered Prince George ceramics and immediately below deposits containing shell-tempered Mockley ceramics (Malpass 1976). Although no radiocarbon assays were obtained from the site, the stratigraphic context of the structural feature suggests a Middle Woodland I date. Prince George ware is thought to be contemporaneous with Pope's Creek ware, a similar pottery lacking large pebble inclusions (Egloff and Potter 1982:103). The lack of postmold evidence limits the comparability of this structure with others in the James River Valley.

The Hampton University Sites (44HT36 and 44HT37)
Colonial Williamsburg Foundation's block excavations at two precontact sites located near the confluence of the Hampton and James rivers in the outer Coastal Plain yielded excavation data of a considerable Middle Woodland I phase component (Edwards et al. 1989). The sites appear to represent small, residential bases occupied over multiple occasions circa A.D. 1–450 (Hodges 1989). As estuarine "base camps," the sites included evidence of shellfish acquisition and the processing of mast and wild seed "crops" in addition to a diverse array of pit features indicative of food processing and storage (Hodges 1989:247–248). Although the excavators identified no architectural patterns and artifact densities at the sites were low, the range of feature types and volume of storage pits indicate that Middle Woodland settlement in the outer Coastal Plain entailed a focusing of residential settlement. A secondary burial at 44HT37 containing at least two individuals suggests that residents invested a symbolic importance in the location as well as enough time to accomplish at least part of a complex, multistage mortuary ritual. Hodges (1989:48) reasonably interprets these sites as indicative of the "intermittent establishment of long-term encampments" by small groups.

As listed in table A-2, feature 42 at 44HT36 returned an uncalibrated radiocarbon date of 1930 ± 70 B.P., which calibrates to the two-sigma range of 50 B.C.–A.D. 245. Twelve additional features present at the site contained Mockley ceramics. These features may represent multiple occupations, an interpretation suggested by the scattered feature distribution. Features at the site fell under the storage and hearth categories. The 44HT37 site included a similar array of pit features, many of which were distributed in two distinct concentrations (Hodges 1989:47). Four features clustered near feature 1003, a small, circular pit with an uncalibrated radiocarbon date of 1910 ± 80 B.P. and a two-sigma calibrated range of 50 B.C.–A.D. 261. Twenty-five meters to the south, a second cluster of three precontact pits included feature 1024 with an uncalibrated radiocarbon date of 1650 ± 80 B.P. and a two-sigma calibrated range of A.D. 234–601. Tests of radiocarbon date contemporaneity indicate that the dates are significantly different at the .05 level (F = 5.28, t = 2.30). Following the interpretation of the site's excavators (Hodges 1989:48), these feature clusters are treated as evidence of two distinct site components, the second of which dates to the Middle Woodland II phase.

Middle Woodland II (A.D. 200–900)

While survey data (e.g., Steponaitis 1987) and shell midden excavation (Waselkov 1982) lend support for the notion that a subsistence shift toward the intensive exploitation of freshwater and saltwater shellfish began as early as the Late Archaic period, excavation data reflecting a heavy reliance on this resource appear with the Middle Woodland II phase. An abrupt Middle Woodland II shift in pottery design from sand-tempered Pope's Creek ware to shell-tempered Mockley ware may signal the in-migration of new groups in the Costal Plain region, possibly the Algonquin predecessors of the Indians first encountered by European colonists. Whether the choice of shell as a ceramic tempering agent resulted solely out of its functional advantages or out of the importance of this material in subsistence and symbolic systems remains an unexplored question. Coastal Plain contexts dated to the Middle Woodland II phase in the James River Valley include components of the Hampton University sites described above, the Reynolds-Alvis site in the inner Coastal Plain, and the Great Neck site (44VB7) near the mouth of the James River.

The Reynolds-Alvis Site (44HE470)

Excavations at the inner Coastal Plain site of Reynolds-Alvis by Virginia Commonwealth University archaeologists opened a large area on a floodplain terrace of the Chickahominy River (Gleach 1986, 1987). The site produced evidence of occupations ranging from Early Archaic through Late Woodland, though radiocarbon dates suggest three prominent components dating to the Middle Woodland I, Late Woodland I, and Late Woodland II phases. The site provides evidence of changing ceramic design during the Middle and Late Woodland periods in an inner Coastal Plain location subject to influences from the Piedmont. As a result, a variety of lithic-, sand-, and shell-tempered wares occur in Reynolds-Alvis features.

Middle Woodland II features represent the most intensive occupation at Reynolds-Alvis. A cluster of pits located near two postmold patterns included features 8 and 11 with uncalibrated radiocarbon dates of 1675 ± 85 B.P. and 1615 ± 85 B.P., respectively. Tests indicate no difference at the .05 significance level between the dates ($F = 0.25, t = 0.50$), implying their contemporaneity. The two dates average to 1645 ± 60 B.P. with a two-sigma calibrated range of A.D. 254–551. Pebble-tempered Prince George ceramics appear in high frequencies in feature 8 and the adjacent feature 10, which is comprised of a pit feature surrounded by a circular pattern of 17 postmolds (Gleach 1986:175–176). At slightly more than 2 meters in diameter, the postmold pattern may represent a small domestic structure or a rack associated with a large fire pit. A second concentration of postmolds within the same cluster of pits measured approximately 3 by 1.5 meters in maximal dimensions with an elliptical shape. Two additional pit features included in the database yielded Middle Woodland II radiocarbon dates.

The Great Neck Site (44vB7)

A series of excavations at the large, multicomponent Great Neck site have produced evidence of pit features, domestic architecture, burials, midden deposits, and a palisaded village dating to the Middle Woodland II through Late Woodland II phases. Hodges's (1993) invaluable synthesis of the complex data sets produced by these excavations comprises the definitive record of late pre-contact excavation data for southeastern Virginia. The site is located 2 miles (3 kilometers) from Cape Henry in the city of Virginia Beach and is divided into several "lots" labeled according to planned residential development of the location.

Evidence of a Middle Woodland presence occurs in several areas of the Great Neck site, including a dense array of features within a single excavation unit and dispersed features in the context of domestic architectural patterns. Unit 106 at lot M3 exposed an approximately 25-square-meter block that included four hearths, three storage pits, a burial, and two unidentified shallow pits containing shell-tempered Mockley ceramics (Hodges 1993:156). Radiocarbon dates from three of the features suggest Middle Woodland II occupations, although tests of radiocarbon date contemporaneity yielded inconsistent results. Thomas's (1986:206) test returned no significant difference at the .05 level (t = 1.85), while Long and Rippeteau's (1974:249) test suggested a significant difference at the .05 level but not at the .10 level (F = 4.01). Despite this discrepancy, a mean date was calculated from the three radiocarbon assays and applied to the undated features within unit 106 in the absence of a means of distinguishing between what may be several temporally close occupations. The mean date of 1590 ± 38 B.P. calibrates to the two-sigma range of A.D. 405–591.

Southeast of lot M3, lot 11 at Great Neck yielded Middle and Late Woodland pit features, structural patterns, and a sheet midden associated with Late Woodland Townsend ceramics (Hodges 1993:218). Six features containing Mockley ceramics were identified at lot 11, including two pits identified as storage features and a hearth. Structure F, assigned to the Middle Woodland occupation, entails an elliptical postmold cluster abutted by a small, rectangular pattern of posts surrounding pit feature 185. Feature 185, which likely represents a large storage facility (Hodges 1993:248), contained Middle Woodland ceramics. Also located adjacent to a feature containing Middle Woodland ceramics, structure G was considerably smaller and more roughly defined in plan.

The Irwin Site (44PG4)

Separate excavations at the Irwin site (44PG4) by the Archaeological Society of Virginia (MacCord 1964) and by a cultural resource management firm (Johnson et al. 1989) uncovered evidence of a large, multicomponent site with Middle and Late Woodland pits. The site is located in the inner Coastal Plain along a floodplain terrace of the Appomattox River, a tributary of the James. Excavations directed by William Johnson in 1984 identified 32 features at Irwin, including midden deposits, trenches, pits, and rock hearths. Johnson et al. (1989:31) describe separate feature concentrations associated with diagnostics of a Middle Woodland II Mockley and a Late Woodland I Townsend occupation that point to considerable horizontal clustering of Irwin site activity. Five shallow pit features containing Mockley ceramics were assigned to the Middle Woodland II phase. The Middle Woodland II presence at the location appears to have been relatively brief given the low density of artifacts from Mockley features and the absence of features larger than small hearths.

Late Woodland I (A.D. 900–1200)

The outset of the Late Woodland period in Tidewater Virginia saw an increased intensity of floodplain settlement (Turner 1976) and the dispersal of small to medium-sized settlements in some areas (Potter 1982). Late Woodland I Coastal Plain groups incorporated domesticates into subsistence patterns as demonstrated by paleobotanical analysis from the Reynolds-Alvis site. Ceramic attributes changed during the Late Woodland with a shift from shell-tempered cord-marked and net-impressed ceramics (i.e., Mockley ware) to shell-tempered fabric-impressed and incised ceramics (i.e., Townsend ware). Contrasting with the Late Woodland I Piedmont in the James River Valley, quite limited excavation data comes from contemporaneous sites in the Coastal Plain. No Late Woodland I architectural data may be drawn from Coastal Plain excavations, and relatively few pit feature contexts from only two sites have been excavated.

The Irwin Site (44PG4)

A Late Woodland I component at the Irwin site containing storage features suggests the likelihood of a more intensive occupation than that represented by the Middle Woodland II features. MacCord's (1964) excavations at Irwin identified two closely spaced storage features with Townsend ceramics. These included feature 3, yielding an uncalibrated radiocarbon date of 910 ± 120 B.P., which calibrates to the two-sigma range of A.D. 890–1300. Johnson (1989) also obtained a radiocarbon date from a storage feature containing Townsend ceramics. Bell-shaped feature III returned an uncalibrated date of 1110 ± 40 B.P., which calibrates to the two-sigma range of A.D. 880–1015. Test of radiocarbon date contemporaneity between these assays produced inconsistent results, with Thomas's (1986:206) approach indicating no significant difference at the .05 level ($t = 1.58$) and Long and Rippeteau's (1974:249) approach indicating a difference at that significance level ($F = 6.94$). Given these results and the spatial separation of the two excavation areas, the two dates were not averaged in the James River database.

The Reynolds-Alvis Site (44HE470)

Feature 9 at the Reynolds-Alvis site returned an uncalibrated radiocarbon date of 1030 ± 75 B.P., which calibrates to the two-sigma range of A.D.

883–1178. Paleobotanical evidence from this Late Woodland I roasting pit included domesticated bean and cucurbit seeds in addition to large quantities of nutshell and seeds of open-field plants (Gleach 1987:174). This feature provides the earliest evidence of horticulture from a sealed feature context in the James River Coastal Plain and suggests floodplain clearance practices related to horticulture. The pit contained ceramics with sand and crushed lithic temper associated with contemporary sites in the Piedmont rather than shell-tempered Mockley or Townsend wares common to the Tidewater region.

Thus the earliest appearance of domesticates in the Coastal Plain occurs in association with ceramics common to the Piedmont, implying that food production was introduced into the Coastal Plain from the interior. The presence of identical ceramic attributes on either side of the fall line highlights the dynamic and permeable nature of this boundary during the Middle and Late Woodland periods. Apparently, groups and ceramic stylistic innovations frequently moved between the Piedmont and Coastal Plain during these periods, providing the material correlates to a scenario whereby Indians from the Piedmont brought horticulture to the inner Coastal Plain. An additional feature at Reynolds-Alvis, feature 2, returned a radiocarbon date of 630 ± 100 B.P., which calibrates to the two-sigma range of A.D. 1225–1449.

Late Woodland II (A.D. 1200–1500)

The Late Woodland II phase in the Virginia Coastal Plain saw the appearance of large, palisaded village sites on the floodplains of major rivers (Turner 1992). Ceramic type distributions became increasingly localized during the Late Woodland period in the Coastal Plain, when Townsend ware no longer dominated the coastal region and four distinct types appeared from the Potomac to the James River drainages (Turner 1993:84). By the end of the Late Woodland II phase in the James River Coastal Plain, simple-stamped Gaston ceramics tempered with sand and crushed quartz dominated the inner Coastal Plain, while shell-tempered simple-stamped Roanoke ceramics occurred in the outer Coastal Plain. Ossuary burial became common during these centuries as well (Boyd and Boyd 1992).

The Newington Site (44KQ6)

Located 12 miles (20 kilometers) north of the James River drainage along the Mattaponi River, the Newington site (44KQ6) was excavated in 1966 by avocational archaeologist R. Westwood Winfree (1969). His report provides a detailed account of the excavations, including feature contents and morphologies and an artifact analysis based on an understanding of Late Woodland material culture that was current during the 1960s. My reanalysis of this material allowed refinement of the site's chronology, indicating that a Townsend component produced a substantial record of pit features and postmold patterns. No radiocarbon dates were obtained from the site.

Winfree's block excavations recovered material from stratified deposits and 22 pit features. As depicted in figure A-20, postmold patterns occur in the context of 10 pit features containing Townsend ceramics. Application of Klein's (1994:321) equation for dating Coastal Plain features returned dates ranging from 770 to 550 B.P. (A.D. 1180–1400), with an uncalibrated mean date of 664 ± 84 B.P. (A.D. 1286 ± 84) for the site's Townsend features. Rim sherds from several of the Townsend features fell into the Rappahannock incised varieties described by Griffith (1980:29–33) and dated to the early portion of the Late Woodland II phase, providing independent support for the temporal assignment of Newington site features. In the absence of more precise chronological data from Newington, the Townsend features were assigned the mean date computed using Klein's (1994) equation, which has a two-sigma calibrated range of A.D. 1224–1432 and a calibration curve intercept at A.D. 1301.

Pit features with Townsend ceramics fell into two general categories: deep, straight-sided features and relatively shallow pit features with fire-cracked rock and charcoal. The former appear to represent storage features and the latter hearths. Within area B at Newington, Winfree (1969:222) noted evidence of a possible structure in the form of an elliptical postmold pattern measuring approximately 5 by 3.5 meters. Feature VIII, interpreted as a storage pit, appears within the postmold pattern in what appears as the northern end of a domestic structure.

The Carter's Grove Museum Site (44JC118)

As part of a project to mitigate the impact of museum construction at Carter's Grove Plantation near Williamsburg, the Colonial Williamsburg Foundation conducted excavations along the James River floodplain that identified Middle and Late Woodland components (Muraca 1989). In addition to shallow features lacking diagnostic artifacts, the excavators identified one particularly large oval-shaped pit (Muraca 1989:17–19). The pit measured 1.75 meters in diameter, had sloping walls to a depth of 42 centimeters, and had a flat bottom lined with fire-cracked rocks. Excavators recovered charred remains

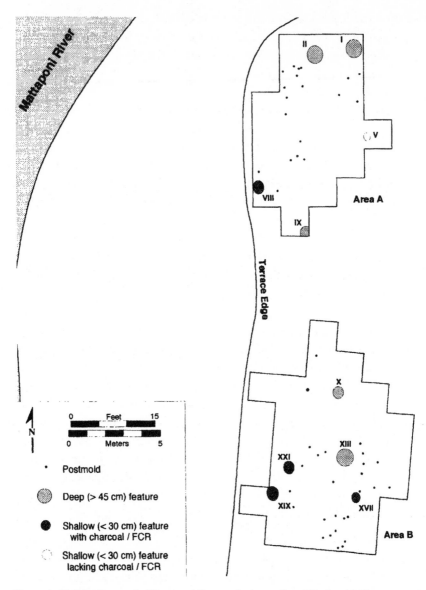

Figure A-20. Newington site Townsend features (redrawn from Winfree 1969)

of animal bones and oyster shell from the feature in addition to shell-tempered ceramics. Two uncalibrated radiocarbon dates obtained from the feature (table A-2) did not differ significantly (F = 1.61, t = 1.14). The dates produce the mean uncalibrated date of 618 ± 55 B.P. with a two-sigma calibrated range of A.D. 1285–1428. The feature appears to represent a sizeable roasting pit.

The Great Neck Site (44VB7)

Three distinct areas within the Great Neck site yielded evidence of Late Woodland II components containing a palisade, domestic architecture, and a variety of pit features associated with Roanoke simple-stamped ceramics. Excavation area B within lot 16 included postmold patterns suggesting an elliptical structure, with burials of an infant and an adolescent located beneath opposite walls of the structure (Hodges 1993:86). One of the burials, feature 29, returned a radiocarbon date of 620 ± 80 B.P., which calibrates to the two-sigma range of A.D. 1270–1441. Three additional pit features occurred in the vicinity of the structure and contained ceramics similar to those found in the burial. These features were dated with reference to the feature 29 radiocarbon assay.

At lot 11 excavators identified Late Woodland II deposits amid the Middle Woodland features described previously. Roasting pit feature 163, containing shell-tempered simple-stamped ceramics, returned a radiocarbon date of 440 ± 50 B.P., a date with a two-sigma calibrated range of A.D. 1409–1627. Evidence of two domestic structures occurred in the context of shell-tempered simple-stamped ceramics, suggesting a Late Woodland II date roughly contemporaneous with the dated feature. One burial near the west wall of structure D, a subadult approximately six to eight years of age, contained the same diagnostic ceramics. These features were dated with reference to the feature 163 assay.

Lot 16 area A excavations identified the southwest portion of a palisaded Native American settlement. Two lines of postmolds suggest the presence of multiple palisades at the site, with two primary interments located immediately within the outer palisade. If the outer line of posts was circular, a 30-meter-diameter palisade would have existed (Hodges 1993:67–68). Three copper ornaments accompanied one of the burials, an adult female. The second burial, an adult male, contained a tubular clay smoking pipe and a rolled copper tube bead. An ossuary containing Roanoke simple-stamped ceramics occurred immediately outside of the palisade. Although not fully excavated, structure A provides evidence of a particularly large, elliptical building within the palisade measuring 6.3 meters in width and at least 12.2 meters in length. Hodges (1993:264) suggested that the palisaded settlement at Great Neck and the lot 11 features were likely contemporaneous based on their ceramics and structural arrangements, an interpretation followed here.

The Great Neck site's Late Woodland II remains provide some of the clearest evidence for the emergence of marked social differentiation in the late precontact James River Valley (Hodges 1993:264). Primary and secondary burials occurred at the site, with primary burials located either adjacent to a palisade or a domestic structure. Male and a female adults were buried next to the palisade, while burial features beneath house floors all contained subadults. The copper items placed with the two primary interments located within the palisade suggest the presence of high-status burials. The secondary ossuary interments reflect mortuary practices involving mass burial that differed considerably from those that produced the burial features near the palisade. The three categories of burial at Great Neck—primary adult burial next to the palisade, primary subadult burial beneath houses, and secondary ossuary interment—do not necessarily correlate neatly or simply with a tripartite social hierarchy (cf. Hodges 1993:264). Nonetheless, the appearance of varying burial forms during the terminal Late Woodland does imply the expression and ritual enactment of important distinctions and a rather heterogeneous social context.

Protohistoric (A.D. 1500–1607) and Contact (A.D. 1607–1650) Periods
During the Protohistoric and Contact periods, the James River Coastal Plain witnessed some of the earliest contact between Europeans and Native Americans north of Florida. Native American pottery throughout the James River Coastal Plain at that time was predominantly simple stamped, with sand-tempered Gaston ware in the inner Coastal Plain and shell-tempered Roanoke ware in the outer Coastal Plain. A limited number of sites have been excavated in Virginia that have securely dated feature contexts within the Protohistoric or Contact period. As Hodges (1993:24) has pointed out, not all Protohistoric or Contact period settlements necessarily contained European trade goods.

Jordan's Journey (44PG302, 44PG307) and Jordan's Point (44PG300) Sites
Multiple excavations in the vicinity of Jordan's Point, a small prominence reaching into a bay formed by the confluence of the James and Appomattox rivers, have identified Native American and European colonial set-

tlements from the sixteenth and seventeenth centuries (e.g., Mouer et al. 1992; McLearan and Mouer 1994; Morgan et al. 1995). Virginia Commonwealth University's large-scale excavations at the Jordan's Journey sites (44PG302 and 44PG307) documented an early-seventeenth-century English settlement superimposed on a dispersed, Protohistoric Native American settlement. Jordan's Journey graphically records the early-seventeenth-century English strategy of establishing plantations in the same prime agricultural land that previously had been cleared and farmed by Native Americans (Turner 1993:87). The settlement at Jordan's Point, likely a Weyanoke village, consisted of houses, pit features, and burials spread around Jordan's Point beyond the boundaries of several numbered archaeological sites. The sites yielded evidence of well-defined domestic structures, 28 of which are included in the James River database. The structures vary widely, although most are elliptical in plan and lack evidence of associated storage pits, burials, or other subsurface features. This patterning suggests the likelihood that storage had been relocated to above-ground facilities.

No radiocarbon dates are available from the sites, yet the predominance of Gaston simple-stamped ceramics, the lack of European trade goods, and the spatial correlation of the Native American settlement with the early-seventeenth-century English one suggest that the Weyanoke village has a sixteenth-century date and precedes Jamestown colony (Mouer et al. 1992:161).

The Paspahegh Site (44JC308)

Large-scale excavations at the Paspahegh site, located along the Chickahominy River near its confluence with the James, uncovered extensive evidence of a Paspahegh village dating to the early years of the Jamestown colony (Lucketti et al. 1994). The Paspaheghs and their settlement at 44JC308 offer some of the best archaeological evidence of a group under Powhatan's influence living in close proximity to Jamestown. Located 6 miles (10 kilometers) upstream from Jamestown, the Paspaheghs at the site interacted intensively with English colonists, as recorded in the written history and in the presence of European copper artifacts in burial contexts. Radiocarbon dates, the predominance of Roanoke simple-stamped ceramics, and the general absence of artifacts diagnostic of earlier periods indicate that Paspahegh's archaeological deposits date almost exclusively to the early Contact period (Lucketti et al. 1994:183).

Excavators identified evidence of 48 structures across the site. With the exception of 25 burials, the site lacked pit features dating to the Contact period settlement. Two of the largest structures at the site contained internal partitions conforming to ethnohistorical descriptions of chiefs' houses (Luck-etti et al. 1994:307). In addition, the varied mortuary patterning at the site suggests the expression of social differentiation not unlike that witnessed in the context of the fifteenth-century palisaded Great Neck settlement. Cop-per grave goods were included with 3 of the 21 excavated burial features, prompting the excavators to suggest that the site's mortuary rituals expressed different levels of social ranking.

Floodplain Archaeology of the Woodland Period James River Ridge and Valley

The late precontact archaeology of the Ridge and Valley province in the vicinity of the James River's headwaters reflects an overall trajectory simi-lar to those identified in the Piedmont and Coastal Plain. During the Late Woodland period, the addition of domesticates to a riverine-focused set-tlement pattern resulted in the dispersal of hamlet-sized settlements on the floodplains of major rivers (Walker and Miller 1992). A Late Woodland II proliferation of large, nucleated, and sometimes palisaded villages suggests altered social dynamics during the final precontact centuries. The Ridge and Valley province's culture history differs in a number of important ways from areas east of the Blue Ridge as well. Mound burial appears somewhat earlier in the Ridge and Valley than it does in the Piedmont, beginning during the Late Woodland I phase and ending sometime during the final precon-tact centuries. Ceramic traditions reflecting northern and western influences differ from the Chesapeake-focused traditions of the James River Piedmont and Coastal Plain. The high frequency of palisaded village sites identified in Virginia's Ridge and Valley may be the result of the region's location at the hub of a disparate range of social interaction and cultural influences. Researchers have produced overviews of the archaeology in the vicinity of the James River's Ridge and Valley headwaters (e.g., Walker and Miller 1992; Egloff 1992; Gardner 1986), yet no detailed study of the region's rich culture history has been undertaken.

Middle Woodland II (A.D. 200–900)

At least two prominent cultural changes distinguish the Middle Woodland I phase from the Middle Woodland II phase in the Ridge and Valley. The stone burial mounds found in the Shenandoah and Potomac river basins during the Middle Woodland I phase disappeared by A.D. 200, implying a collapse of a "big man sphere" (Blanton 1992:82) of exchange and elite interaction centered to the west and north. Second, a shift in ceramic surface treatment from net impression to fabric impression occurred, resulting in the quartz-tempered Albemarle fabric-impressed type.

The Cement Plant Site (44AU51)

The Cement Plant site (44AU51) is located 15 miles (24 kilometers) north of the James River drainage, near the Shenandoah River headwaters. Archaeological Society of Virginia members identified a dense scatter of postmolds and 14 shallow features in block excavations at the site (Valliere and Harter 1986). Plow zone deposits contained primarily Albemarle ceramics, and a small number of Albemarle sherds were recovered from feature contexts. As listed in table A-3, feature 10 returned a radiocarbon date of 1340 ± 60 B.P. (uncalibrated) with a two-sigma calibrated range of A.D. 615–790.

Late Woodland I (A.D. 900–1200)

Late Woodland survey data from Virginia's Ridge and Valley province indicate an expansion of settlement onto floodplain levees with the best agricultural soils (Gardner 1986:77) as occurred in the Piedmont and Coastal Plain, although in some areas survey data suggest that a rising population made use of all environmental zones (Egloff 1992:211). Radiocarbon dates from accretional burial mounds in the region record mound burial practices that commenced during Late Woodland I centuries, practices subsumed by MacCord (1986) under the "Lewis Creek Mound Culture." Ceramics in the Late Woodland Ridge and Valley suggest a complex blending of traditions and influences. Early in the Late Woodland I phase Albemarle ceramics predominated, followed by the incorporation of limestone-tempered Page (or Radford) ceramics.

The Cement Plant Site (44AU51)

Feature 1 at the Cement Plant site contained Albemarle ceramics and returned a date of 1030 ± 60 B.P. (uncalibrated). This date differs significantly from the earlier dated Cement Plant feature at the .05 level (F = 16.84, t = 4.96) and calibrates to the two-sigma range of A.D. 892–1160. Following the excavators' interpretation (Valliere and Harter 1986:90), other pits and postmold patterns at the site were assigned this date. From the proliferation of postmolds at the site, Valliere and Harter (1986) identified 12 possible patterns. Nine well-identified and relatively complete circular or elliptical

patterns were included in the James River database. The overlapping distribution of structural patterns at the site point to multiple occupations of the
location. Low artifact densities in feature contexts and an overall absence of
large, deep pits suggest that the Cement Plant site saw only brief settlement.

The Huffman Site (44BA5)

Located along the Jackson River, the Huffman site (44BA5) is one of several
large floodplain sites near the James River headwaters excavated by James
Madison University archaeologists in conjunction with the construction of
Gathright Dam (Geier and Warren 1982a). Prior to these excavations, Archaeological Society of Virginia members conducted fieldwork at the site
(L. Johnson 1982). Together, these excavations exposed a substantial Late
Woodland settlement with domestic architecture, associated clusters of pit
features, and several burials. Paleobotanical analysis identified maize and beans
in four storage pits (Geier and Warren 1982a:138). The abundance of wild
plant remains accompanying these cultigens points to the pursuit of a mixed
subsistence economy.

Eighty-two of Huffman's features that contained predominantly Page
cord-marked ceramics were included in the data set. While the excavators
interpret the spatial patterning at the site as indicative of a single settlement,
four radiocarbon dates from the sites ranged from 1065 ± 65 B.P. (uncalibrated) to 730 ± 65 B.P. (uncalibrated), implying multiple Late Woodland I
occupations (Geier and Warren 1982a:122). For my database, Huffman features containing Page cord-marked ceramics that lacked radiocarbon assays
were assigned the composite mean of the radiocarbon dates from the site,
867 ± 34 B.P., which has a two-sigma calibrated range of A.D. 1047–1258.
While this method of dating the Huffman site's features introduces some
imprecision, the radiocarbon assays and diagnostic ceramics do provide solid
evidence for settlement circa A.D. 1050–1250.

James Madison University's excavations uncovered two clearly defined
circular postmold patterns at Huffman in association with storage pits. House
2 contained evidence of two internal storage pits in addition to external
features. This pattern may indicate that Ridge and Valley groups had begun to
shift storage pits to internal locations by the end of the Late Woodland I phase,
as did groups to the east. Twenty primary interments at the site offer evidence
that mortuary practices in the region did not always entail mound burial. The
burials contained no associated grave goods. The Archeological Society of

Virginia's excavations at the site identified a similar range of features amid a dense scatter of approximately 450 postmolds. Larry Johnson (1982:40) proposed that an arc of postmolds at the site reflected a palisade with a diameter of approximately 30 meters based on the exposed section.

Late Woodland II (A.D. 1200–1500)

The Late Woodland II establishment of large floodplain villages was accompanied by changes in the distribution of ceramic wares. Although frequently associated with the Protohistoric and Contact periods in the northern Ridge and Valley (Walker and Miller 1992:173), palisade construction appeared during the Late Woodland II phase within at least one settlement in the James River headwaters (Whyte and Thompson 1989) and within a number of settlements from southwest Virginia (Egloff 1992:207). Albemarle ceramics declined in use in the Ridge and Valley province during these centuries, to be replaced in much of the region by limestone-tempered pottery. Sand-tempered net-impressed Dan River ceramics occurred at the Late Woodland II Bessemer site (44BO26) described below, suggesting the movement of groups from the Roanoke River drainage into the James River headwater region. As indicated by radiocarbon dating of mound contexts (MacCord 1986:4), mound burial continued into Late Woodland II centuries in the Ridge and Valley, contemporary with its appearance in the Piedmont.

The 44WR300 Site

Included in this study due to its well-preserved evidence of household organization, 44WR300, or the "Areas 2/3" site, is located along the floodplain of the South Fork of the Shenandoah River (Snyder and Fehr 1984). The Thunderbird Research Corporation's large-scale machine stripping of the site produced evidence of two domestic structures, pit features, and several burials. Albemarle and Page cord-marked ceramics were recovered, with the former in dominant frequencies. Uncalibrated radiocarbon dates from the site ranged from 1030 ± 100 B.P. to 630 ± 50 B.P. Despite the wide temporal distribution of these dates, the excavators argue rather convincingly that the uniformity of the ceramic complex and the spatial coherence of the feature layout support the interpretation that most features derive from a single component (Snyder and Fehr 1984:225). The site's radiocarbon assays produced a mean radiocarbon date of 769 ± 28 B.P. with a calibrated two-sigma range of A.D. 1226–1291.

The architectural patterns at 44wr300 appeared in the context of a group of spatially proximate pit features that appear to form household clusters. Three interior features occurred within both structures, and storage pits were located immediately outside of each house. A variety of mortuary practices are suggested by the five burial features that were recorded. A large pit contained the disarticulated bones of one individual, the articulated bones of a second, and two bundle burials. The bundle burials were accompanied by two pipes, a beaver incisor, and two flaked tools.

Not unlike at the Huffman site dated to roughly the same era, the 44wr300 excavations produced evidence of horticultural settlement with a dense array of pits in close proximity to domestic structures. Community patterning at the two sites entails small settlements comprised of several houses situated on the floodplain (Snyder and Fehr 1984:i).

The Noah's Ark Site (44ba15)

James Madison University archaeologists also excavated the Noah's Ark site (44ba15) to mitigate the impact of the Gathright Dam construction (Geier and Warren 1982b). Located on the Jackson River upstream from Huffman, the site produced four burials and evidence of two circular structures associated with hearths and storage pits. Ceramics from the site were predominantly limestone tempered. Excluding one date with a high error factor interpreted by the excavators as anomalous (Geier and Warren 1982b:141), the remaining four uncalibrated radiocarbon dates cluster tightly between 700 ± 85 B.P. and 645 ± 80 B.P. Tests of contemporaneity indicate no significant difference between these dates at the .05 level (F = 0.29, t = 0.47). Geier and Warren (1982b:141) suggest that the Noah's Ark site reflects a number of hamletlike reoccupations over a brief period of time. A mean date of 678 ± 37 B.P. resulted from the Noah's Ark site's radiocarbon dates, a date with a calibrated two-sigma range of A.D. 1279–1395.

Excavations identified four spatially distinct activity areas containing postmolds, pits, and artifact concentrations that may reflect the presence of a small number of households at the site (Geier and Warren 1982b:143). Two postmold patterns interpreted as house patterns surrounded interior storage features, while no storage features occurred around the exterior areas of these houses. The four burials occurred in shallow pits with two flexed skeletons and one bundle burial identifiable. No accompanying grave goods were recovered. The site resembles Huffman and 44wr300 in its size and household cluster arrangements, although the consistent location of storage features in house interiors does provide evidence of altered household organization.

The Bessemer Site (44B026)

Located on the floodplain at the confluence of the James River and Craig Creek, the Bessemer site includes evidence of two distinct but spatially overlapping cultural components: a palisaded village with Dan River ceramics and a second occupation marked by Page ceramics. Two separate excavations conducted by James Madison University archaeologists identified domestic architecture, pit features, burials, and midden deposits (Whyte and Thompson 1989; Geier and Moldenhauer 1977). Radiocarbon assays from these contexts place both occupations during the fourteenth century, with the Page component immediately following the Dan River occupation (Whyte and Thompson 1989:ii). Excluding two radiocarbon assays that returned anomalous dates (Whyte and Thompson 1989:145), the uncalibrated mean date for features associated with the Dan River occupation is 648 ± 27 B.P. (A.D. 1302 ± 27), which has a two-sigma calibrated range of A.D. 1291–1398. The uncalibrated mean date for Page features is 608 ± 23 B.P. (A.D. 1342 ± 23), which calibrates to the two-sigma range of A.D. 1303–1406.

The first excavations at Bessemer uncovered evidence of an elliptical structure measuring approximately 15 by 6 meters in plan and associated with Dan River ceramics (Geier and Moldenhauer 1977:17). This unusually long structure contained evidence of interior partitions and was located within the palisade in an area otherwise devoid of architectural evidence. Thompson (1989:34) raises the possibility that the structure represents communal, nondomestic architecture. One other postmold pattern associated with the Dan River occupation also had an elliptical floor plan but with considerably smaller dimensions.

The second set of Bessemer excavations uncovered evidence that the Dan River settlement was surrounded by an elliptical or D-shaped palisade encompassing an area of approximately 20,700 square meters (Whyte and Thompson 1989:289). Two Dan River burials, both primary interments lacking grave items, appear to have been placed close to the palisade. Paleobotanical analysis of Dan River features identified substantial evidence of maize horticulture in addition to botanical evidence of occupations during the spring, summer, and fall. Excavations of features dating to the Page occupation of the site identified two structures with circular floor plans, each considerably smaller than the Dan River structure 1. A cluster of pit features surrounded both structures. Page component features also contained evidence of maize horticulture. The seven burials associated with the Page occupation were all primary interments, two with grave goods. Red ocher and black bear canine teeth were placed with one burial, and a second burial was associated with a triangular projectile point and three pieces of galena (Thompson 1989:65, 68).

The Bessemer site illustrates that Late Woodland II social interaction in the Ridge and Valley included population replacement by culturally distinct groups and, assuming that the palisade served as a fortification, intergroup hostilities. The palisaded Dan River settlement, exhibiting cultural links to the Roanoke River Piedmont, was followed by a settlement lacking a palisade and marked by limestone-tempered Page ceramics.

Protohistoric (A.D. 1500–1607) and Contact (A.D. 1607–1650) Periods
Palisaded settlements became prominent fixtures on the Ridge and Valley floodplain landscape after A.D. 1500. The Perkins Point (44BA3) and Beaver Pond (44BA39) sites provide evidence of this development in the James River drainage. From a broader perspective, a striking proliferation of settlements surrounded by some form of stockade is apparent throughout the Virginia Ridge and Valley after A.D. 1500. Palisaded settlements located along the Shenandoah River that have been subject to excavations include Miley (44SH2) (MacCord and Rodgers 1966), Cabin Run (44WR3) (Snyder and Fehr 1984), and Quicksburg (44SH3) (MacCord 1973). In the Roanoke River drainage, the palisaded Thomas Sawyer site (44RN39) has returned radiocarbon dates straddling the sixteenth and early seventeenth centuries (Barber 1988). Survey data (e.g., Custer 1980; Hoffman and Foss 1980) indicate that settlement away from floodplain terraces decreased in frequency and became more transient during this time. Ridge and Valley residents introduced shell-tempered Keyser ceramics into the Shenandoah River area during this period. These ceramics appear alongside limestone-tempered pottery at the Perkins Point site considered below.

The Perkins Point Site (44BA3)
Excavations at the Perkins Point site by Archaeological Society of Virginia members (MacCord 1982) and later by James Madison University archaeologists involved with Gathright Dam mitigation (Whyte and Geier 1982) identified an oval palisaded settlement measuring approximately 135 by 90 meters. Although differential preservation of postmolds limited evidence of

architectural patterning at the site, structural patterns, burials, and pit features were identified within the palisade. Three radiocarbon dates (listed in table A-3) did not differ significantly at the .05 level (F = 1.49, t = 0.87). The average of these dates, 392 ± 37 B.P., calibrates to the two-sigma range of A.D. 1438–1635, not a particularly useful result in deciding whether to assign the occupation to the Late Woodland II phase, the Protohistoric period, or the Contact period. Glass beads occurred within features 62 and 69, which returned the earliest radiocarbon dates. Citing the beads as the sole evidence of European contact, Whyte and Geier (1982:113) favor placing the site in the Protohistoric period, an interpretation followed here. Ceramics from the site included a mix of limestone-tempered and shell-tempered Keyser series ceramics.

A structure with an elliptical floor plan measuring approximately 15 by 6 meters and an internal partition at Perkins Point suggests parallels with the large Dan River house at Bessemer. Storage pits occurred in association with the remaining postmold patterns, which were predominantly circular in plan. Information concerning 11 house patterns and more than 100 pit features was obtained from the Perkins Point site, including examples of storage, roasting, and hearth pits.

The Beaver Pond Site (44BA39)
Located 550 meters upstream from the Perkins Point site, the Beaver Pond site is another palisaded site on the Jackson River that appears to date to the Protohistoric period (Geier and Dutt 1978). The absence of radiocarbon dates from the site makes temporal placement difficult. Affinities between Perkins Point and Beaver Pond in settlement organization and in ceramics led Walker and Miller (1992:180) to suggest a Protohistoric date of circa A.D. 1600 for the latter site, an interpretation followed here. Most of the ceramics were limestone tempered.

The site is remarkable for its unusually shaped palisade and low artifact density. The palisade matched the shape of the triangular terrace landform. Excavators recovered fewer than 100 ceramic sherds in the context of 11 structural patterns and 25 pit features. The domestic architectural patterns, all circular in plan, generally lacked evidence of rebuilding or associated pit features. With maximal dimensions of 120 meters north-south and 65 meters east-west, the site exhibited a particularly low number of pit features.

Calculation of Residential
Stability and Use-Duration Indices

Site No.	Date A.D.	Feature Richness	Lithic Evenness	Mean House Floor Area	Mean Post Diameter	Mean No. Structure Wall Posts	Mean No. Interior Features
44jc26	0	1	0.18	4.69	—	—	1.00
44ht36	75	2	0.04	—	—	—	—
44ht37	100	2	0.00	—	—	—	—
44he470	400	3	0.25	3.27	0.10	15.00	0.50
44vb7	400	3	0.00	—	—	—	—
44vb7	400	2	0.00	9.59	0.09	29.00	0.50
44ht37	425	1	0.00	—	—	—	—
44pg4	650	1	0.00	—	—	—	—
44fv134	675	3	0.22	—	—	—	—
44ne143	900	2	0.19	—	—	—	—
44pg4	975	3	0.00	—	—	—	—
44ne4	1025	3	0.22	14.23	—	44.00	0.00
44au51	1025	1	0.01	8.57	0.08	19.00	0.50
44ah193	1125	4	0.19	—	—	—	—
44pg4	1150	1	0.00	—	—	—	—
44fv134	1175	3	0.20	—	—	—	—
44ne143	1175	4	0.06	16.98	0.11	33.60	0.60
44ba5	1200	4	0.15	58.86	0.10	52.50	3.00
44ah193	1250	4	0.18	—	—	—	—
44hr1	1250	3	0.34	—	0.11	47.00	1.75
44go30	1275	3	0.04	16.85	—	42.00	2.00
44wr300	1275	4	0.13	29.22	—	20.00	3.00
44kq6	1300	2	0.25	13.74	0.07	22.00	1.00
44ba15	1300	4	0.21	37.85	0.11	31.00	3.50
44bo26	1325	5	0.16	50.05	0.09	172.00	0.00
44vb7	1350	2	—	27.92	0.09	52.00	1.00
44bo26	1350	5	—	33.17	0.12	60.00	1.00
44hr1	1425	4	0.49	20.15	0.10	37.00	3.00
44vb7	1450	4	—	76.66	0.11	38.00	3.00
44vb7	1450	3	—	58.38	—	109.00	1.50
44pg302	1550	2	0.00	24.37	0.08	40.38	0.13
44go30	1575	4	0.63	—	0.13	—	—
44ba3	1600	5	0.24	26.61	0.10	48.33	0.54
44ba39	1600	3	0.37	28.22	0.13	47.00	0.56
44jc308	1610	3	0.34	18.59	0.06	36.06	0.00

Mean Pit Volume	Feature Density	Postmold Density	Burial Density	Artifact Density	Burial to House Ratio	Residential Stability	Use Duration
0.00	3.13	—	0.00	—	0.00	0.26	0.39
0.20	1.41	—	0.00	101.30	0.00	0.36	0.27
0.03	2.00	—	0.50	103.53	0.00	0.17	0.45
0.26	1.20	22.80	0.00	108.71	0.00	0.40	0.27
0.28	27.27	48.48	3.03	265.28	—	0.43	0.83
0.16	2.07	67.93	0.00	132.14	0.00	0.27	0.45
0.15	2.00	—	0.00	27.31	0.00	0.20	0.28
0.01	5.62	—	0.00	912.67	0.00	0.10	0.60
0.29	1.60	—	0.00	197.45	0.00	0.63	0.38
0.14	1.07	8.55	0.00	184.18	0.00	0.40	0.28
0.39	5.62	—	0.00	54.21	0.00	0.49	0.39
0.07	3.33	43.79	0.00	223.13	0.00	0.40	0.47
0.01	16.75	261.96	0.00	37.97	0.00	0.15	0.53
0.31	1.39	—	0.00	161.80	0.00	0.69	0.32
0.73	4.30	—	0.00	84.93	0.00	0.41	0.38
0.34	1.60	—	0.00	398.61	0.00	0.63	0.45
0.11	5.65	44.89	0.00	319.51	0.00	0.46	0.56
0.16	3.27	31.90	0.60	225.11	2.50	0.70	0.65
0.45	1.42	—	—	103.89	0.00	0.74	0.30
0.69	3.34	54.94	1.67	118.52	4.00	0.75	0.71
0.27	8.00	72.00	—	33.65	0.00	0.51	0.51
0.22	4.43	14.77	0.57	280.97	2.50	0.58	0.68
0.13	7.83	36.01	0.00	523.84	0.00	0.35	0.55
0.12	2.27	11.96	0.17	235.11	2.00	0.64	0.57
0.16	1.78	30.19	0.15	539.55	0.67	0.58	0.59
0.05	4.24	215.25	1.69	435.79	2.00	0.44	0.85
0.44	1.59	6.08	0.40	—	3.50	0.82	0.51
0.54	8.70	412.96	0.00	75.75	0.00	0.71	0.54
0.43	1.54	215.90	1.03	166.44	1.00	0.80	0.67
0.23	1.03	110.69	0.34	—	0.50	0.71	0.56
0.34	0.10	7.93	0.13	127.94	0.56	0.37	0.36
0.06	5.00	37.50	1.67	249.39	—	0.73	0.70
0.22	1.76	58.81	0.20	214.27	2.60	0.61	0.64
0.07	0.51	97.60	0.83	—	0.00	0.61	0.36
0.36	0.07	40.73	0.00	91.19	0.52	0.45	0.44

Calculation of Households per Settlement from Feature Sherd Frequencies

Site	Occupation Date A.D.	Feature Sherds	Residential Stability	Use Duration	Portion of Settlement Excavated	Portion of Feature Remaining
44JC26	1	397	0.26	0.39	1.00	1.00
44HT36	75	189	0.36	0.27	1.00	0.75
44HT37	100	23	0.17	0.45	—	0.75
44HE470	400	89	0.40	0.27	0.25	0.75
44VB7	400	892	0.43	0.83	0.75	0.75
44VB7	400	101	0.27	0.45	0.25	0.75
44HT37	425	11	0.20	0.28	—	0.75
44PG4	650	29	0.10	0.60	0.25	0.75
44FV134	675	213	0.63	0.38	0.25	0.75
44NE143	900	40	0.40	0.28	0.15	0.75
44PG4	975	39	0.49	0.39	—	—
44NE4	1025	29	0.40	0.47	0.10	0.75
44AU51	1025	4	0.15	0.53	—	0.75
44AH193	1125	1,054	0.69	0.32	1.00	0.75
44PG4	1150	124	0.41	0.38	—	0.75
44FV134	1175	308	0.63	0.45	0.50	0.75
44NE143	1175	161	0.46	0.56	0.15	0.75
44BA5	1200	3,208	0.70	0.65	1.00	0.75
44AH193	1250	639	0.74	0.30	0.50	0.75
44HR1	1250	1,970	0.75	0.71	—	0.75
44GO30B	1275	62	0.51	0.51	—	0.75
44WR300	1275	2,148	0.58	0.68	0.80	0.75
44KQ6	1300	507	0.35	0.55	0.25	0.75
44BA15	1300	1,086	0.64	0.57	0.60	0.75
44BO26	1325	393	0.58	0.59	0.10	0.75
44VB7	1350	35	0.44	0.85	—	0.75
44BO26	1350	1,141	0.82	0.51	0.25	0.75
44HR1	1425	483	0.71	0.54	—	0.75
44VB7	1450	123	0.80	0.67	—	0.75
44VB7	1450	234	0.71	0.56	—	0.75
44PG302	1550	227	0.37	0.36	0.70	—
44GO30	1575	44	0.73	0.70	0.02	0.75
44BA3	1600	1,843	0.61	0.64	0.75	0.75
44BA39	1600	76	0.61	0.36	—	0.75
44JC308	1610	1,077	0.45	0.44	0.50	0.75
31OR231	1701	7,787	0.81	0.86	1.00	0.75

Est. Portion of Sherds Disposed in Features	Total Disposal Assemblage	Households per Settlement
0.75	529	3.283
0.75	336	12.174
0.75	—	—
0.75	633	3.686
0.75	2,114	3.726
0.75	718	3.718
0.75	—	—
0.75	206	2.162
0.75	1,515	3.979
0.75	474	2.662
0.75	—	—
0.75	516	1.725
0.75	—	—
0.75	1,874	5.338
0.75	—	—
0.75	1,095	2.430
0.75	1,908	4.659
0.75	5,703	7.884
0.75	2,272	6.437
0.75	7,004	—
0.75	—	—
0.75	4,773	7.612
0.75	3,605	11.780
0.75	3,218	5.548
0.75	6,987	12.842
0.75	—	—
0.75	8,114	12.203
0.75	3,435	—
0.75	—	—
0.75	—	—
0.75	—	—
0.75	3,911	4.814
0.75	4,369	7.038
0.75	—	—
0.75	3,829	12.164
0.75	13,844	12.500

Notes

Preface

1. While there is currently some dispute over the use of the labels "Indian" and "Native American," neither term conveys the diversity of practices and experiences among the original inhabitants of the Americas. I have opted to follow the common practice among descendants of Virginia's Native community who use the term "Indian" in self-reference.

3. Archaeological Approaches

1. Sahlins's (1963) "man of renown" and Strathern's (1969) financier serve as inspiration for the network/exclusionary model, as do the dynamics of prestige-good exchange systems (e.g., Friedman and Rowlands 1978) and "wealth finance" (D'Altroy and Earle 1985).

2. Sahlins's (1963) "center man" and Strathern's (1969) home producer flesh out the corporate strategy in that a broad coalition of followers is generated through economic relations focused on a localized setting.

3. The network and corporate distinction describes a political axis similar to the one highlighted in Renfrew's (1974) contrast between "group-oriented" and "individualizing" chiefdoms in third millennium Europe. The group-oriented chiefdoms produced monumental architecture that defined spaces devoted to communal ritual and mass interments with few associated grave goods (Renfrew 1974:74–79). Contrasting the "faceless and anonymous" remains of group-oriented chiefdoms, the archaeology of individualizing chiefdoms in Europe reflected the aggrandizement of leaders in the form of impressive tombs filed with wealth items. These mortuary patterns and the remains of fortified settlements suggest that individualizing chiefdoms produced a political arena of competition, warfare, personal wealth, and prestige-good exchange (Blanton et al. 1996:6).

4. The probabilistic nature of radiocarbon dating and absolute seriation permits comparison of feature dates. Those dates that appear on statistical and archaeological grounds to be contemporaneous may be combined. I applied Long and Rippeteau's (1974:206) and Thomas's (1986:249) modified t tests to radiocarbon assays in order to evaluate whether the dated contexts represented a single "instant" in time or if differences between assays indicated the probability of distinct time periods. Even when the features contain identical diagnostic artifacts, statistical indications that two dated features have equivalent dates do not necessarily imply simultaneous feature use. Rather, given the precision of the available methods, the dated contexts could not be distinguished statistically or archaeologically. On the ground, this may be conceived in terms of a single settlement, with the recognition that features on some of the sites were used over different occupations that were close in time. Long and Rippeteau (1974:206–210) also provide a method of averaging multiple

dates that allowed me to calculate mean ages for such settlements. The features considered as contemporaneous using this approach appear on statistical and archaeological grounds to represent the facilities of a temporally, spatially, and culturally distinct presence.

4. Sedentariness and Village Settlement

1. In order to prevent variables with particularly high ranges from "swamping" the index, the values of the seven variables were converted to fractional ranks prior to being combined as part of the index. This was done by taking the rank of a case and dividing by the number of cases with valid values so that ranks are expressed as fractional values from 0 to 1. This approach standardizes the values of variables and allows consideration of fractional values that are readily interpretable.

2. Residential stability and occupation date are positively and significantly correlated (Pearson's $r = 0.632$ with a probability [p] less that 0.001 and a sample size of 35 settlements with the necessary information).

3. Coastal Plain: $r = 0.610$, $p = 0.006$, $n = 16$; Piedmont: $r = 0.482$, $p = 0.067$, $n = 11$; Ridge and Valley: $r = 0.523$, $p = 0.092$, $n = 8$.

4. Use duration correlates positively with occupation date ($r = 0.341$, $p = 0.023$, $n = 35$).

5. Piedmont: $r = .614$, $p = 0.022$, $n = 11$; Coastal Plain: $r = 0.313$, $p = 0.119$, $n = 16$.

6. The quadratic regression line drawn through the data in figure 4-3 results in a low significance level and a relatively high r^2 value, suggesting a relatively good fit with the data ($r^2 = 0.430$, $p = 0.005$, $n = 22$).

5. Domestic Economy

1. Boxplots summarize the central tendency and range of variability in groups of cases. The "box" represents the interquartile range containing the central 50 percent of values. A heavy line across the box indicates the median value. The "whiskers" are lines that extend from the box to the highest and lowest values, excluding outliers (circles) and extreme values (asterisks). Boxplots allow easy comparison of groups of cases according to the middle value (i.e., the median), cases close to this value (the interquartile range), the general range of variation (as depicted by the whiskers), and any unusually low or high values (outliers and extremes).

2. The Late Woodland II increase over Late Woodland I values in the Piedmont ($t = -2.296$, $p = 0.020$) and in the Ridge and Valley ($t = -1.931$, $p = 0.037$) is statistically significant. The Coastal Plain data, which lack Late Woodland I cases, indicate a significant increase of Late Woodland II values over Middle Woodland ones ($t = -2.646$, $p = 0.015$).

3. $r = 0.515$, $p < 0.001$, $n = 42$.

4. The difference between Late Woodland II floor areas and combined Protohistoric/Contact values in the Coastal Plain is not statistically significant ($t = -1.375$, $p = 0.240$). Similarly, the difference between Late Woodland II and Protohistoric values in the Ridge and Valley province is not statistically significant ($t = -1.442$, $p = 0.161$).

5. Centuries missing in the graph reflect the absence of household clusters dating

to those intervals in the James River data set. The Late Woodland II increase over the Late Woodland I is statistically significant (t = -2.107, p = 0.022), and during the late Precontact period the number of interior features correlates positively with occupation date (r = 0.363, p = 0.008, n = 35).

6. The number of exterior features correlates positively with interior feature frequency: r = 0.490, p < 0.001, n = 112.

7. Measurement methods followed those employed by Klein (1994) using a "Starrett" dial indicator and Plog's (1985:145) vessel diameter estimation method.

8. r = -0.233, p = 0.001, n = 197.

9. During the precontact centuries, associated storage volumes increased through time in a statistically significant manner. Associated storage volume correlates positively with occupation date prior to A.D. 1500 (r = 0.290, p = 0.046, n = 35). The difference between Late Woodland II and Protohistoric values is not statistically significant (t = 3.233, p = 0.655), again suggesting an interruption of a late precontact trend without showing clear evidence of its reversal.

10. Comparison of the presence or absence of external storage features between Late Woodland I and Middle Woodland II household clusters using Fisher's Exact Test indicates that the observed frequencies are not significantly different than those expected if the variables were independent and only random chance were operating (p = .231). Small sample sizes may play a role in this lack of statistical significance. Statistically significant differences between Late Woodland I and Late Woodland II frequencies (p = .033) support the conclusion that the presence or absence of external storage is dependent upon a household cluster's chronological placement during the Late Woodland period.

11. Comparison of the frequencies of household clusters with and without internal storage during the Late Woodland II phase with the preceding period using Fisher's Exact Test produces a probability that approaches significance at the 0.10 level (p = 0.108), indicating a likelihood of frequencies different than those expected if the variables were independent. Comparison of Late Woodland II and Protohistoric household clusters using Fisher's Exact Test returns a probability of p = .033, a statistically significant result.

12. These data do not appear to result from sample size differences measured in terms of the number of excavated houses per occupation, since house frequency and floor area range do not correlate in a statistically significant manner. Nor does the pattern closely match changes in the mean house sizes depicted in figure 5-1. Apparently, floor area range provides a measure of differentiation in domestic architecture in the James River Valley relatively free of sampling biases.

13. r = 0.526, p = 0.022, n = 15.

14. The quadratic regression line depicted in the chart results in an r^2 value of 0.3703. For the linear regression, $r^2 = 0.2767$.

15. Range (the distance between the highest and lowest values in a distribution) and standard deviation (a measure of approximately 68 percent of the dispersion around the mean) are absolute measures expressed in units of measurement identical with the raw variate (i.e., square meters of house floor area). With regard to house floor areas, these

measures gauge variability in terms of real-world living space. However, both are less useful for comparing groups of cases with different means, such as those associated with the floor areas of different eras in the James River Valley. The magnitude of standard deviation is a direct function of the mean, and range values can be particularly unstable as they relate only to two extreme values. On the other hand, range values may be appropriate in detecting the occurrence of extreme values associated with unusually large houses. The coefficient of variation, by contrast, expresses group variability as measured by standard deviation in terms that are relative to the sample mean. As a "pure measure," coefficient of variation is expressed as a percentage rather than in the absolute units in which the variable was measured.

16. $r = 0.435, p = 0.060, n = 14$.

17. This standardization is necessary for comparing data across multiple occupations in the sample, since the mean house floor area and dispersion around this mean differ substantially between occupations. Z scores for the James River sample were calculated based on each occupation's mean and standard deviation. Based on the distribution of these values, z scores greater than 0.7 appear to represent the floor areas of particularly large houses. This distinction separates the houses larger than roughly 70 percent of the domestic structures in a community as large structures.

18. $r = 0.345, p = 0.027, n = 44$.

19. $X^2 = 3.866, p = .049$.

6. Community Organization

1. $r = -0.617, p = 0.016, n = 12$.

2. $r = 0.357, p = 0.012, n = 49$.

3. This evaluation of feature use computes the percentage of principal pit feature types (hearths, storage pits, roasting pits, and burials) for each occupation in the sample. The percentages reflect the relative proportions of different feature categories within individual settlements.

4. $r = -0.288, p = 0.050, n = 34$.

5. $r = 0.374, p = 0.015, n = 34$.

7. Regional Interaction

1. Ceramic sherd counts came from features containing at least 10 sherds with identifiable surface treatments.

2. $r^2 = 0.651$.

3. The locations of the fall line and Blue Ridge Mountains are referenced with dashed lines on the charts. The scatterplots depict multiple cases with the same X and Y values using "sunflowers," such that each "petal" (i.e., a line extending from the point) represents an additional case with the same surface treatment and distance values.

4. $r = 0.101, r^2 = 0.010, p = 0.386$.

5. $r = 0.074, r^2 = 0.006, p = 0.524$.

6. $r = -0.108, r^2 = 0.012, p = 131$.

7. Fisher's Exact Test returns a probability of 0.664.

8. $X^2 = 1.500$.

9. Fisher's Exact Test returns a probability of 0.545 for the Coastal Plain–Piedmont comparison and 0.580 for the Coastal Plain–Ridge and Valley comparison.

10. Fisher's Exact Test returns a probability of 0.010.

11. $X_c^2 = 19.544$. This value was adjusted with Yates Correction for Continuity, which is necessary when the smallest expected value is less than 10 (Thomas 1986:298). Fisher's Exact Test returns a probability of less than 0.001 for the Protohistoric frequencies.

12. For the frequencies of Late Woodland I and II features with and without chert debitage, $X_c^2 = 4.464$. Due to sample size considerations (Thomas 1986:289), the chi-square value has been altered with Yates Correction for Continuity. Fisher's Exact Test produces a probability of 0.018.

13. $X_c^2 = 8.980$.

14. The Late Woodland I to Late Woodland II increase is statistically significant (t = -3.075, p = 0.003). One-way analysis of variance indicates that Middle Woodland, Late Woodland, and combined Protohistoric and Contact era surface treatment diversity differed in a statistically significant manner (F = 3.441, p = 0.036).

Bibliography

Alvord, Clarence W., and Lee Bidgood

    1912   *The First Explorations of the Trans-allegheny Region by the Virginians, 1650–1674.* Cleveland: Arthur H. Clark.

Archer, Gabriel

    1998a   A Relation. In *Jamestown Narratives: Eyewitness Accounts of the Virginia Colony,* edited by E. W. Haile. Champlain VA: Roundhouse.

    1998b   A Brief Description of the People. In *Jamestown Narratives: Eyewitness Accounts of the Virginia Colony,* edited by E. W. Haile. Champlain VA: Roundhouse.

Axtell, James

    1988   At the Water's Edge: Trading in the Sixteenth Century. In *After Columbus: Essays in the Ethnohistory of Colonial North America,* edited by James Axtell. Oxford: Oxford University Press.

    2000   *Natives and Newcomers.* Oxford: Oxford University Press.

Banister, John

    1970   *John Banister and His Natural History of Virginia, 1678–1692,* edited by J. Ewan and N. Ewan. Urbana: University of Illinois Press.

Barber, Michael B.

    1988   The Thomas Sawyer Site (44RN39B) Salem, Virginia: A Progress Report on Emergency Excavations. Manuscript on file, Virginia Department of Historic Resources, Richmond.

Barker, Alex

    1992   Powhatan's Pursestrings: On the Meaning of Surplus in a Seventeenth Century Algonquin Chiefdom. In *Lords of the Southeast: Social Inequality and Native Elites of Southeastern North America,* edited by Alex W. Barker and Timothy R. Pauketat. Archaeological Papers of the American Anthropological Association No. 3. Washington DC: American Anthropological Association.

Benedict, Ruth

    1959   *Patterns of Culture.* Boston: Houghton Mifflin.

Beverley, Robert

    1947   *The History and Present State of Virginia,* edited by L. B. Wright. Chapel Hill: University of North Carolina Press.

Binford, Lewis R.

    1964   *Archaeological and Ethnohistorical Investigations of Cultural Diversity and Progressive Development among the Aboriginal Cultures of Coastal Virginia and North Carolina.* Ph.D. dissertation, University of Michigan. Ann Arbor: University Microfilms.

    1983   *In Pursuit of the Past: Decoding the Archaeological Record.* New York: Thames and Hudson.

Binford, Lewis, and R. J. Chasko
    1976   Nunamuit Demographic History: A Provocative Case. In *Demographic Archaeology*, edited by E. B. W. Zubrow. Albuquerque: University of New Mexico Press.

Blanton, Dennis
    1992   Middle Woodland Settlement Systems in Virginia. In *Middle and Late Woodland Research in Virginia: A Synthesis*, edited by T. Reinhart and M. E. Hodges. Richmond: Archaeological Society of Virginia.
    1999   *The Potomac Creek Site (44ST2) Revisited.* Research Report Series No. 10. Richmond: Virginia Department of Historic Resources.
    2000   Drought as a Factor in the Jamestown Colony, 1607–1612. *Historical Archaeology* 34:74–81.

Blanton, Richard
    1994   *Houses and Households: A Comparative Study.* New York: Plenum Press.

Blanton, Richard E., Gary M. Feinman, Stephen A. Kowalewski, and Peter N. Peregrine
    1996   A Dual Process Theory for the Evolution of Mesoamerican Civilization. *Current Anthropology* 37(1):1–14.

Boehm, Christopher
    1993   Egalitarian Behavior and Reverse Dominance Hierarchy. *Current Anthropology* 34(3):227–254.

Bourdieu, Pierre
    1973   The Berber House. In *Rules and Meanings*, edited by M. Doublas. Harmondsworth, England: Penguin.
    1977   *Outline of a Theory of Practice.* Cambridge: Cambridge University Press.

Boyd Donna C., and C. Clifford Boyd
    1992   Late Woodland Mortuary Variability in Virginia. In *Middle and Late Woodland Research in Virginia: A Synthesis*, edited by T. Reinhart and M. E. Hodges. Richmond: Archaeological Society of Virginia.

Bragdon, Kathleen J.
    1996   *Native People of Southern New England: 1500–1650.* Norman: University of Oklahoma Press.

Braun, David P.
    1980   Experimental Interpretations of Ceramic Vessel Use on the Basis of Rim and Neck Formal Attributes. In *Museum of Northern Arizona Research Paper No. 11*, edited by D. C. Giero et al. Flagstaff: Museum of Northern Arizona.
    1983   Pots as Tools. In *Archaeological Hammers and Theories*, edited by J. Moore and A. Keene. New York: Academic Press.
    1985   Absolute Seriation: A Time Series Approach. In *For Concordance in Archaeological Analysis: Bridging Data Structure, Quantitative Technique, and Theory*, edited by C. Carr. Westport CT: Westport Publishers.
    1991   Why Decorate a Pot? Midwestern Household Pottery, 200 B.C.–A.D. 600. *Journal of Anthropological Archaeology* 10:360–397.

Braun, David P., and Stephen Plog
    1982   Evolution of "Tribal" Social Networks: Theory and Prehistoric North American Evidence. *American Antiquity* 47:504–525.

Braun, E. Lucy
    1950   *The Deciduous Forests of Eastern North America.* Philadelphia: Blakiston.

Brown, A. G.
    1997   *Alluvial Geoarchaeology: Floodplain Archaeology and Environmental Change.* Cambridge: Cambridge University Press.

Brumfiel, E. M., and J. W. Fox
    1993   *Factional Competition and Political Development in the New World.* Cambridge: Cambridge University Press.

Brumfiel, Elizabeth
    1992   Distinguished Lecture in Archaeology: Breaking and Entering the Ecosystem—Gender, Class, and Faction Steal the Show. *American Anthropologist* 94:551–567.

Brush, G. S.
    1986   Geology and Paleoecology of Chesapeake Bay. *Journal of the Washington Academy of Sciences* 76(3):140–160.

Byrd, Brian F.
    1994   Public and Private, Domestic and Corporate: The Emergence of the Southwest Asian Village. *American Antiquity* 59:639–666.

Callahan, Errett H.
    1985   Pamunkey Housebuilding: An Experimental Study of Late Woodland Construction Technology in the Powhatan Confederacy. Ph.D. dissertation, Department of Anthropology, Catholic University of America.

Canuto, Marcello A., and Jason Yaeger
    2000   *Archaeology of Communities: A New World Perspective.* New York: Routledge

Carbone, Victor I.
    1976   Environment and Prehistory in the Shenandoah Valley. Ph.D. dissertation, Department of Anthropology, Catholic University of America.

Carneiro, Robert L.
    1981   The Chiefdom: Precursor of the State. In *The Transition to Statehood in the New World*, edited by G. D. Jones and R. R. Kautz. New York: Cambridge University Press.

Casteel, Richard W.
    1979   Relationships between Surface Area and Population Size: A Cautionary Note. *American Antiquity* 44:803–807.

Certeau, Michel de
    1988   *The Practice of Everyday Life.* Berkeley: University of California Press.

Charles, Douglas K., and Jane E. Buikstra
    1983   Archaic Mortuary Sites in the Central Mississippi Drainage: Distribution, Structure, and Implications. In *Archaic Hunters and Gatherers in the Midwest*, edited by J. Phillips and J. Brown. New York: Academic Press.

Chase, Joan
   1988   A Comparison of Signs of Nutritional Stress in Prehistoric Populations of
           the Potomac Piedmont and Coastal Plain. Ph.D. dissertation, Department of
           Anthropology, American University.
Chayanov, Alexander V.
   1966   *The Theory of Peasant Economy*, edited by D. Thorner et al. Homewood IL:
           American Economic Association.
Clark, Wayne E.
   1980   The Origins of the Piscataway and Related Indian Cultures. *Maryland Historical
           Magazine* 75(1):8–22.
Clastres, Pierre
   1989   *Society against the State*. New York: Zone Books.
Clayton, John
   1968   Another Account of Virginia. *Virginia Magazine of History and Biography* 76:415–
           436.
Conkey, Margaret W.
   1978   Style and Information in Cultural Evolution: Toward a Predictive Model for
           the Paleolithic. In *Social Archaeology*, edited by C. L. Redman et al. New York:
           Academic Press.
Cook, Samuel R.
   2000   *Monacans and Miners: Native American and Coal Mining Communities in Ap-
           palachia*. Lincoln: University of Nebraska Press.
Cook, Sherburne F.
   1972   *Prehistoric Demography*. McCaleb Module in Anthropology 16. Reading MA:
           Addison-Wesley.
Coupland, Gary, and E. B. Banning
   1996   Introduction: The Archaeology of Big Houses. In *People Who Lived in Big
           Houses: Archaeological Perspectives on Large Domestic Structures*. Madison WI: Pre-
           history Press.
Cowgill, George L.
   1975   On Causes and Consequences of Ancient and Modern Population Changes.
           American Anthropologist 77:505–525.
Crumley, Carole L.
   1987   A Dialectical Critique of Hierarchy. In *Power Relations and State Formation*,
           edited by T. C. Patterson and C. W. Gailey. Washington DC: American Anthro-
           pological Association.
Cunningham, C.
   1964   Order in the Atoni House. *Bijdragen tot de Taaal-Land-en Volkenkunde* 120:34–
           68.
Curry, Dennis C.
   1999   *Feast of the Dead: Aboriginal Ossuaries in Maryland*. Crownsville: Maryland His-
           torical Trust Press.

Custer, Jay F.

 1980 Settlement-Subsistence Systems in Augusta County, Virginia. *Quarterly Bulletin of the Archaeological Society of Virginia* 35:1–27.

 1984 A Controlled Comparison of Late Woodland Settlement Patterns in Augusta County, Virginia. In *Upland Archaeology in the East*, Symposium 2, edited by C. R. Geier et al. Washington DC: United States Forest Service.

 1986 Late Woodland Cultural Diversity in the Middle Atlantic: An Evolutionary Perspective. In *Late Woodland Cultures of the Middle Atlantic Region*, edited by J. F. Custer. Newark: University of Delaware Press.

 1987 Late Woodland Settlement Diversity in the Middle Shenandoah Valley: Some Thoughts on MacCord's "Lewis Creek Mound Culture." *Quarterly Bulletin of the Archaeological Society of Virginia* 42:146–149.

D'Altroy, Terence N., and Timothy Earle

 1985 Staple Finance, Wealth Finance, and Storage in the Inka Political Economy. *Current Anthropology* 26:187–206.

Deal, Michael

 1983 Pottery Ethnoarchaeology among the Tzeltal Maya. Ph.D. dissertation, Department of Anthropology, Simon Fraser University.

DeBoer, Warren R.

 1974 Ceramic Longevity and Archaeological Interpretation: An Example from Upper Ucayali, Peru. *American Antiquity* 39:335–342.

 1988 Subterranean Storage and the Organization of Surplus: The View from Eastern North America. *Southeastern Archaeology* 7(1):1–20.

DeBoer, Warren R., and D. W. Lathrap

 1979 The Making and Breaking of Shipibo-Conibo. In *Ethnoarchaeology: Implications of Ethnography for Archaeology*, edited by C. Kramer. New York: Columbia University Press.

Dent, Richard J.

 1995 *Chesapeake Archaeology: Old Traditions, New Traditions*. New York: Plenum Press.

Dickens, Roy S.

 1985 The Form, Function, and Formation of Garbage-filled Pits on Southeastern Aboriginal Sites: An Archaeobotanical Analysis. In *Structure and Process in Southeastern Archaeology*, edited by Roy Dickens and H. Trawick Ward. Birmingham: University of Alabama Press.

Dietler, Michael, and Brian Hayden (editors)

 2001 *Feasts: Archaeological and Ethnographic Perspectives on Food, Politics, and Power.* Washington DC: Smithsonian Institution Press.

Dobyns, Henry F.

 1983 *Their Numbers Become Thinned: Native American Population Dynamics in Eastern North America.* Knoxville: University of Tennessee Press.

Dunham, Gary H.

 1994 Common Ground, Contesting Visions: The Emergence of Burial Mound Ritual in Late Prehistoric Central Virginia. Ph.D. dissertation, Department of Anthropology, University of Virginia.

1999   Marking Territory, Making Territory: Burial Mounds in Interior Virginia. In *Material Symbols: Culture and Economy in Prehistory*. Carbondale: Center for Archaeological Investigations, Southern Illinois University.

Earle, Timothy
1978   Chiefdoms in Archaeological and Ethnohistorical Perspectives. *Annual Review of Anthropology* 16:279–308.

Edwards, Andrew C., William E. Pittman, Gregory J. Brown, Mary Ellen N. Hodges, Marley R. Brown III, Eric E. Voight
1989   *Hampton University Archaeological Project: A Report on the Findings*. Williamsburg VA: Colonial Williamsburg Foundation.

Egloff, Keith T.
1985   Spheres of Cultural Interaction across the Coastal Plain in the Woodland Period. In *Structure and Process in Southeastern Archaeology*, edited by R. Dickens and H. T. Ward. Birmingham: University of Alabama Press.

1992   The Late Woodland Period in Southwest Virginia. In *Middle and Late Woodland Research in Virginia: A Synthesis*, edited by T. Reinhart and M. E. Hodges. Richmond: Archaeological Society of Virginia.

Egloff, Keith T., and Stephen Potter
1982   Indian Ceramics from Coastal Plain Virginia. *Archaeology of Eastern North America* 10:95–117.

Ehrenreich, Robert M., Carole L. Crumley, and Janet E. Levy
1995   *Heterarchy and the Analysis of Complex Societies*. Archaeological Papers of the American Anthropological Association No. 6. Washington DC: American Anthropological Association.

Evans, Clifford
1955   *A Ceramic Study of Virginia Archaeology*. Bureau of American Ethnology, Smithsonian Institution, Bulletin 160. Washington DC.

Fausz, J. Frederick
1977   The Powhatan Uprising of 1622: A Historical Study of Ethnocentrism and Cultural Conflict. Ph.D. dissertation, Department of History, College of William and Mary.

1985   Patterns of Anglo-Indian Aggression and Accommodation along the Mid-Atlantic Coast, 1584–1634. In *Cultures in Contact: The European Impact on Native Cultural Institutions in Eastern North America, A.D. 1000–1800*, edited by W. W. Fitzhugh. Washington DC: Smithsonian Institution.

Feest, Christian F.
1966   Powhatan, a Study in Political Organization. *Wiener Völkerklundliche Mitteilungen* 13:69–83.

1978   Virginia Algonquins. In *Northeast*, edited by B. G. Trigger. *Handbook of North*

American Indians, vol. 15, W. C. Sturtevant, general editor. Washington DC: Smithsonian Institution.

Feinman, Gary M.

   1995   The Emergence of Inequality: A Focus on Strategies and Processes. In *Foundations of Social Inequality*, edited by T. D. Price and G. M. Feinman. New York: Plenum Press.

Feinman, Gary M., and Jill Neitzel

   1984   Too Many Types: An Overview of Sedentary Prestate Societies in the Americas. *Advances in Archaeological Method and Theory*, vol. 7, edited by M. Schiffer. New York: Academic Press.

Ferguson, R. Brian, and Neil L. Whitehead (editors)

   1992   *War in the Tribal Zone: Expanding States and Indigenous Warfare.* Santa Fe NM: School of American Research Press.

Flanagan, James G.

   1989   Hierarchy in "Egalitarian" Societies. *Annual Review of Anthropology* 18:245–266.

Flannery, Kent

   1972   The Origins of the Village as a Settlement Type in Mesoamerica and the Near East: A Comparative Study. In *Man, Settlement, and Urbanism*, edited by P. Ucko et al. London: Duckworth.

Ford, Richard I.

   1974   Northeastern Archaeology: Past and Future Directions. *Annual Review of Anthropology* 3:385–413.

Foster, George M.

   1960   Life Expectancy of Utilitarian Pottery in Tzintzuntzan, Michoacan, Mexico. *American Antiquity* 25:606–609.

Fowke, Gerard P.

   1894   *Archaeologic Investigations in James and Potomac Valleys.* Bureau of American Ethnology, Smithsonian Institution, Bulletin 23. Washington DC.

Fried, Morton H.

   1967   *The Evolution of Political Society: An Essay in Political Economy.* New York: Random House.

Friedman, Jonathan, and M. J. Rowlands

   1978   Notes Toward and Epigenetic Model of the Evolution of "Civilization." In *The Evolution of Social Systems*, edited by J. Friedman and M. J. Rowlands. Pittsburgh: University of Pittsburgh Press.

Gallivan, Martin D.

   1994   Excavation of a Late Woodland Site in the James River Piedmont. Paper presented at the Archaeological Society of Virginia Conference, Norfolk.

   1995   Interpreting Late Woodland Site Structure in the Virginia Piedmont. Paper presented at the South Eastern Archaeological Conference, Knoxville TN.

1997a   The Leatherwood Creek Site: A Dan River Phase Site in the Southern Virginia Piedmont. *Quarterly Bulletin of the Archaeological Society of Virginia* 52:150–171.

1997b   Spatial Analysis of John Smith's 1612 Map of Virginia. *Journal of Middle Atlantic Archaeology* 13:145–160.

1999   *The Late Precontact James River Village: Household, Community, and Regional Dynamics.* Ph.D. dissertation, University of Virginia. Ann Arbor: University Microfilms.

2002   Measuring Sedentariness and Settlement Population: Accumulations Research in the Middle Atlantic Region. *American Antiquity* 67:535–557.

2003   *Early Horticultural Settlement in the James River Piedmont: The Partridge Creek Site (44AH193).* Virginia Department of Historic Resources Research Report Series No. 12. Richmond: Virginia Department of Historic Resources.

Gallivan, Martin D., and Jeffrey L. Hantman

1996   Rethinking Chieftaincy: Powhatan and Monacan Ethnohistory and Archaeology. Paper presented at the Society for American Archaeology Conference, New Orleans.

1998   Stratified Deposits in the Central Virginia Piedmont: Excavations at the Spessard Site (44FV134). Manuscript on file, Department of Anthropology, University of Virginia, Charlottesville.

Gardner, Peter M.

1991   Foragers' Pursuit of Individual Autonomy. *Current Anthropology* 32:543–572.

Gardner, William M.

1986   *Lost Arrowheads and Broken Pottery: Traces of Indians in the Shenandoah Valley.* Manassas VA: Thunderbird Publications.

1987   Comparison of Ridge and Valley, Blue Ridge, Piedmont, and Coastal Plain Archaic Period Site Distribution: An Idealized Transect (Preliminary Model). *Journal of Middle Atlantic Archaeology* 3:49–128.

Geier, Clarence R., and Kathleen M. Dutt

1978   *Archaeological Activity at BA-14, BA-39, BA-40, in the Gathright Reservoir Area, Bath County, Virginia.* Submitted to the U.S. Army Corps of Engineers, Norfolk VA.

Geier, Clarence R., and Joey Moldenhauer

1977   *The Bessemer Site 44-(BO-26): A Late Woodland Dan River Cultural Component in Central Western Virginia.* Harrisonburg VA: James Madison University.

Geier, Clarence R., and J. Craig Warren

1982a   *The Huffman Site 44(BA5): A Late Woodland Site on the Jackson River, Bath County, Virginia.* Harrisonburg VA: Archaeological Research Center, James Madison University.

1982b   *The Noah's Ark Site 44(BA15): A Late Woodland and Protohistoric Site on the Jackson River, Bath County, Virginia.* Harrisonburg VA: Archaeological Research Center, James Madison University.

Gerard, William R.
 1907   Virginia's Indian Contributions to English. *American Anthropologist*, n.s., 9:87–
         112.
Giddens, Anthony
 1979   *Central Problems in Social Theory: Action, Structure and Contradiction in Social Anal-
         ysis*. London: Macmillan.
Gleach, Frederic W.
 1986   "... Where the Pale ran": Sir Thomas Dale's Palisades in Seventeenth-
         Century Virginia. *Quarterly Bulletin of the Archaeological Society of Virginia*
         41:160–168.
 1987   The Reynolds-Alvis Site 44(HE470): A Summary Report. *Quarterly Bulletin of
         the Archeological Society of Virginia* 42:205–232.
 1997   *Powhatan's World and Colonial Virginia: A Conflict of Cultures*. Lincoln: University
         of Nebraska Press.
Gold, Debra L.
 1998   Emergent Social Inequality in Late Woodland Interior Virginia: A Bioarchae-
         ological Perspective. Paper presented at the Society for American Archaeology
         Conference, Seattle.
 2000   "Utmost Confusion" Reconsidered: Bioarchaeology and Secondary Burial in
         Late Prehistoric Interior Virginia. In *Bioarchaeological Studies of Life in the Age
         of Agriculture: A View from the Southeast*, edited by P. M. Lambert. Tuscaloosa:
         University of Alabama Press.
Gradie, Charlotte M.
 1993   The Powhatans in the Context of the Spanish Empire. In *Powhatan Foreign
         Relations: 1500–1722*, edited by H. C. Rountree. Charlottesville: University
         Press of Virginia.
Gravely, Richard P.
 1971   The Leatherwood Creek Site: 44 HR 1. *Eastern States Archaeological Federation
         Bulletin* 30:11–12.
 1983   Archaeological Sites in the Upper Dan River Drainage System. In *Piedmont
         Archaeology*, edited by J. M. Wittkofski and L. Browning. Richmond: Archae-
         ological Society of Virginia.
Gregory, Chris A.
 1982   *Gifts and Commodities*. London: Academic Press.
Griffith, Daniel
 1980   Townsend Ceramics and the late Woodland of Southern Delaware. *Maryland
         Historical Magazine* 75(1):23–41.
Grove, Jean M.
 1990   *The Little Ice Age*. New York: Routledge.
Haile, Edward W. (editor)
 1998   *Jamestown Narratives: Eyewitness Accounts of the Virginia Colony*. Champlain VA:
         Roundhouse.

Hantman, Jeffrey L.

1983   Stylistic Distributions and Social Networks in the Prehistoric Plateau South-west. Ph.D. dissertation, Department of Anthropology, Arizona State University.

1984   Regional Organization of the Northern Mogollon. *American Archaeology* 4:171–80.

1985   *The Archaeology of Albemarle County.* Archaeological Survey Monograph 2. Charlottesville: Department of Anthropology, University of Virginia.

1987   Cultural Boundaries and Lithic Procurement in Central Virginia. In *Upland Archaeology in the East: A Third Symposium*, edited by M. B. Barber. Washington DC: United States Forest Service.

1989   Surplus Production and Complexity in the Upper Little Colorado Province, East-Central Arizona. In *Sociopolitical Structure of Prehistoric Southwestern Societies*, edited by S. Upham et al. Boulder CO: Westview Press.

1990   Between Powhatan and Quirank: Reconstructing Monacan Culture and History in the Context of Jamestown. *American Anthropologist* 92:676–690.

1993   Powhatan's Relations with the Piedmont Monacans. In *Powhatan Foreign Relations: 1500–1722*, edited by H. C. Rountree. Charlottesville: University Press of Virginia.

1998   Ancestral Monacan Society. Paper presented at the Society for American Archaeology Conference, Seattle.

Hantman, Jeffrey L., Martin D. Gallivan, and Daniel Hayes

1993   Contact Period Settlement in the Virginia Piedmont. Paper presented at the Southeastern Archaeological Conference, Raleigh NC.

Hantman, Jeffrey L., and Debra Gold

2000   The Woodland in the Middle Atlantic: Ranking and Dynamic Political Stability. In *The Woodland Southeast*, edited by D. G. Anderson and R. C. Mainfort. Tuscaloosa: University of Alabama Press.

Hantman, Jeffrey L., and Michael Klein

1992   Middle and Late Woodland Archaeology in Piedmont Virginia. In *Middle and Late Woodland Research in Virginia: A Synthesis*, edited by T. Reinhart and M. E. Hodges. Richmond: Archaeological Society of Virginia.

Hantman, Jeffrey L., and Stephen Plog

1982   The Relationship of Stylistic Similarity to Patterns of Material Exchange. In *Contexts for Prehistoric Exchange*, edited by T. K. Earle and J. E. Ericson. New York: Academic Press.

Hariot, Thomas

1972   *A Briefe and True Report of the New Found Land of Virginia.* New York: Dover.

Hart, John P.

1995   Storage and Monongahela Subsistence-Settlement Change. *Archaeology of Eastern North America* 23:41–56.

Hassan, Fekri A.

1981   *Demographic Archaeology.* New York: Academic Press.

Hayden, Brian

1993   *Archaeology: The Science of Once and Future Things.* New York: W. H. Freeman.

Hayden, Brian, and A. Cannon

1983   Where the Garbage Goes: Refuse Disposal in the Maya Highlands. *Journal of Anthropological Archaeology* 2:117–163.

Hayes, Daniel R., and G. William Monaghan

1998   The Down and Dirty Approach to a Variable Archaeological Record: A Geomorphological Framework for Archaeological Site Formation, Preservation, and Discovery in the James and Potomac River Basins. Paper presented at the Society for American Archaeology Conference, Seattle.

Hegmon, Michelle

1986   Information Exchange and Integration on Black Mesa, Arizona, A.D. 931–1150. In *Spatial Organization and Exchange: Archaeological Survey on Northern Black Mesa,* edited by S. Plog. Carbondale: Southern Illinois University Press.

1989   Risk Reduction and Variation in Agricultural Economies: A Computer Simulation of Hopi Agriculture. *Research in Economic Anthropology* 11:89–121.

Hendon, Julia A.

1996   Archaeological Approaches to the Organization of Domestic Labor: Household Practice and Domestic Relations. *Annual Review of Anthropology* 25:45–61.

Herz, Norman, and Ervan G. Garrison

1998   *Geological Methods for Archaeology.* New York: Oxford University Press.

Hill, James N.

1970   *Broken K Pueblo: Prehistoric Social Organization in the American Southwest.* Tucson: University of Arizona Press.

Hitchcock, Robert K.

1987   Sedentism and Site Structure: Organizational Changes in Kalahari Basarwa Residential Locations. In *Method and Theory for Activity Area Research: An Ethnoarchaeological Approach,* edited by S. Kent. New York: Columbia University Press.

Hodder, Ian

1977   The Distribution of Material Culture Items in the Baringo District, Western Kenya. *Man* 12:239–269.

1990   *The Domestication of Europe.* Oxford: Blackwell.

Hodges, Mary E.

1989   The Prehistoric Sites. In *Hampton University Archaeological Project: A Report on the Findings,* edited by Andrew C. Edwards et al. Williamsburg VA: Colonial Williamsburg Foundation.

1993   Middle and Late Woodland Settlement at Great Neck, Site 44vB7 in Virginia

Beach, Virginia. Master's thesis, Department of Anthropology, University of Tennessee.

Hoffman, Michael A., and Robert W. Foss

　1980   Blue Ridge Prehistory: A General Perspective. *Quarterly Bulletin of the Archaeological Society of Virginia* 34:185–210.

Holland, C. Gilly

　1978   Albemarle County Settlements: A Piedmont Model. *Quarterly Bulletin of the Archaeological Society of Virginia* 33:29–44.

Holland, C. Gilly, Clifford Evans, and Betty Meggers

　1983   The Rapidan Mound Revisited: A Test Excavation of a Prehistoric Burial Mound. *Quarterly Bulletin of the Archaeological Society of Virginia* 38:1–42.

Hulton, Paul

　1984   *American 1585: The Complete Drawings of John White.* Chapel Hill: University of North Carolina Press.

Huntington, Richard, and Peter Metcalf

　1979   *Celebrations of Death: The Anthropology of Mortuary Ritual.* Cambridge: Cambridge University Press.

Jirikowic, Christine A.

　1990   The Political Implications of a Cultural Practice: A New Perspective on Ossuary Burial in the Potomac Valley. *North American Archaeologist* 11:353–374.

Johnson, Gregory A.

　1978   Information and the Development of Decision-making Organizations. In *Social Archaeology: Beyond Subsistence and Dating*, edited by C. L. Redman et al. New York: Academic Press.

　1982   Organizational Structure and Scalar Stress. In *Theory and Explanation in Archaeology: The Southampton Conference*, edited by C. Renfrew et al. New York: Academic Press.

　1983   Decision-making and Pastoral Nomad Groups. *Human Ecology* 11(2):175–199.

　1989   Dynamics of Southwestern Prehistory: Far Outside-Looking In. In *Dynamics of Southwestern Prehistory*, edited by Linda Cordell and George Gummerman. Washington DC: Smithsonian Institution Press.

Johnson, Larry D.

　1982   The Huffman Site. In *Prehistory of the Gathright Dam Area, Virginia*, edited by Howard A. MacCord. Privately printed.

Johnson, William C., Jeffrey P. Blick, and D. Scott Speedy

　1989   *Preliminary Report on the 1984 Archaeological Investigations at the Irwin Site (44PG4), Prince George County, Virginia.* Richmond: Virginia Division of Historic Landmarks.

Kapches, Mima

　1990   The Spatial Dynamics of Ontario Iroquoian Longhouses. *American Antiquity* 55:49–67.

Kavanahaugh, Maureen
    1983   Prehistoric Occupation of the Monacacy River Region, Maryland. In *Piedmont Archaeology: Recent Research and Results*, edited by J. M. Wittkofski and L. E. Browning. Richmond: Archaeological Society of Virginia.

Kelly, John E.
    1990   Range Site Community Patterns and the Mississippian Emergence. In *The Mississippian Emergence*, edited by B. D. Smith. Washington DC: Smithsonian Institution Press.

Kent, Susan
    1984   *Analyzing Activity Areas: An Ethnoarchaeological Study of the Use of Space*. Albuquerque: University of New Mexico Press.
    1989   And Justice for All: The Development of Political Centralization among Newly Sedentary Foragers. *American Anthropologist* 91:703–712.

Kent, Susan (editor)
    1990   *Domestic Architecture and the Use of Space: An Interdisciplinary Cross-Cultural Study*. Cambridge: Cambridge University Press.

Kintigh, Keith W.
    1989   Sample Size, Significance, and Measures of Diversity. In *Quantifying Diversity in Archaeology*, edited by R. D. Leonard and G. T. Jones. Cambridge: Cambridge University Press.

Kintigh, Keith W., and Albert J. Ammerman
    1982   Heuristic Approaches to Spatial Analysis in Archaeology. *American Antiquity* 47:31–63.

Klatka, Thomas
    1988   *Archaeological Survey in Fluvanna County*. Archaeological Survey Monograph 5. Charlottesville: Department of Anthropology, University of Virginia.

Klatka, Thomas, Michael Klein, Jeffrey Hantman, and Gary Dunham
    1986   *Archaeological Survey in Buckingham County*. Archaeological Survey Monograph 3. Charlottesville: Department of Anthropology, University of Virginia.

Klein, Michael
    1986   Settlement Patterns in Prehistoric Virginia. Master's thesis, Department of Anthropology, University of Virginia.
    1987   *The Montpelier Periphery: An Archaeological Survey*. Archaeological Survey Monograph 4. Charlottesville: Department of Anthropology, University of Virginia.
    1994   An Absolute Seriation Approach to Ceramic Chronology in the Roanoke, Potomac and James River Valleys, Virginia and Maryland. Ph.D. dissertation, Department of Anthropology, University of Virginia.
    1997   The Transition from Soapstone Bowls to Marcey Creek Ceramics in the Middle Atlantic Region: A Consideration of Vessel Technology, Ethnographic Data, and Regional Exchange. *Archaeology of Eastern North America* 25:143–158.

Klein, Michael, and Martin Gallivan
    1997   Houses, Households, and Late Prehistoric Transformation in Virginia. Paper

presented at the Eastern States Archaeological Federation Conference, Mount Laurel NJ.

Klein, Michael, and Thomas Klatka

1991   Late Archaic and Early Woodland Demography and Settlement Patterns. In *Late Archaic and Early Woodland Research in Virginia: A Synthesis*, edited by T. Reinhart and M. E. Hodges. Richmond: Archaeological Society of Virginia.

Klein, Michael, and Stevens J. Sanderson

1996   Ceramic Attributes and Accokeek Creek Chronology: An Analysis of Sherds from the Falcon's Landing (18 PR 131) and the Accotink Meander (44 FX 1908) Sites. *North American Archaeologist* 17:113–141.

Kohler, Timothy A., and Eric Blinman

1987   Solving Mixture Problems in Archaeology: Analysis of Ceramic Materials for Dating and Demographic Reconstruction. *Journal of Anthropological Archaeology* 6:1–28.

Kraft, J. C., and G. S. Brush

1981   A Geological-Paleoenvironmental Analysis of Sediments in St. John's Pond and the Nearshore Zone Near Howard's Wharf at St. Mary's City, Maryland. Manuscript on file, Virginia Department of Historic Resources, Richmond.

Kramer, Carol

1979   An Archaeological View of a Contemporary Kurdish Village: Domestic Architecture, Household Size, and Wealth. In *Ethnoarchaeology: Implications of Ethnography for Archaeology*. New York: Columbia University Press.

Kupperman, Karen O.

2000   *Indians and English: Facing off in Early America*. Ithaca NY: Cornell University Press.

Lane, Ralph

1955   Discourse on the First Colony. In *The Roanoke Voyages, 1584–1590*, edited by D. B. Quinn. Cambridge: Hakluyt Society.

Lawson, John

1967   *A New Voyage to Carolina*. Chapel Hill: University of North Carolina Press.

Leach, Edmund

1973   Concluding Address. In *The Explanation of Culture Change*, edited by Colin Renfrew. London: Duckworth.

Leacock, Eleanor, and Richard Lee (editors)

1982   *Politics and History in Band Societies*. Cambridge: Cambridge University Press.

Lederer, John

1958   *The Discoveries of John Lederer*. Charlottesville: University Press of Virginia.

Lee, Richard B.

1979   *The !Kung San*. Cambridge: Cambridge University Press.

1981   Is There a Foraging Mode of Production? *Canadian Journal of Anthropology* 2(1):13–19.

1982   Politics, Sexual and Non-sexual, in an Egalitarian Society. In *Politics and History in Band Societies*, edited by E. Leacock and R. Lee. Cambridge: Cambridge University Press.

1990   Primitive Communism and the Origin of Social Inequality. In *The Evolution of Political Systems*, edited by Steadman Upham. Cambridge: Cambridge University Press.

Levi-Strauss, Claude

1969   *The Elementary Structures of Kinship.* Boston: Beacon Press.

Lewis, Clifford M., and Albert Loomie (editors)

1953   *The Spanish Jesuit Mission in Virginia, 1570–1572.* Chapel Hill: University of North Carolina Press.

Lightfoot, Kent G.

1984   The Occupation Duration of Duncan. In *The Duncan Project: A Study of the Occupation Duration and Settlement Pattern of an Early Mogollon Pithouse Village*, edited by K. G. Lightfoot. Tempe: Office of Cultural Resource Management, Arizona State University.

Lightfoot, Kent G., and Gary M. Feinman

1982   Social Differentiation and Leadership Development in Early Pithouse Villages in the Mogollon Region of the American Southwest. *Society for American Antiquity* 47:64–86.

Lightfoot, Kent G., and Roberta Jewett

1986   The Shift to Sedentary Life: A Consideration of the Occupation Duration of Early Mogollon Pithouse Villages. In *Mogollon Variability*, edited by C. Benson and S. Upham. University Museum Occasional Papers No. 15. Las Cruces: New Mexico State University.

Lindstrom, Lamont

1984   Doctor, Lawyer, Wise Man, Priest: Big-men and Knowledge in Melanesia. *Man* 19:291–309.

Lipe, W. D., and Michelle Hegmon

1989   *The Architecture of Social Integration in Prehistoric Pueblos.* Cortez CO: Crow Canyon Archaeological Center.

Long, Austin, and Bruce Rippeteau

1974   Testing Contemporaneity and Averaging Radiocarbon Dates. *American Antiquity* 39:205–215.

Longacre, William A.

1964   Archaeology as Anthropology: A Case Study. Ph.D. dissertation, Department of Anthropology, University of Chicago.

Lowie, Robert

1948   *Social Organization.* New York: Holt.

Lucketti, Nicholas M., Mary Ellen N. Hodges, and Charles T. Hodges (editors)

1994   *Paspahegh Archaeology: Data Recovery Investigations of Site 44JC308 at the Gov-*

ernor's Land at Two Rivers, James City County, Virginia. Williamsburg VA: James River Institute for Archaeology.

MacCord, Howard A.

1964   The Irwin Site, Prince George County, Virginia. *Quarterly Bulletin of the Archaeological Society of Virginia* 19:37–42.

1973   The Quicksburg Site, Shenandoah County, Virginia. *Quarterly Bulletin of the Archaeological Society of Virginia* 27:121–140.

1974   The Wingina Site, Nelson County, Virginia. *Quarterly Bulletin of the Archaeological Society of Virginia* 28:169–180.

MacCord, Howard A. (editor)

1982   *Prehistory of the Gathright Dam Area, Virginia.* Privately printed.

1986   The Lewis Creek Mound Culture in Virginia. Manuscript on file, Virginia Department of Historic Resources, Richmond.

MacCord, Howard A., and C. Lanier Rodgers

1966   The Miley Site, Shenandoah County, Virginia. *Quarterly Bulletin of the Archaeological Society of Virginia* 21:9–20.

Mallios, Seth

1998   Give and Let Die. Paper presented at the Middle Atlantic Archaeological Conference, Ocean City MD.

Malpass, Michael A.

1976   Analysis of the Ceramic Artifacts from the Powhatan Creek Site. *Quarterly Bulletin of the Archaeological Society of Virginia* 31:66–82.

Marx, Karl

1977   *Capital: Volume One.* New York: Vintage Books.

Mauss, Marcel

1990   *The Gift.* New York: W. W. Norton.

McGhee, Robert

1984   Speculations on Climatic Change and Thule Culture Development. *Folk* 11–12:172–184.

McGuire, Randall H.

1983   Breaking Down Cultural Complexity: Inequality and Heterogeneity. In *Advances in Archaeological Method and Theory*, vol. 6, edited by M. Schiffer. New York: Academic Press.

1992   *Death, Society, and Ideology in a Hohokam Community.* Boulder CO: Westview Press.

McGuire, Randall H., and Robert McC. Netting

1982   Leveling Peasants? The Demographic Implications of Welath Differences in an Alpine Community. *American Ethnographer* 9:269–290.

McGuire, Randall H., and Dean J. Saitta

1996   Although They Have Petty Captains, They Obey Them Badly: The Dialectics of Prehispanic Western Pueblo Social Organization. *American Antiquity* 61:197–216.

McGuire, Randall H., and Michael B. Schiffer

    1983   A Theory of Architectural Design. *Journal of Anthropological Archaeology* 2:277–303.

McLearan, Douglas C.

    1991   Late Archaic and Early Woodland Material Culture in Virginia. In *Late Archaic and Early Woodland Research in Virginia: A Synthesis*, edited by T. Reinhart and M. E. Hodges. Richmond: Archaeological Society of Virginia.

    1992   Virginia's Middle Period: A Regional Perspective. In *Middle and Late Woodland Research in Virginia: A Synthesis*, edited by T. Reinhart and M. E. Hodges. Richmond: Archaeological Society of Virginia.

McLearan, Douglas C., and L. Daniel Mouer

    1994   *Jordan's Journey III: A Preliminary Report on the 1992–1993 Excavations at Archaeological Site 44PG307.* Richmond: Archaeological Research Center, Virginia Commonwealth University.

Mehrer, Mark M.

    1995   *Cahokia's Countryside: Household Archaeology, Settlement Patterns, and Social Power.* DeKalb: Northern Illinois University Press.

Merrill, James H.

    1991   *The Indians' New World: Catawbas and Their Neighbors from European Contact through the Era of Removal.* New York: W. W. Norton.

Miller, Christopher L., and George R. Hamell

    1986   A New Perspective on Indian-White Cultural Contact: Cultural Symbols and Colonial Trade. *Journal of American History* 73(2):311–328.

Mintz, Sidney W.

    1985   *Sweetness and Power: The Place of Sugar in Modern History.* New York: Penguin.

Mooney, James P.

    1907   *The Siouan Tribes of the East.* Bureau of American Ethnology, Smithsonian Institution, Bulletin 22. Washington DC.

Moore, Henrietta L.

    1986   *Space, Text and Gender: An Anthropological Study of the Marakwet of Kenya.* Cambridge: Cambridge University Press.

    1992   Households and Gender Relations: The Modeling of the Economy. In *Understanding Economic Processes: Monographs in Economic Anthropology*, edited by S. Ortiz and S. Lees. Lanham MD: University Press of America.

Moore, Lawrence E.

    1993   Piscataway, Doeg, and the Potomac Creek Complex. *Journal of Middle Atlantic Archaeology* 19:117–138.

Moretti-Langholtz, Danielle

    1998   Other Names I Have Been Called: Political Resurgence among Virginia Indians in the Twentieth Century. Ph.D. dissertation, Department of Anthropology, University of Oklahoma.

Morgan,Tim, Nicholas M. Luccketti, Beverly Straube, S. Fiona Bessey and Annette Loomis
  1995   *Archaeological Excavations at Jordan's Point: Sites 44PG151, 44PG300, 44PG302, 44PG303, 44PG315, 44PG333*, vol. 1. Williamsburg VA: Virginia Company Foundation.

Mouer, L. Daniel
  1981   Powhatan and Monacan Settlement Hierarchies. *Quarterly Bulletin of the Archaeological Society of Virginia* 36:1–21.

  1983   A Review of the Ethnohistory and Archaeology of the Monacans. In *Piedmont Archaeology: Recent Research and Results*, edited by J. M. Wittkofski and L. E. Browning. Richmond: Archaeological Society of Virginia.

  1990   The Formative Transition in Virginia. In *Late Archaic and Early Woodland Research in Virginia: A Synthesis*. Richmond: Archaeological Society of Virginia.

  n.d.   DMZ or Deer Park? Buffer Zones as Boundary Systems. Manuscript on file, Virginia Department of Historic Resources, Richmond.

Mouer, L. Daniel, Fredrick W. Gleach, and Douglas C. McLearen
  1986   A Ceramics Temporal Typology in Progress for Central Virginia. In *Introduction to Phase 2 and Phase 3 Archaeological Investigations of the Henrico County Regional Wastewater System*, edited by L. Daniel Mouer. Richmond: Archaeology Research Center, Virginia Commonwealth University.

Mouer, L. Daniel, Douglas C. McLearan, R. Taft Kiser, Christopher P. Egghart, Beverley J. Binns, and Dane T. Magoon
  1992   *Jordan's Journey: A Preliminary Report on Archaeology at Site 44PG302*. Richmond: Archaeological Research Center, Virginia Commonwealth University.

Mouer, L. Daniel, Robin L. Ryder, and Elizabeth G. Johnson
  1981   Down to the River in Boats: The Late Archaic/Transitional in the Middle James River Valley, Virginia. *Quarterly Bulletin of the Archaeological Society of Virginia* 36:29–48.

Muraca, David
  1989   *The Carter's Grove Museum Site Excavation*. Williamsburg VA: Colonial Williamsburg Foundation.

Murdock, George P.
  1949   *Social Structure*. New York: MacMillan.

Naroll, Raoul
  1962   Floor Area and Settlement Population. *American Antiquity* 27:587–589.

Nass, John P., and Richard W. Yerkes
  1995   Social Differentiation in Mississippian and Fort Ancient Societies. In *Mississippian Communities and Households*, edited by J. Daniel Rogers and Bruce Smith. Tuscaloosa: University of Alabama Press.

Nelson, Ben A., Timothy Kohler, and Keith Kintigh
  1994   Demographic Alternatives: Consequences for Current Models of Southwestern Prehistory. In *Understanding Complexity in the Prehistoric Southwest*, edited by G. Gummerman and M. Gell-Mann. Reading MA: Addison-Wesley.

Nelson, Nels C.
  1909   Shellmounds of San Francisco Bay Region. In *Publications in American Archaeology and Ethnology* 7. Berkeley: University of California.
Netting, Robert McC.
  1982   Some Home Truths on Household Size and Wealth. *American Behavioral Scientist* 25(6):641–662.
  1990   Population, Permanent Agriculture, and Polities: Unpacking the Evolutionary Portmanteau. In *The Evolution of Political Systems*, edited by Steadman Upham. Cambridge: Cambridge University Press.
Netting, Robert McC., Richard Wilk, and Eric Arnould
  1984   *Households: Comparative and Historical Studies of the Domestic Group.* Berkeley: University of California Press.
Parker, Scott
  1989   Prehistoric Lithic Exchange in Virginia. Master's thesis, Department of Anthropology, University of Virginia.
Pauketat, Timothy R.
  1989   Monitoring Mississippian Homestead Occupation Span and Economy Using Ceramic Refuse. *American Antiquity* 54:288–310.
  1994   *The Ascent of Chiefs.* Tuscaloosa: University of Alabama Press.
Pauketat, Timothy R. (editor)
  2001   *The Archaeology of Traditions: Agency and History Before and After Columbus.* Gainesville: University Press of Florida.
Paynter, Robert
  1989   The Archaeology of Equality and Inequality. *Annual Review of Anthropology* 18:369–399.
Percy, George
  1998   Observations Gathered Out of Discourse. In *Jamestown Narratives: Eyewitness Accounts of the Virginia Colony*, edited by E. W. Haile. Champlain VA: Roundhouse.
Peregrine, Peter
  1992   Social Change in the Woodland-Mississippian Transition: A Study of Household and Community Patterns in the American Bottom. *North American Archaeologist* 13:131–147.
Petherick, Gary L.
  1987   Architecture and Features at the Fredericks, Wall, and Mitchum Sites. In *The Siouan Project: Seasons I and II*, edited by Roy Dickens, H. Trawick Ward, and R. P. Stephen Davis. Chapel Hill: University of North Carolina Research Laboratories of Anthropology.
Plog, Stephen
  1985   Estimating Vessel Orifice Diameters: Measurement Methods and Measurement Error. In *Decoding Prehistoric Ceramics*, edited by B. A. Nelson. Carbondale: Southern Illinois University Press.

1986   Change in Regional Trade Networks. In *Spatial Organization and Exchange: Archaeological Survey on Northern Black Mesa*, edited by S. Plog. Carbondale: Southern Illinois University Press.

1989   Ritual, Exchange, and the Development of Regional Systems. In *The Architecture of Social Integration in Prehistoric Pueblos*, edited by W. D. Lipe and Michelle Hegmon. Cortez CO: Crow Canyon Archaeological Center.

1990a   Agriculture, Sedentism, and Environment in the Evolution of Political Systems. In *The Evolution of Political Systems*, edited by Steadman Upham. Cambridge: Cambridge University Press.

1990b   Sociopolitical Implications of Stylistic Variation in the American Southwest. In *The Uses of Style in Archaeology*, edited by M. W. Conkey and C. A. Hastdorf. Cambridge: Cambridge University Press.

1995a   Equality and Hierarchy: Holistic Approaches to Understanding Social Dynamics in the Pueblo Southwest. In *Foundations of Social Inequality*, edited by T. D. Price and G. M. Feinman. New York: Plenum Press.

1995b   Approaches to Style: Complements and Contrasts. In *Style, Society, and Person: Archaeological and Ethnological Perspectives*, edited by C. Carr and J. E. Neitzel. New York: Plenum Press.

Plog, Stephen, and Jeffrey L. Hantman

1990   Chronology Construction and the Study of Prehistoric Culture Change. *Journal of Field Archaeology* 17:439–456.

Potter, Stephen R.

1982   An Analysis of Chicacoan Settlement Patterns. Ph.D. dissertation, Department of Anthropology, University of North Carolina, Chapel Hill.

1989   Early English Effects on Virginia Exchange and Tribute Systems in the Seventeenth Century: An Example from the Tidewater Potomac. In *Powhatan's Mantle: Indians in the Colonial Southeast*, edited by P. Wood, G. Waselkov, and T. Hatley. Lincoln: University of Nebraska Press.

1993   *Commoners, Tribute, and Chiefs: The Development of Algonquin Culture in the Potomac Valley.* Charlottesville: University Press of Virginia.

Preucel, Robert W., and Ian Hodder

1996   *Contemporary Archaeology in Theory: A Reader.* Oxford: Blackwell.

Prezzano, Susan C.

1988   Spatial Analysis of Post Mold Patterns at the Sackett Site, Ontario County, New York. *Man in the Northeast* 35:27–45.

Price, T. Douglas, and Gary M. Feinman

1995   *Foundations of Social Inequality.* New York: Plenum Press.

Purchas, Samuel (compiler and editor)

1617   *Purchas His Pilgrimage.* 3rd ed. London.

Quinn, David Beers

1985   *Set Fair for Roanoke: Voyages and Colonies, 1584–1606.* Chapel Hill: University of North Carolina Press.

Rafferty, Janet E.
    1985   The Archaeological Record on Sedentariness: Recognition, Development, and
            Implication. In *Advances in Archaeological Method and Theory*, vol. 8, edited by
            M. Schiffer. New York: Academic Press.

Ramenofsky, Ann F.
    1987   *Vectors of Death*. Albuquerque: University of New Mexico Press.

Rapoport, Amos
    1982   *The Meaning of the Built Environment: A Nonverbal Communication Approach.*
            Beverly Hills CA: Sage.

Rappaport, Roy A.
    1979   *Ecology, Meaning, and Religion*. Richmond CA: North Atlantic Books.

Read, Dwight W.
    1978   Towards a Formal Theory of Population Size and Area of Habitation. *Current
            Anthropology* 19:312–317.

Reinhart, Theodore R.
    1976   Excavations at the Powhatan Creek Site. *Quarterly Bulletin of the Archaeological
            Society of Virginia* 31:37–65.

Renfrew, Colin
    1974   Beyond a Subsistence Economy: The Evolution of Social Organization in
            Prehistoric Europe. In *Reconstructing Complex Societies: An Archaeological Collo-
            quium*, edited by Charlotte B. Moore. Cambridge MA: American Schools of
            Oriental Research.

Renfrew, Colin, and John F. Cherry (editors)
    1986   *Peer Polity Interaction and Socio-political Change*. Cambridge: Cambridge Uni-
            versity Press.

Ritchie, William A., and Robert E. Funk
    1973   *Aboriginal Settlement Patterns in the Northeast*. Albany: New York State Museum
            and Science Service Memoir.

Rogers, J. Daniel, and Bruce Smith (editors)
    1995   *Mississippian Communities and Households*. Tuscaloosa: University of Alabama
            Press.

Roseberry, William
    1982   Balinese Cockfights and the Seduction of Anthropology. *Social Research*
            49(4):1013–1028.

Rountree, Helen C.
    1989   *The Powhatan Indians of Virginia: The Traditional Culture*. Norman: University of
            Oklahoma Press.
    1990   *Pocahontas' People: The Powhatan Indians of Virginia through Four Centuries*. Nor-
            man: University of Oklahoma Press.
    1993   Summary and Implications. In *Powhatan Foreign Relations: 1500–1722*, edited
            by H. C. Rountree. Charlottesville: University Press of Virginia.

Rountree, Helen C., and E. Randolph Turner
  1994   On the Fringe of the Southeast: The Powhatan Paramount Chiefdom in Virginia. In *The Forgotten Centuries: Indians and Europeans in the American South, 1521–1704*, edited by C. Hudson and C. Tesser. Athens: University of Georgia Press.
  2002   *Before and after Jamestown: The Powhatans and Algonquians of Virginia*. Gainesville: University Press of Florida.

Rousseau, Jean-Jacques
  1968   *The Social Contract*. Middlesex: Penguin Classics.

Sackett, James R.
  1986   Style, Function and Assemblage Variability: A Reply to Binford. *American Antiquity* 51:628–634.

Sahlins, Marshall D.
  1963   Poor Man, Rich Man, Big Man, Chief: Political Types in Melanesia and Polynesia. *Comparative Studies in Society and History* 5:285–303.
  1972   *Stone Age Economics*. Chicago: Aldine.
  1985   *Islands of History*. Chicago: University of Chicago Press.

Saitta, Dean J., and Arthur S. Keene
  1990   Primitive Communism and the Origin of Social Inequality. In *The Evolution of Political Systems* edited by Steadman Upham. Cambridge: Cambridge University Press.

Schiffer, Michael B.
  1975   Archaeology as Behavioral Science. *American Anthropologist* 77:836–848.
  1976   *Behavioral Archeology*. New York: Academic Press.
  1987   *Formation Processes of the Archaeological Record*. Albuquerque: University of New Mexico Press.

Schmitt, Karl
  1965   Patawomeke: An Historic Algonkian Site. *Quarterly Bulletin of the Archeological Society of Virginia* 20:1–36.

Service, Elman R.
  1975   *Origins of the State and Civilization*. New York: W. W. Norton.

Shanks, Michael, and Christopher Tilley
  1982   Ideology, Symbolic Power and Ritual Communication: A Reinterpretation of Neolithic Mortuary Practices. In *Symbolic and Structural Archaeology*, edited by I. Hodder. Cambridge: Cambridge University Press.

Silberbauer, George
  1982   Political Process in G/wi Bands. In *Politics and History in Band Societies*, edited by Eleanor Leacock and Richard Lee. Cambridge: Cambridge University Press.

Smith, Bruce D.
  1986   The Archaeology of the Southeastern United States: From Dalton to de Soto, 10,500 to 500 B.P. *Advances in World Archaeology* 5:1–92.

Smith, John

    1986a   A True Relation. In *The Complete Works of Captain John Smith*, vol. 1, edited by P. L. Barbour. Chapel Hill: University of North Carolina Press.

    1986b   A Map of Virginia. In *The Complete Works of Captain John Smith (1580–1631)*, vol. 1, edited by P. L. Barbour. Chapel Hill: University of North Carolina Press.

    1986c   The Proceedings. In *The Complete Works of Captain John Smith (1580–1631)*, vol. 1, edited by P. L. Barbour. Chapel Hill: University of North Carolina Press.

    1986d   The Generall Historie of Virginia. In *The Complete Works of Captain John Smith (1580–1631)*, vol. 2, edited by P. L. Barbour. Chapel Hill: University of North Carolina Press.

Smith, Marvin T.

    1987   *Archaeology of Aboriginal Culture Change: Depopulation during the Early Historic Period*. Gainesville: University Press of Florida.

Snow, Dean R.

    1989   The Evolution of Mohawk Households, A.D. 1400–1800. In *Households and Communities: Proceedings of the 21st Annual Chacmool Conference*, edited by S. MacEachern, D. J. W. Archer, and R. Garvin. Calgary: University of Calgary Archaeological Association.

Snyder, Kimberly A., and April M. Fehr

    1984   *Data Recovery Excavations at 44WR3, 44WR299, 44WR300, and 44WR301*. Front Royal VA: Thunderbird Research Corporation.

Southall, Aidan W.

    1988   On Mode of Production Theory: The Foraging Mode of Production and Kinship Mode of Production. *Dialectical Anthropology* 12:165–192.

Spelman, Henry

    1998   Relation of Virginia. In *Jamestown Narratives: Eyewitness Accounts of the Virginia Colony*, edited by E. W. Haile. Champlain VA: Roundhouse.

Stahle, David W., Malcom K. Cleaveland, Dennis B. Blanton, Matthew D. Therrell, and David A. Gay

    1998   The Lost Colony and Jamestown Droughts. *Science* 280:564–567.

Steponaitis, Laurie C.

    1987   Prehistoric Settlement Patterns in the Lower Patuxent Drainage, Maryland. Ph.D. dissertation, Department of Anthropology, State University of New York at Binghamton.

Steponaitis, Vincas

    1978   Location Theory and Complex Chiefdoms: A Mississippian Example. In *Mississippian Settlement Patterns*, edited by B. D. Smith. New York: Academic Press.

Stewart, R. Michael

    1984   South Mountain (Meta) Rhyolite: A Perspective on Trade and Exchange in the Middle Atlantic Region. In *Prehistoric Lithic Exchange Systems in the Mid-*

dle Atlantic Region, edited by J. F. Custer. Newark: Center for Archaeological Research, University of Delaware.

1989   Trade and Exchange in Middle Atlantic Prehistory. *Archaeology of Eastern North America* 17:47–78.

1991   Clemson Island Studies in Pennsylvania: A Perspective. *Pennsylvania Archaeologist* 60(1):79–107.

Strachey, William

1953   *The Historie of Travell into Virginia Britania*. Glasgow: University Press.

1999   *A Dictionary of Powhatan*. American Language Reprint Series 8. Bristol PA: Arx.

Strathern, Andrew J.

1969   Finance and Production: Two Strategies in New Guinea Highland Exchange Systems. *Oceania* 40:42–67.

Stuiver, M., and Reimer, P. J.

1993   Extended 14C Data Base and Revised CALIB 3.0 14C Age Calibration Program. *Radiocarbon* 35:215–230.

Sullivan, Alan P.

1980   Prehistoric Settlement Variability in the Grasshopper Area, East-central Arizona. Ph.D. dissertation, Department of Anthropology, University of Arizona.

Testart, Alain

1982   The Significance of Food Storage among Hunter-Gatherers: Residence Patterns Population Densities, and Social Inequalities. *Current Anthropology* 23: 523–537.

Thomas, David H.

1986   *Refiguring Anthropology: First Principles of Probability and Statistics*. Prospect Heights IL: Waveland Press.

Thompson, Steven M.

1989   Post Structures. In *Archaeological Investigations at the Bessemer Site (44B026): A Late Woodland Period Dan River and Page Component Village Site on the Upper James River, Virginia*, edited by T. R. Whyte and S. M. Thompson. Harrisonburg VA: Archaeological Research Center, James Madison University.

Tourtellotte, Perry

1990   The Partridge Creek Site 44(AH193) Amherst County, Virginia: Report on the Excavations, December 1985–June 1986. Manuscript on file, Virginia Department of Historical Resources, Richmond.

Trigger, Bruce

1990   Maintaining Economic Equality in Opposition to Complexity: An Iroquoian Case Study. In *The Evolution of Political Systems*, edited by Steadman Upham. Cambridge: Cambridge University Press.

1991   Constraint and Freedom: A New Synthesis for Archaeological Explanation. *American Anthropologist* 93:551–569.

Trimble, Carmen

1996   Paleodiet in Virginia and North Carolina as Determined by Stable Isotope

Analysis of Skeletal Remains. Master's thesis, Department of Anthropology, University of Virginia.

Turner, E. Randolph

1976   An Archaeological and Ethnohistorical Study of the Evolution of Rank Societies in the Virginia Coastal Plain. Ph.D. dissertation, Department of Anthropology, Pennsylvania State University.

1978   An Intertribal Deer Exploitation Buffer Zone for the Virginia Coastal Plain-Piedmont Regions. *Quarterly Bulletin of the Archaeological Society of Virginia* 32:42–48.

1982   A Reexamination of Powhatan Territorial Boundaries and Population, Ca. A.D. 1607. *Quarterly Bulletin of the Archaeological Society of Virginia* 37:45–64.

1992   The Virginia Coastal Plain during the Late Woodland Period. In *Middle and Late Woodland Research in Virginia: A Synthesis*, edited by T. Reinhart and M. E. Hodges. Richmond: Archaeological Society of Virginia.

1993   Native American Protohistoric Interactions in the Powhatan Core Area. In *Powhatan Foreign Relations: 1500–1722*, edited by H. C. Rountree. Charlottesville: University Press of Virginia.

Turner, Victor W.

1969   *The Ritual Process: Structure and Antistructure.* Chicago: Aldine.

Ubelaker, Douglas H.

1974   Reconstruction of Demographic Profiles from Ossuary Skeletal Samples: A Case Study from the Tidewater Potomac. *Smithsonian Contributions to Anthropology* 18. Washington DC.

Valliere, Oliver D., and John C. Harter

1986   The Cement Plant Site, Augusta County, Virginia. In *The Lewis Creek Mound Culture in Virginia*, edited by H. A. MacCord Sr. Privately published.

Varien, Mark D.

1999   *Sedentism and Mobility in a Social Landscape: Mesa Verde and Beyond.* Tucson: University of Arizona Press.

Varien, Mark D., and Barbara J. Mills

1997   Accumulations Research: Problems and Prospects for Estimating Site Occupation Span. *Journal of Archaeological Method and Theory* 4:141–191.

Walker, Joan M., and Glenda F. Miller

1992   Life on the Levee: The Late Woodland Period in the Northern Great Valley of Virginia. In *Middle and Late Woodland Research in Virginia: A Synthesis*, edited by T. Reinhart and M. E. Hodges. Richmond: Archaeological Society of Virginia.

Wallerstein, Immanuel M.

1974   *The Modern World System.* New York: Academic Press.

Ward, H. Trawick

1985   Social Implications of Storage and Disposal Patterns. In *Structure and Process in Southeastern Archaeology*, edited by R. S. Dickens and H. T. Ward. Tuscaloosa: University of Alabama Press.

1993   Barbeque Rituals on the North Carolina Piedmont. Paper presented at the Southeastern Archaeological Conference, Raleigh NC.

Ward, H. Trawick, and R. P. Steven Davis

1988   Archaeology of the Historic Ocaneechi Indians. *Southern Indian Studies* 36.

1991   The Impact of Old World Diseases on the Native Inhabitants of the North Carolina Piedmont. *Archaeology of Eastern North America* 19:171–181.

1993   *Indian Communities of the North Carolina Piedmont:* A.D. *1000-*A.D. *1700.* Chapel Hill NC: Research Laboratories of Anthropology.

1999   *Time Before History: The Archaeology of North Carolina.* Chapel Hill: University of North Carolina Press.

Warrick, Gary A.

1988   Estimating Ontario Iroquoian Village Duration. *Man in the Northeast* 36:21–61.

1996   Evolution of the Iroquoian Longhouse. In *People Who Lived in Big Houses: Archaeological Perspectives on Large Domestic Structures.* Madison WI: Prehistory Press.

Waselkov, Gregory A.

1982   Shellfish Gathering and Shell Midden Archaeology. Ph.D. dissertation, Department of Anthropology, University of North Carolina, Chapel Hill.

Waters, Michael R.

1992   *Principles of Geoarchaeology: A North American Perspective.* Tucson: University of Arizona Press.

Wattenmaker, Patricia

1998   *Household and State in Upper Mesopotamia: Specialized Economy and the Social Uses of Goods in an Early Complex Society.* Washington DC: Smithsonian Institution Press.

Weber, Max

1993   *The Sociology of Religion.* Boston: Beacon Press.

1996   *The Protestant Ethic and the Spirit of Capitalism.* Los Angeles: Roxbury.

Welch, Paul D.

1991   *Moundville's Economy.* Tuscaloosa: University of Alabama Press.

Whyte, Thomas, and Clarence R. Geier

1982   *The Perkins Point Site (44 BA 3): A Protohistoric Stockaded Village on the Jackson River, Bath County, Virginia.* Harrisonburg VA: Archaeological Research Center, James Madison University.

Whyte, Thomas R., and Steven M. Thompson

1989   *Archaeological Investigations at the Bessemer Site 44 (BO 26): A Late Woodland Period Dan River and Page Component Village Site on the Upper James River, Virginia.* Harrisonburg VA: Archaeological Research Center, James Madison University.

Wiessner, Pauline W.

1974   A Functional Estimator of Population from Floor Area. *American Antiquity* 39:343–350.

1977   Hxaro: A Regional System of Reciprocity for Reducing Risk among the

!Kung San. Ph.D. dissertation, Department of Anthropology, University of Michigan.

1985   Style or Isochrestic Variation? A Reply to Sackett. *American Antiquity* 50:160–166.

Wilk, Richard R.

1984   Households in Process: Agricultural Change and Domestic Transformation among the Kekchi Maya of Belize. In *Households: Comparative and Historical Studies of the Domestic Group*, edited by R. McC. Netting, R. R. Wilk, and E. J. Arnould. Berkeley: University of California Press.

1989   Decision Making and Resource Flows within the Household: Beyond the Black Box. In *The Household Economy: Reconsidering the Domestic Mode of Production*. Boulder CO: Westview Press.

Wilk, Richard R., and William L. Rathje

1982   Household Archaeology. *American Behavioral Scientist* 25(6):617–640.

Williamson, Margaret Holmes

1979   Powhatan Hair. *Man* 14:392–413.

Wills, Wirt H.

1992   Foraging Systems and Plant Cultivation During the Emergence of Agriculture Economies in the Prehistoric American Southwest. In *Transitions to Agriculture in Prehistory*, edited by A. B. Gebaurer and T. D. Price. Monographs in World Archaeology No. 4. Madison WI: Prehistory Press.

Winfree, R. Westwood

1969   Newington, King and Queen County. *Quarterly Bulletin of the Archeological Society of Virginia* 22:2–26.

Winter, Marcus C.

1976   The Archaeological Household Cluster in the Valley of Oaxaca. In *The Early Mesoamerican Village*, edited by K. V. Flannery. New York: Academic Press.

Wobst, H. Martin

1977   Stylistic Behavior and Information Exchange. In *Papers for the Director: Research Essays in Honor of James B. Griffin*, edited by C. E. Cleland. Anthropological Papers No. 61. Ann Arbor: Museum of Anthropology, University of Michigan.

Woodburn, James

1982   Egalitarian Societies. *Man* 17:431–451.

Wright, Henry T.

1984   Prestate Political Formations. In *On the Evolution of Complex Societies: Essays in Honor of Harry Hoijer 1982*, edited by T. Earle. Malibu CA: Undena.

Yanagisako, Sylvia J.

1979   Family and Household: The Analysis of Domestic Groups. *Annual Review of Anthropology* 8:161–205.

Index

CPSIA information can be obtained at www.ICGtesting.com
Printed in the USA
BVOW08*0506191016

465339BV00013B/23/P